20 SECRETS TO SUCCESS FOR

NCAA STUDENT-ATHLETES

WHO WON'T GO PRO

Ohio University Sport Management Series

Dr. Norm O'Reilly, Series Editor

20 Secrets to Success

for NCAA Student-Athletes Who Won't Go Pro

Rick Burton

Jake Hirshman

Norm O'Reilly, PhD

Andy Dolich

Heather Lawrence, PhD

Foreword by Oliver Luck
Afterword by Pat O'Conner

OHIO UNIVERSITY PRESS • ATHENS

Ohio University Press, Athens, Ohio 45701
ohioswallow.com
© 2018 by Ohio University Press

Printed in the United States of America
Ohio University Press books are printed on acid-free paper ∞ ™

28 27 26 25 24 23 22 21 20 19 18   5 4 3 2 1

Library of Congress Cataloging-in-Publication Data available upon request.
Names: Burton, Rick, author.
Title: 20 secrets to success for NCAA student-athletes who won't go pro /
 Rick Burton, Jake Hirshman, Norm O'Reilly, Andy Dolich, Heather Lawrence ;
 foreword by Oliver Luck ; afterword by Pat O'Conner.
Other titles: Twenty secrets to success for NCAA student-athletes who won't go pro
Description: Athens, Ohio : Ohio University Press, 2017. | Series: Ohio
 university sports management book series | Includes bibliographical
 references and index.
Identifiers: LCCN 2017043931| ISBN 9780821422946 (hardback : alk. paper) |
 ISBN 9780821422953 (pb : alk. paper) | ISBN 9780821446171 (pdf)
Subjects: LCSH: College athletes--Education--United States. | College
 athletes--United States--Life skills guides. | BISAC: SPORTS & RECREATION
 / General. | EDUCATION / Counseling / Vocational Guidance.
Classification: LCC LC2581 .B87 2017 | DDC 796.04/3092--dc23
LC record available at https://lccn.loc.gov/2017043931

Contents

Foreword

We are human; therefore, we make mistakes—all of us. But what sets us apart is acknowledging the mistake and correcting it. I learned this lesson while participating in intercollegiate athletics, and it has served me well in the rough-and-tumble world of business.

Let me share with you my biggest mistake in my career in the professional sports business and how my boss helped me quickly rectify it.

In the waning months of 2005, the Anschutz Entertainment Group (AEG), owner of the San Jose Earthquakes—one of the founding members of Major League Soccer—decided to relocate the franchise to Houston. I was offered the position of president/general manager of the franchise and on New Year's Day in 2006 my tenure began.

Of course, there were dozens of tasks in front of us—hiring a staff, finding office space, negotiating a stadium lease, identifying a practice facility, relocating players and coaches, securing sponsorships, selling season tickets. The list was endless and we had only a few weeks before the opening match.

Naturally, the most pressing issue was deciding on the team name. After conducting just a handful of meetings with local soccer officials as well as the MLS office, we decided—in a nod to the European tradition of naming clubs after the year in which they were founded (think Schalke 04 or Hannover 96)—to name the new club Houston 1836, which was the year the City of Houston was established by charter.

Almost immediately there was negative feedback bordering on outrage. Why? Well, 1836 was "annus horribilis" in the eyes of a sizable portion of the Houston community. Three significant military battles took place that year—Alamo, Goliad, and San Jacinto. And in that last battle, which was fought just outside what is now Houston, General Sam Houston defeated General Santa Anna and Mexico lost its province of Texas.

Very quickly I realized that our brand new franchise had a problem. Unintentionally, we had just insulted a hugely important demographic—the

Hispanic fan of Mexican descent—by rolling out the team name without a proper vetting. A week or so into this imbroglio, my cell phone rang.

It was Phil Anschutz, owner of AEG, my boss, and a man of few words. He wanted to know my assessment of the situation. I told him it was serious. He pushed back a bit, saying "my folks in Los Angeles (AEG executives) think this will blow over and that the team can ride it out." "No," I responded, "it won't. This is like a burr under the saddle and it will only get worse." There were a few seconds of silence, then Phil said matter-of-factly, "Well, change the name."

Mr. Anshutz, a man I had not yet met, trusted in me, and his decisiveness allowed us to cut our losses, rectify the error, and return to promoting the team and the inaugural season. And that inaugural season ended with a bang—the Houston Dynamo as MLS Cup Champions!

In this book, you will read about how being a student-athlete teaches you how to recognize your mistakes and correct them. Being a student-athlete also gives you the skill set to manage and prioritize time demands. Like most student-athletes, you will go pro in something other than sport. This experience truly equips you for life after sport in your career, family, and personal growth.

There are several anecdotes in this book about the value of being a student-athlete and playing intercollegiate athletics. In my case, I would not have had my career opportunities if sport had not been part of my early foundation. Transitioning into the business world was as fundamental as playing college football. It gave me the confidence, determination, and spirit to excel in life.

Oliver Luck
Executive Vice President, NCAA

Acknowledgments

The writing of a book such as this requires the input, support, and expertise of many. Even with a core writing team of five authors with varied backgrounds and experiences, a topic as vast and complicated as this book's necessitates the contributions of many others. We are fortunate to have received input from sixty-four external contributors in the writing of this book. Their experiences, perspectives, and advice played a vital and significant role in the compilation of this book.

We would further like to acknowledge recent Ohio University graduate Kevin Fagin, now with the Cincinnati Reds, for his efforts in supporting the data collection required for this book.

Thank you also to Syracuse University's Margie Chetney and students Arek Olson and Sierra Shafer, former student-athletes, who helped in the research and reviewing process.

Within the book, the names of the interviewees are noted where they are quoted or where their input was included. The interviewees come from many backgrounds, including former student-athletes, coaches, athletic directors, sport administrators, other professionals, and former professional athletes. All interviewees, along with their sport and school if they are former student-athletes, plus their current title, are listed in Appendix C at the back of the book. We would like to express our most sincere appreciation for their support, time, and expertise, which informed and helped shape this book.

The authors would also like to thank the team at Ohio University Press, particularly Gillian Berchowitz, for their support, informative reviews, and strong push for a high-quality product that can improve the student-athlete experience for all.

Finally, all five of us would like to expressly thank our families, friends, and colleagues who supported the long nights, big pushes, and tough conversations that are always required in the process of writing a book of this nature.

Introduction

When business author Stephen Covey wrote his landmark text *The 7 Habits of Highly Effective People* in 1989, he drew from more than twenty-five years of observing what made leaders successful. That book has never been out of print, and we suspect a major reason is that Covey made the concept of simple, straightforward advice (built around just seven habits) easy for everyone to grasp. Covey believed businesspeople, future leaders, and students alike could all become more effective and accomplished by reading his book.

As a group of authors, we came together wanting to emulate that concept but for a very specific audience: collegiate student-athletes. We wanted to prepare high school seniors getting ready to go to college as student-athletes and to assist those NCAA student-athletes already enrolled at a university or college who will soon find out there is more to adult life than just playing a sport. Many have the dream of playing sports professionally or competing at the Olympics, but many others have the dream of becoming a doctor, lawyer, or CEO.

So this book is a handbook. Not a textbook. It has been specifically written for student-athletes. It is intended for the locker room, the dorm room, the house off campus, the cafeteria, the bus, the plane, or the study hall, as well as the classroom.

The reason we want this book read in those locations is that after a few years as a college student-athlete, reality always sets in. Being an intercollegiate student-athlete means enduring a rigorous schedule of practices, classes, labs, tutorial sessions, weight training, road trips, and academic counseling.

We also wanted this book to work for every type of NCAA student-athlete. Not just students whose families have gone to college for generations . . . but also students for whom a grant-in-aid scholarship will make them the first ever in their family to go to college. Similarly, we wanted this book to serve not just students who have grown up in a highly developed American system of sport (i.e., Amateur Athletic Union teams, elite travel teams, private

1

sport academies) but also the thousands of international students who are recruited to play for NCAA schools and must adapt not only to the myriad rules by which NCAA athletes are governed but also to living in a new country.

But why stop there? We also wanted to make sure this book was not subliminally written for a particular gender, race, sexual orientation, socioeconomic privilege, or level of skill. In fact, we wanted to consistently recognize that playing sports at a US institution of higher education is incredibly demanding. We appreciate that every student-athlete is different and will face numerous physical, emotional, social, spiritual, and mental health challenges during his or her tenure at a university.

Mental health for NCAA student-athletes is not to be taken lightly. The NCAA's chief medical officer, Brian Hainline, who is responsible for running the NCAA's Sport Science Institute, has been tireless in telling athletic administrators, athletes, and parents that understanding and supporting student-athlete mental wellness (as well as addressing sexual assault and interpersonal violence) are a mandate for the NCAA as a governing body as well as for all of the NCAA's member institutions.

Like mental health, diversity and inclusion are foundational (but also confounding) issues for anyone who enters the college sports experience. Not all student-athletes, however, feel confident that the invitation to the party included their name. As one sage recently noted, diversity is getting invited to the party, while inclusion is getting asked to dance.

Most student-athletes will make their way through college and find individuals like themselves. But not everyone gets comfortable in every situation.

So we should be clear in our intention. We want everyone who reads this book to find value or to be provoked to think differently. But how individuals read a handbook, and in particular whether an individual seeks clarity for an issue specific to her or him, varies widely. Students who might come from greater disadvantage than others they see around them need to use this book as a starting block toward seeking assistance.

To draw upon the work of the acclaimed writer and social scientist Malcolm Gladwell, author of the seminal book *Outliers* (2008), the difference between those who succeed and those who fail is "not something expensive or impossible to find; not something encoded in DNA or hardwired into the circuits of [young] brains." What those who fail lack is "something that could have been given to them if we'd only known they needed it: a community around them that prepared them properly for the world."

You, the reader, may or may not have enjoyed great support, encouragement, and endorsement at home. But chances are very good that either way, most readers of this book will have needed to adapt to a new setting (college) and then find a supportive community there. We hope this book is a literary version of that process—a simple book that can provide insight, advice, and counsel, much of it from others just like you, who made this same journey.

Why tell you this? Well, at the end of the college continuum, for more than 98 percent of all NCAA student-athletes, the dream of playing professionally or for a national or Olympic team . . . of leveling up (if you are a video gamer) . . . will not happen. The end of college is the end of the elite sports journey for most student-athletes. Life after graduation awaits, and the world can be harsh.

This book is for student-athletes (and perhaps their parents or guardians) who will encounter some confusion and yearn for solutions to an age-old conundrum that collegiate student-athletes have faced since the NCAA was formally named in 1910. And that is: How do I prepare for what I am going to do next? And a corollary: How do I leverage my strengths and turn my weaknesses into learning moments?

The answers are in this book.

We wrote the book in such a way that any student-athlete can pick it up and prowl or browse through any chapter. You don't have to read it sequentially or in one sitting or during any particular semester. Rather, you can use this book according to your specific needs. In other words, our aim was to write a self-help book for elite student-athletes. That's you.

We believe most student-athletes arrive at their goal of playing intercollegiate sports through a great deal of hard work and discipline that allows for both athletic and academic success. To help you build on those accomplishments, we wanted to make this book flow, starting with the first secret of creating and following a student-athlete plan that could prepare any student-athlete for a more successful future.

From there, nineteen more secrets follow. They have all been written by our team of five authors, including four former collegiate athletes, two of whom captured championships; a university faculty athletics representative; a dynamic young scholar; and an executive who has worked his entire career in professional sports, rubbing shoulders with the greatest athletes of all time. We have worked together to make sure this book is easy to read and easy to benefit from.

The NCAA and its member institutions face the challenge of doing more to support student-athletes. The student-athlete, however, must also accept responsibility for preparing for his or her own future. Choosing a major with your advisor, attending classes, and learning about your chosen profession is the plan you the student-athlete must own. Simply said, "Whatever you put into it, you'll get out of it." This book gives student-athletes the information needed to positively influence their individual outcomes.

In the NCAA's promotional materials, student-athletes proudly proclaim the tag line, "There are over 400,000 NCAA student-athletes, and just about all of us will be going pro in something other than sports." If most student-athletes will go professional in something other than sports, then most student-athletes can take advantage of the secrets we share here.

But don't just take that from us. Thumb through this book and notice the athletic directors, coaches, and former players who have offered their time to make sure student-athletes get the best possible advice.

Any contemporary book must acknowledge the great and profound differences that make all of us unique individuals. Readers will vary by personality, height, weight, intelligence, prior accomplishment, race, religion, socioeconomic status, gender identification, country of origin, historical association with higher education, and types of foods we enjoy (or dislike) . . . just to name a few differences.

To that end, this book is written with everyone in mind and with no single classification featured. All student-athletes are welcome in this book and all are acknowledged. All of us are challenged to do the best we can and to help each other out. We must learn to be interdependent (as Covey wrote). And to encourage one another.

We sincerely hope these pages will unlock a few of the mysteries contained and camouflaged on college campuses. We are confident these "secrets" can make you more successful in college and beyond.

We wish you all the best,

The Authors

How to Use This Book

If you are a high school student-athlete hoping to play collegiate athletics, please read Secrets 1–11 first.

If you are a high school senior who won't compete as a collegiate student-athlete, check out Secrets 12–20.

If you are a college freshman or sophomore, check out Secrets 1–11 and 15 first, then 12–14 and 16–20.

If you are a college junior or senior, check out ALL the Secrets.

If you are a college graduate, check out Secrets 13, 14, and 16–20.

And as a special request to everyone, please review the recommended readings and other resources (found in Appendix B) for your ongoing benefit.

Part 1

Succeeding as a
Student-Athlete

Secret 1 — Create and Follow Your Student-Athlete Plan

There is an old saying that failing to plan is planning to fail. Sure, it's a simple twist on a few words, but the second part of the saying is where the big outcome rests. No plan means you fail. For many that word "plan" is probably mysterious or simply a hassle. Most of us remember in elementary school having to produce an outline that used roman numerals, capital letters, and arabic numerals. Many of us thought it was stupid to be forced to outline a report on birds or the state of Tennessee. Why couldn't we just start writing the report? The reason was that "the plan" (i.e., the outline) would make writing the story so much easier. For student-athletes, the creation of a plan, simple or otherwise, is a massive determinant in achieving post–athletic career success.

CREATE AND FOLLOW YOUR STUDENT-ATHLETE PLAN

When we asked Oliver Luck, Executive Vice President of the NCAA, about career planning for a student-athlete, he succinctly said, "The backup plan is going pro in your sport." Yes, a leader of the NCAA who played in the NFL is suggesting that a career in pro sports is Plan B. Plan A is your life path based on your academic choices.

Steve Cobb, Director of the Arizona Fall League, said, "It is important to have a plan as an athlete, a roadmap. If you don't have a plan, you aren't going to get to where you want to be. And you can have the best game plan of anyone, but if you don't have the right people supporting you or around you, your plan won't be as effective."

Wise words from these two executives are ones to take to heart, and an indication that you should probably start your plan now.

Most young adults arriving on a college campus as recruited student-athletes (or walk-ons) have both specific and vague goals. And the source of these goals has likely come from life experiences, role models, parents, or peers. Commonly held objectives for freshmen student-athletes entering college include the following:

List No. 1

1. Impress the coaching staff and earn "playing time."

2. Beat out others on the team and emerge as a "starter."

3. Take advantage of the university's training facilities to help achieve Goals 1 and 2.

4. Make new friends and settle into college life.

5. Figure out how to balance athletics with academics and a social life and eventually graduate.

6. Make sure to take care of mental health and consistently make good decisions on sleep, food, socializing, and interpersonal relationships.

Unfortunately, for most student-athletes, there are several other desirable goals that never get stated or are formulated so vaguely that they don't register until late in an athlete's senior year. Those goals look a lot more like this:

List No. 2

1. Identify a professional work career that seems exciting and will sustain the lifestyle I want for the many years after I finish playing my sport.

2. Graduate in four or five years with a degree in a major that will enhance the procurement and enjoyment of my future professional career.

3. Graduate with honors or a GPA that will impress future employers or make admission to graduate, medical, or law school possible.

4. Take advantage of every single Athletic Department and University/College offering that makes me more accomplished and more functional for life after college.

5. Build an individual brand that resonates with teachers, administrators, the media, and future employers.

6.   Join professional groups on campus or attend professional presentations that facilitate the development of a well-rounded individual and not "just" a "jock" or athlete.

7.   Take advantage of the travel opportunities related to my sport and get to know the different cities and countries I might visit. Get out and explore.

ROB SMITH
(former student-athlete, Head Baseball Coach at Ohio University)

I didn't have a plan, and I was very misguided early on in the process. I had some struggles, and I didn't really get things going until after my first year in school. I learned how to start prioritizing things like my academics, because the baseball wasn't hard to prioritize.

I was also the first person in my family to graduate from college, so academics wasn't a highly emphasized thing in our house, and I got buried early on because of that.

The plan component is probably more important than the goal-setting component because you can't reach your goals without a plan. It's important to understand what your tasks are and what needs to be done to execute them. As Herm Edwards, former NFL star, would say, "a goal without a plan is just a wish." The plan is far more important than the goal.

If all you are concerned with is the endgame with no real process, then more often than not, you will fail. If you're like the 99 percent of us who walk on the planet who can't just show up and play, or have great skills without training as much, you must think about the process.

You already know which of the two lists above you naturally gravitated toward. And, granted, as a seventeen- or eighteen-year-old landing on a college campus for the first time (carrying the weight of an athletic scholarship and the pride of parents, guardians, or an entire "village"), the reason you were recruited as a student-athlete was because of your athletic skill. So, logically, it makes sense to "stick to what got you here."

But here's what makes that natural inclination to simplify tricky. Media coverage of student-athletes around you will reveal many starters or prized recruits who believe they will go pro in their sport. Since they believe they will go to the NFL, NBA, WNBA, NHL, MLB, MLS, LPGA, PGA, WTA, or the Olympics, their goals rarely go beyond numbers 1–3 in list 1. So their goal-setting is simple. Get noticed, get media coverage, get drafted/selected. And the faster the better.

But here's the biggest secret of all that we'll keep repeating in this book: 99 percent of all collegiate student-athletes will never play professionally or represent their country in the Olympic Games.[1] Yes, some will . . . and there is nothing wrong with keeping that particular dream alive . . . but if 100 percent believe they will play professionally and 99 percent will fail at that ambition, then a key secret for the 99 percent is to hedge your bet (even just a little) so you have a safety net for the day your ACL tears or the coaching staff starts taking playing time away from you. If trends hold, on average you have a good sixty-ish years to live after you stop playing a high-performance sport.

The idea of a safety net for college athletes is a well-supported idea based on previous research in the area.[2]

Said another way, college (in general) covers four years. That's approximately 1,400 days, between the first day and graduation, and 200 weeks. If you are an elite athlete, you may train, practice, or compete in your sport during each of those 45 months. But how much will you put into preparation for week 201? That's the week after you graduate and realize you aren't going back to College Station (Texas), Collegeville (Minnesota), or State College (Pennsylvania) that next August.

This is where planning comes in. The building of the safety net. It is the effort you put into everything other than your sport. Sure, there are a lot of hours that will disappear. If you average eight hours of sleep for 1,400 days, you will lose 467 days (almost 16 months) sleeping. That's right . . . 33 percent of your college career will be spent sleeping. Eating won't take up another year but it will take up entire days and months when all the hours are added up.

And how about your sport? If you average three hours a day (every day) in pursuit of your goal of more playing time, you will lose another 175 days. The bottom line? There is less time than you imagine available for establishing and actually accomplishing that "other" priority, professional career success.

So how do you create a plan that lets you master this initial secret?

The very first thing to do is to really understand your schedule. Many around you will assume you are not disciplined enough to set a schedule that fits your long-term goals . . . or even the goals of your head coach. That's why forces beyond your control will set practice times, conditioning times, eating times (Training Table), class times, study times (mandatory Study Hall), injury rehabilitation times, and sometimes even bedtimes.

All of a sudden, one thing missing in your calendar is free time. This is a hard realization for many and it often comes as a surprise to learn that one day you wake up and realize there is no time to hear a guest speaker on campus or to join a campus organization featuring a topic or profession that interests you. The choice has been made for you. Classes, practice, eat, study, sleep. Repeat for seasons on end.

This is not to say that you won't have any free time at all . . . but free time is often not "free" and it is sometimes the hardest time to spend wisely. So, a part of this first secret is learning how to schedule your free time to plan and accomplish the bigger-picture goals you want to achieve.

One trick is developing lists of things you want to do or see. Lists are also fun because you can throw them away as soon as you make them or you can carry them around for years. Lists can be created in spare time, boring time, while eating or, as some people do, as your day starts. They can be "Must Do" lists or "Dreaming to Do" notations. Here are a few to consider:

- Places I Would Like to Visit on Vacation
- Places Where I Would Like to Live
- Dream Jobs
- Books I Would Like to Read
- People I Would Like to Meet
- Potential Mentors I Should Connect With
- Musical Acts I Want to See before I Am 30
- 10 Celebrities I Would Invite to Dinner
- Cars I Would Like to Fix Up and Own
- Hobbies I Would Like to Have
- Grad Schools I Would Consider Attending
- Meals I Would Eat if the Zombie Apocalypse Was Starting in One Week
- Locations Where I Could Outlast the *Walking Dead* Zombies

Your "Dream Jobs" consideration may be the last thing most readers would construct, but in reality, should probably be among the first. Instead, responses such as the ones below are something you may catch yourself saying . . .

- I don't have a dream job. I've never thought about that.
- I want to own the Dallas Cowboys or get hired as the general manager of the New York Rangers.
- My dream job is to work for _____ but I know I could never get them to hire me.
- None of my dream job companies recruit at my university.
- What do you mean by dream job? Do you mean like working for someone cool or just doing a task that's easy?
- What's the difference between a dream job and a dream company?
- Dream jobs don't exist. That's fantasy for people who believe that stuff that if you follow your dreams, you can be happy. Where I come from, there are no dream jobs. Just stupid jobs.

For some, the "Dream Jobs" list would include the following companies:

- Apple or Samsung
- Google or Mozilla Firefox
- Facebook or Twitter
- EA Sports or Activision

- The NFL, WNBA, MMA, WTA, NASCAR, or USOC
- Under Armour or Adidas
- Microsoft or Dell
- Nike or Abercrombie & Fitch
- New York Liberty or the LA Clippers
- ESPN, NBC Sports, or Fox Sports
- Disney or 20th Century Fox

As you can see, the list can feature many potential careers, but the power of the list is that it functions as a vehicle for imagination, creativity, and accomplishment. The old adage that "it won't happen unless you write it down" is true for many and is a strong rationale for lists and plans in general.

One list that is not shown in the many already suggested above is this:

What I Want Out of My Four Years at _____ University.

As an exercise, try making such a list in which you limit yourself to only ten achievements. Then let's see if the hypothetical list we created here (during our imaginary freshman year) would have any similarity to something you might create:

1. Graduate in four years with a 3.5 GPA.

2. Get hired by Nike to work in an area connected to my sport.

3. Make friends with at least four professors who are intellectually stimulating and committed to my success through introductions and networking.

4. Become a member of at least one campus organization that has nothing to do with sports.

5. Participate in an overseas course that is either a semester abroad or a shorter study tour in another country (less than twenty-one days).

6. Give back to my sport or college community by coaching or using my team's access to less-privileged individuals.

7. Make three lifelong friends who will be there for me when times are tough (and for whom I will be there when they need me).

8. Get real about how much I will owe in college loans or in appreciation for those who helped me get through college for free.

9. Read four books that were not assigned but that will stretch my imagination or stimulate my intellectual curiosity.

10.   Dominate my friends in video games such as *EA SPORTS FIFA, Madden NFL,* or *Call of Duty: Black Ops.*

Bonus Extra: Cure cancer, walk on the moon, get my screenplay purchased, record with Beyoncé.

Bonus Plus: Actually take the time to do another Top 10 list.

Again, you should see that the creation of the list is not hard, but committing to the plan that will deliver the itemized outcomes requires long-term awareness. The other piece in the puzzle is figuring out how to evaluate progress toward your various goals. When a student starts his or her freshman year, graduation seems light years away. Four years. At least 120 credits. So many term papers and final exams.

Sheesh. It's hard, then, to write "Graduate in four years with a 3.5 GPA." But if that is the goal, the 3.5 GPA allows for semester-by-semester evaluation. Like an athlete, you will have either exceeded your goal or missed it. If you are ahead, you make plans for leveraging that success. If you are behind, you need to make adjustments. GPA is a great example of the kind of thing to evaluate since it is measurable semester by semester, course by course.

Football movies are famous for their stirring halftime speeches in which the coach convinces the players to put their first half mistakes behind them, to overcome their distrust of each other, to block out the distractions of the crowd and "win one for the Gipper" or some other clichéd personage (how about the speech in *Rudy* or inspirational words said to Michael Oher in *The Blind Side)*. Sometimes players get chewed out at halftime. Sometimes players get the silent treatment. But invariably, the announcers covering the game, witnessing a great comeback, suggest that adjustments "must've gotten made at halftime and would you look at how this team is responding!"

You should feel the same about your ability to adjust. Traditionally, school years are usually broken into semesters (two) or quarters (three) and after final exams there is a point when you know your GPA for the grading period and therefore for your academic career so far. You know whether you are meeting NCAA academic progress requirements, are eligible, are likely to get announced as having made the Dean's List, or maybe have a shot at making an All-Conference Academic list.

If your grades aren't what you want, then adjustments must be made. Perhaps your adjustments include one or more of the following:

• Paying more attention to course details

• Skipping fewer classes

• Changing studying habits

- Working with different tutors
- Studying with different friends
- Allowing more time for homework and test prep
- Making more time to meet professors and getting to know them
- Asking for help earlier in the semester
- Making a commitment to do better by working harder
- Allocating more time to studying

Perhaps, as you read this, you have never had, nor expect to have, grades that fall below your expectations. If that's the case, you can move on to any of the other items listed above in "What I Want Out of My Four Years at _____ University."

The second bullet point is getting a job at Nike, and while we randomly selected that particular company, the goal can be evaluated just like grades. If you want to work in athletic apparel and equipment when you graduate (or technology, media, medicine, or music), the same approach to accomplishment can be evaluated regularly (and often with the help of a list that is focused on the goal):

- Whom did I meet from my desired industry this term?
- What did I read about my desired company this month?
- Who at my school knows someone working in the field I want to enter?
- How can I get networked to an employee at my dream company?
- What more did I learn about the field I want to work in?
- Will I be ready for a job interview (or internship opportunity) if one suddenly materializes?

Interim measurable goals could be a class project opportunity, a consulting project, a practicum, or an internship with that company or one in its field.

CHAPTER SUMMARY

One of the most important secrets to learn during your time in college is how to create a plan for success that that leads to a desirable outcome. It is not as simple as creating random lists (although that can certainly help) or banking on the hope that things will fall into place for you. An essential element is establishing concrete goals and having a true desire to accomplish those goals and "check them off." This is what will lay the foundation for you to position yourself for career success.

ERIK PRICE
(Associate Commissioner at the Pac-12 Conference)

I think it's very important to have an academic plan, do internships, and travel during the summer. Traveling exposes you to new perspectives and provides you with new experiences. You don't necessarily have to have a plan that is divorced from being an athlete, such as coaching, training, or strength and conditioning. I have seen a lot of student-athletes be successful and go into ancillary careers such as those. Every student-athlete should have two paths that they want to follow that are not "playing sports" related, so that the last time you suit up, you are not in a crisis afterwards. For example, one of the most important parts of your plan is graduating, and having a graduate school plan because advanced degrees are what help you get the jobs that you can sit in for life, generally speaking.

Goals may change and dreams may get upended . . . but failing to plan is planning to fail. Why let that happen when a little effort can set anyone on a path to a much more fulfilling future?

Secret 2 Understand Who a Student-Athlete Is

Author Viewpoint—DR. NORM O'REILLY

I was fortunate enough to be a student-athlete during both my undergraduate degree (Nordic skiing at the University of Waterloo) and master degrees (swimming at the University of Ottawa). Although they are two major Canadian universities, Waterloo and Ottawa would be the equivalent of Division II colleges in the United States (from an athletics perspective). Both have formal and resourced athletic departments and a full slate of sports, but scholarships are low, facilities sufficient (but not great), and ticket sales for events low or nonexistent in some sports.

I believe I was successful as a student-athlete: getting named an Academic All-Canadian, requiring both academic and athletic success. Life as a student-athlete was challenging, to say the least, and full of sacrifices, mostly on the social front. Parties missed, events declined, hanging-out with my roommates at a minimum.

As an undergraduate student, in a challenging science program, I was very focused on individual learning (lots of studying) and a large amount of class time: 15 hours in class and 15 hours in labs. Five days a week of classes, including Friday afternoon labs. As a graduate student, less class time but enormous responsibilities as teaching assistant, research assistant, and reading.

As an athlete, I focused efforts on competing and performing at a high level. My sports were both individual but with training and competition as part of a team. Between 15 and 25 hours per week training and at least 10 weekends away each academic year for competition, sometimes more. 5 a.m. practices regularly. Friday night practice. Saturday/Sunday morning practice. Team meetings. Coach consultations. All on top of challenging academic schedules.

I don't believe my experience is atypical for most student-athletes.

THE SECRET IN A FEW WORDS

Secret 1 told you to follow a plan. This is vital to the student-athlete or really to anyone with any objective at all. This leads us to Secret 2, which will give context to your plan. You are a student-athlete. Being a student-athlete is a special experience, and a privileged one. Yes, a small percentage of student-athletes are super-privileged and may go professional, but this book is not for them. It is for you, someone who will live four years of your life in a unique way. Like Spider-Man and Peter Parker, you've got a double role, even a double personality.[1] And, you need to be very good at and focused on each.

On one hand, you are a high-performance athlete. Respected by other students, under massive pressure from your coach and teammates, fortunate to have a scholarship (in many cases), and surrounded by support structures that few athletes of your level outside of the NCAA can even dream about. On the other hand, you're a student, one of more than sixteen million college students in the USA, a learner making your way in the world, trying to get ahead, and seeking a job one day. You have to approach each role separately, find time for each, and be successful in each. Get poor grades and you are off the team. Bad performance on the field, no more scholarship. Yes, your privileged role is coupled with a lot of pressure. And, wow, you get to do this for four amazing years. Many of those sixteen million would change spots with you in a heartbeat. So, the secret is simple: know who you are, relish it, and leverage it to the max. It will be, for many if not most of you, the best years of your life.

UNDERSTAND WHO A STUDENT-ATHLETE IS: A STUDENT-ATHLETE OR AN ATHLETE-STUDENT?

This book and the secrets within it are written for student-athletes who will not go pro. Several of the authors of the book were athletes in this situation. The gender of student-athletes is a factor to consider because—although male and female athletes alike rarely manage to become professional athletes—there are statistically more opportunities (though still very few) for male student-athletes, so female student-athletes often have a better understanding than their male counterparts of the reality of being a typical student-athlete.

There are many contexts comparable to this reality. Think about music, where very few who dream of performing professionally ever establish a career as a professional musician. And, of those who do, few achieve the success they dreamed of. The same can be said for fashion designers, authors, journalists, and artists. Although some do "make it," most need to find another path to a sustainable career and a life outside of their passion.

As a full-time student in college in the United States,[2] you are one of sixteen million. However, as an NCAA student-athlete, you are one of fewer than five hundred thousand. Yes, only 1 in 32 students in the USA has the status you do. You are special. You have earned privileges.

However, with great power comes great responsibility.

So, "special" and "privileged" are coupled with "pressure" and "risk." Let us explain.

The path for most student-athletes in most sports is similar (and we're quite certain you can relate). As a high school student, you were likely the big fish. Academically you did very well (or well enough), and athletically you were a star. You won championships, you captained your team, other teams in your district feared facing you, the media attention in school and local publications piled up, and you've got boxes of awards, medals, and honors that most of your friends covet.

Yes, you were a big deal. And, because you were that big deal, fortune shone on you and you got the chance to become an NCAA student-athlete. Perhaps you're a Division I, Division II, or Division III recruit. You might be on a "full-ride" scholarship or you might have "walked on" and barely made the team. Whatever the path, you delivered the academic and athletic credentials to become a 1-in-32 student-athlete.

Very cool. You have the "power." But, the pond just got bigger. You're still a big fish but with a lot more swimming to do! And let's be clear, there are fish bigger than you. There always are.

So, what exactly is the great responsibility you face? Well, it manifests itself as pressure, and it has multiple sources:

1. Your parents (grandparents, guardians): You are the apple of their eyes, they brag about you at their local curling club, golf club, favorite pub, and with their friends. They have likely invested in you over the years (athletically, academically, and even financially) to help with your training and your studies. They may also be the type of parents who exerted pressure on you to perform. And, even if they don't directly exert any pressure, the perception of such is likely there. If you need clarification on this point, just imagine what would happen if you failed two classes one semester, lost your scholarship, and got kicked off your team. How would you tell your parents (or grandparents or guardians)? How hard would that be? How disappointed would they be?

2. Your friends (who are not teammates): Your core social group, your high school group of friends, will love you no matter what,

but you've likely built your image and your "self" around being a star athlete, and now a student-athlete, so that expectation is there. You'll feel the pressure here if anything starts to slip . . .

3. Your college coach: You were likely comfortable with your high school or club coach as you developed, but now you're in college. Your coach likely recruited you, selected you over others, and helped you get that amazing scholarship. But now put yourself in your coach's shoes. College coaches are fired often; turnover is frequent and the pressure on them to win is extremely high. This pressure is transferred to the athletes (you), who often feel a need and a pressure to perform "for their coach."

4. Your college teammates: Again, back home, in high school or club, you were likely with your buddies or boy/girlfriends. Now, you're with a bunch of teammates, some older than you, some competing with you, some who may rely on you for their success or who may hope you fail so they can play more. Some teammates will probably become lifelong friends and may even have the same academic major as you. Other teammates may not; they may be rivals or live a completely different life (in a different academic program). Whether friend (counting on you) or foe (wanting your playing time), teammates will be a source of pressure as well.

5. Your partner (if you have one): This is a relationship that we will delve into in much detail in a later "secret" in this book, but it is one to be cautious about. Either a relationship from home or a new one at college is a source of major pressure and can compromise any student-athlete who must already live two lives. Only a very supportive partner can work, even if that partner is also a student-athlete, and even then, this is a source of stress.

6. Your hometown media: If you are from a city of more than a million people, you can skip this one. But if you represent a small hometown, this is a big commitment and an important responsibility. You could find, like one of this book's authors who comes from a town of fifteen thousand people, that you remain a media personality in your town's local publications many years after your athletic career. This manifests itself in pressure to represent your town, pressure to continue to perform for and contribute to family and friends, and time pressure from the requirements of setting up calls, giving interviews, responding to questions, and maintaining a social media presence.

7. Your Athletic Department: Off-the-field commitments will come from many sources in your university's athletic department.

Media interviews. Pep rallies. Athlete councils (like SAAC). Team meetings. Anti-doping seminars. Marketing. And much more.

Be wary of these commitments: they are "time-eaters" and bring their own political pressure.

These seven sources of responsibility (aka pressure) are certainly not an exhaustive list, but they are ones we believe will affect almost all student-athletes. Depending on your particular situation, you will have other sources of responsibility (e.g., a part-time job, a sick parent) and pressure (e.g., a need to travel home, sleep deprivation) that you need to deal with.

MAX DITTMER (former swimming student-athlete at the University of Iowa, Associate Business and Store Planner at Under Armour)

My parents for the most part were hands-off and supportive for whatever/whenever I needed them. I can't imagine the extra pressure added if they weren't the way they are, and I am thankful for that.

Academics were never a problem for me personally, so as long as I was maintaining good grades as expected, I had almost no conversations or pressure from my parents about the academic side of things. However, the pressure from them was put on me at a young age to maintain good grades. Therefore, the pressure of getting good grades just became an internal pressure.

The pressure I received from athletics was more just wanting myself to succeed and be happy. I was always very positive, and never negative. I never felt any pressure from anyone else's end if I didn't succeed or do as well as I hoped.

My friends didn't add any academic or athletic pressure, but more social pressure. I always got the "come out with us," "skip practice," or "go to practice hung over." From the coaches' standpoint, it depends on the coach, but for the most part they were supportive in both areas, but definitely they were more focused on the athletic side.

For academics, the coaches would give me relative accommodations, but practice/competitions for the most part trumped all. Everything else should be scheduled around these. I remember receiving pressure during finals weeks from coaches for missing practices when we were on "break" and "no required practices" to allow for academic focus during finals week. Essentially you would be shamed for missing unless your test was during finals. That was hard to deal with. For swimming, there was lots of pressure to perform, but never negatively stated if you performed bad, just positive reinforcement when you performed well.

Teammates would pressure me to just stay eligible, that's it. Athletically, there was pressure and expectations to perform well, come to practice and try hard. If you were slacking for any reason, your teammates would let you know about it.

The hometown media for Iowa didn't have any backlash academically because the swim team had a great GPA, and athletically, it was mainly positive because we were never under the scrutiny that a football or basketball team would be under. But, the swim team constantly improved over my 4 years, and I do know that there was some media backlash in later years after I left with all the new facilities and a small decline in performance.

The pressures from the Athletic Department were definitely vocalized more on the academics side than the athletics. Our academic help was need-based in the sense that if you sustained above a 3.0 for consecutive semesters, you did not have to log study hours, but if you were below you would need anywhere from four to twelve hours a week. For athletics, not a huge showing from the AD for swimming. During the fundraising years for the new pool, it was more noticeable, but being a non-revenue sport, we were not the main focus so expectations weren't as big as for other revenue-generating sports.

Even for the most successful student-athletes, life is challenging and full of sacrifices.

To delve further into the student-athlete role, we interviewed Anson Dorrance, currently the head coach of the women's soccer program at the University of North Carolina, and the winningest women's soccer coach of all time. He agreed with the special status of the student-athlete and emphasized the importance of realizing the opportunity and how fragile it can be. He emphasized that "there are so many things you can feed that will derail you if you have ambitions academically and athletically but also in terms of character development." Each of your sources of responsibility must be planned for and managed in the context of the "double objective" of academic success and athletic excellence. Clearly, Secret 1 relies on understanding Secret 2!

So, what can you do? What is Secret 2 really telling us?

From our perspective, there are five things you need to do.

1.   *Realize that you are special and fortunate.* The opportunity to both continue to progress your life (i.e., study toward the pursuit of a career) and concurrently be a high-performance athlete in arguably the top sport development system in the world is an experience to cherish and one you will miss (and often talk about) when you are older. The combination of your two lives will help you build character. Embrace the student-athlete status role and put your focus on those two outcomes, little else. Dan Butterly, Senior Associate Commissioner for the Mountain West Conference, explains very clearly why you want to realize the unique student-athlete role.

Student-athletes continue to be outstanding leaders. That has not changed over the years. There are tremendous traits student-athletes have that they often undersell on their resume or during a job interview. Team building, how to deal with adversity, excellent health and wellness, leadership traits and a zest for success. One of the great trends I have seen from this generation of student-athletes compared to previous student-athletes is how they venture outside their own sport, come together with student-athletes in other sports, and have created a significant voice and leadership group not only to make the NCAA better, but by leading, they will make their generation better too. When I was an undergraduate, I heard student-athletes from other teams often complain about all the great resources football and men's basketball received. Now, many of those same benefits are available to all student-athletes because of the voice this generation of student-athletes has put forth.

As Butterly emphasizes, the successful completion of your plan (Secret 1) and deep understanding of the privileged role you are in (this secret) will launch your career.

2. *Be a student AND an athlete.* Many student-athletes in the "other 99 percent," even though they realize that a professional career or Olympic opportunity is not probable, still view themselves as athletes first and not as a student. If you know you will not play professionally, you must view yourself as a student first (or at least tied for first) in all things and all activities. Glenn Schembechler, a former scout and coach, and now counsel to athletes, provides the following support:

High school athletes who earn a college scholarship aren't getting it for the right reason. Many high school athletes don't identify themselves as students first. They see it as this opportunity for just sports, with school on the side; as opposed to getting school paid for and getting to play sports. You need to identify yourself as a student first because you need to have a realistic outlook on where you are going to go after playing sports in college.

However, what Schembechler outlines is much easier to say than to do. So, you must make being a student as important as (if not more important than) being an athlete. A balanced approach is highly recommended.

Schembechler supports a couple of specific points that we want to emphasize within this secret. The first is related to the choice of major or degree or area of concentration. Often, as student-athletes, you are so focused on sport and competition that you just want "a degree." You may not think about where your interest is for a career postcollege. The focus is on picking some classes that fit your training schedule and will allow you to graduate in four years.

But if that's the case, you are not spending enough time thinking about what you should be taking in order set yourself up for a career postgraduation. Student-athletes are often too busy to meet with an advisor or to get to know a professor, or to even consider who their favorite professor is! Setting yourself up for success after college needs to be a priority. You need to find your passion outside of your sport. Schembechler agreed and gave some great advice: "Find something that you are passionate about so that you can wake up and give a 100 percent effort to it each day. If you aren't passionate, you are going to fall behind quickly in anything you do."

This advice is very appropriate, and following it is not beyond the time or resources available to any student-athlete. Before your season starts, or on a quiet weekend, spend some time thinking about what you love, what your favorite class is. Then, get to know a professor or two (or four!) in that area, get some advice, and get into the program you are interested in (one that ideally has job opportunities). And, in this effort, reach out to family members, friends, and others who know those areas, have connections, and can help advise you on great choices.

The second piece of advice we'd like to emphasize is the vital importance to get work experience during your four years as a student-athlete. Of course, this is easier said than done, given your busy schedule of academics and athletics. Schembechler advises that you have to "take advantage of the opportunities to do internships and other experiences so that you can dip your toes into the industry of focus." This is a key point. To get ahead in most fields today (engineering, business, health professions, technical, etc.), the more experiences you have on your resume, the better you will do and the more competitive you will be for jobs.

Quite simply, four years of being a student-athlete cannot compete—in most cases—with a well-prepared graduate who is not an athlete but who has a practicum, two internships, an independent study with an expert in the field, and related summer jobs. This is not to say that one path is better than the other, but just to underline the reality that a student-athlete faces at the end of senior year. So how do you do this? How do you fit these practical experiences into your busy life? Well, a few pieces of advice.

First, you need to network with the right people, inside and outside the university. Inside, this includes career coaches, advisors, faculty members, researchers, and administrators (including deans and support staff). These are people who have your best interests at heart, contacts in your field, and a mandate to help you. But they won't be able to help you unless they know who you are and unless you ask. Get to know them, attend events, join clubs and student organizations. Sure, you have to balance this with your training and competition, but that is no excuse. You have off-seasons, downtime, days off, and free time. The trick is to replace some of the "useless" activities like watching TV and playing video games with positive ones. Instead of going out one night, join a student club in your area of interest. Instead of sleeping in one day, go to a career fair. These are very simple choices, with very significant positive outcomes.

Second, figure out what you want to do. As noted earlier, meet with advisors, professors, and more. Find a mentor. Connect with a professor. Meet a graduate student. But take that a step further and include this in your plan from Secret 1. Write down your career choices. Your "dream job" (in real life, not as an athlete) postgraduation. Outline what you need to do to get competitive for that job at graduation and go do it.

3. *Be responsible for building your own character.* When you are trying to balance the pursuit of academic success and high-performance sport, it becomes difficult to focus on other elements of what it takes to be a successful person. Some student-athletes have these traits and high-quality characters but many do not. UNC's Anson Dorrance provided the following response when we asked him about this:

> From my perspective, the definition of student-athlete is that this is part of a process to become a better human being. A critical quality I think most of us overlook when we are evaluating a student-athlete is character development . . . The main priority for someone coming into college as an athlete is to develop his or her character and there are some fantastic benefits to that. I think there is a direct correlation between developing your own character and having a successful athletic and academic career.

Dorrance went on to explain that it is you, the student-athlete, who needs to take responsibility for your own character development:

> Student-athletes are supervisors of their own development. They get to guide their own development and obviously most critically, their character development. They also are the supervisors of their own academic world and their athletic world as well. . . . [It] is very critical for any [student-athlete] to understand their opportunity to shape their own future based on the standards they set for themselves. The responsibility they take for themselves.

Practically, what Dorrance advises is very important. You need to take responsibility. You need to plan for your career. You need to do the research to determine what career path (major, courses, internships, etc.) is best for you and will get you a job after graduation.

HILLARY (BACH) NELSON
(former softball student-athlete at Arizona State University, Partnerships Manager at Positive Coaching Alliance)

Some people enjoy expectations and some people don't enjoy the added pressure. I would say, for those that do, use it as confidence. Your coach or your parent, whoever is putting those expectations on you, they think you're capable or else they wouldn't be asking you to do this. If they are starting you in a big game, it's because they know you can be successful. I never met a coach who tried to lose. So, if they're putting you in there, take it as a really big sign of confidence and enjoy it. Enjoy that pressure and go out there and show them that they were right, prove them right. If you don't enjoy the expectations, try focusing on smaller goals. If the expectation is to pitch a shutout game against the big rival, try focusing on winning every inning or winning each batter or winning each pitch. I want to throw a curveball outside. Did I hit that spot? No. OK, I lost that pitch, but let me win this next pitch. Focus on those small things that you can control, just like your effort on each play or that positive attitude that will help you keep your mind off of the bigger picture.

---

4.   *Be career focused*. This point builds upon the others and and is quite simple. Think about your career, alongside your training and competition goals, as a focus of your plans, your choices, your efforts. It is about planning for life after graduation right from the get-go. It is about understanding why joining a student

club in your area of interest is better than a night of television each week. In his interview, Schembechler captured this point clearly: "As a student-athlete, you need to realize that you are going to have to change your mindset to be ready for a career. It's all a matter of who you associate yourself with that allows you to change that mindset." In order to accomplish this, he advises that you "have to study what the market is like of the industry you want to go into."

5. *Maintain relationships outside your sport.* When you come to college as a freshman on scholarship, it is very easy to build your entire social network at college around your team and your teammates. You will spend a lot of time with them, and often you won't have any close friends from high school who are nearby. Chris Dawson, a former student-athlete, and associate commissioner at the Pac-12 Conference, explained this very clearly:

> I think student-athletes can best prepare for the transition out of sport by making sure that when they're still an active athlete they maintain other relationships and other interests to the greatest extent possible. If your whole world is your team, which is very easy to do when you're a college athlete, then you lose your support system when your athletics career is over and you lose your sense of identity. I think that the transition can be smoother when you understand that it's going to happen to you at some point. It's going to be a different point for different people.

CHAPTER SUMMARY

The three things you can take out of this chapter (if you remember nothing else from what you just read) are these:

1. Have an understanding of who you are and what opportunity you have in front of you. Focus on the NOW with the future in mind and the past in the rearview mirror.

2. Build your character and take responsibility for your actions. As Jim Rohn once said, "You must take personal responsibility. You cannot change the circumstances, the seasons, or the wind, but you can change yourself."

3. Rise to the challenge, don't let the pressure get to you, focus on your career, be a great student, and create relationships outside of the teammates you are with 24/7.

Secret 3 — Ride Your Success Wheel

Current student-athletes sometimes have trouble succeeding in both athletics and school.[1] Being a student-athlete is like having a full-time job to go along with school. The average person works forty hours in a week, and a student-athlete is putting in at least seventy-five hours of work a week in just school and sports alone. No one said it was easy, but a little help can go a long way. This chapter will provide strategies for how to succeed as a student-athlete and get set up for success in life after sports with your success wheel.

As we've said before, being a student-athlete is a privilege and also a choice. Student-athletes are among the hardest-working students on campus because of their dual commitments, but that doesn't mean they are held to lower standards academically. The institution and athletic department want to be known for having great student-athletes who can succeed in both academics and athletics.

RIDE YOUR SUCCESS WHEEL

If you are a student-athlete who thinks that you don't have time to put a 100 percent effort into both academics and athletics, you are wrong. Colby Targun, a former student-athlete at Texas State University, played both football and baseball for all four years. He now works for the NFL at the league's headquarters in New York City, and says, "Having the proper balance between academics, athletics, and social life is imperative to being successful as a student-athlete. All this while having attention [to] detail, organization, and a drive to succeed will make for a great experience."

Colby says he had three priorities as a student-athlete that led to his success as both a student and an athlete. He summarizes his priorities: "Having my coursework completed in time and receiving good grades, performing on the playing field, and developing myself as a person overall (working on relationships, my future, etc.)." He remembers, "I was always working to get as far ahead as possible with my coursework, therefore allowing me to focus as much as I could on football or baseball, whichever season it may be." One of the greatest things he learned from his success was his "relationship skills in being teammates with all walks of life." He further emphasizes that it "is important to be able to relate to anybody you meet in some way."

Colby advises student-athletes to "have an eye on the future, but also live in the moment. Don't worry about the next chapter so much that you miss out on your junior and senior year. Everything will work out eventually as it should if you are prepared."

THE STUDENT-ATHLETE SUCCESS WHEEL

In writing this chapter, we reviewed previous work in the area (e.g., Comeaux and Harrison 2011),[2] built on our own experiences and backgrounds, brainstormed, and developed our own version of a "success wheel" that you can follow and use to track your efforts and decisions as you progress through your experiences as a student-athlete. The following graphic depicts the wheel.

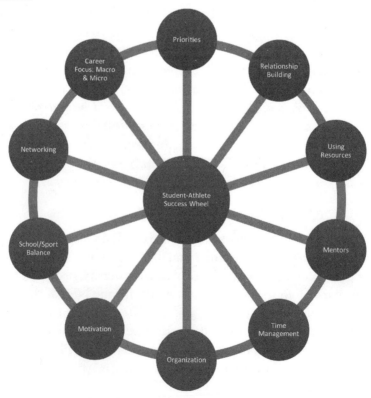

The Success Wheel, shown on the previous page, highlights the top ten aspects of how to succeed as a student-athlete. Each of these aspects, or spokes on the wheel, is discussed in detail in the following paragraphs. The core idea behind the success wheel is that each aspect builds on the others to cumulatively drive your success.

Priorities: Priorities are arguably the step where the success wheel starts to turn. It is extremely important that you prioritize your time—your most important resource. Sleep is incredibly important for an athlete's success, and you should aim to get an average of eight hours a night. That leaves, again on average, sixteen hours in a day to do everything else. Class and homework will take up a minimum of five hours a day. Training, practice, and competitions will occupy close to six hours on average daily. Eating, bio-breaks, and any other obligations get the leftover five hours maximum during the day. If you are dating someone or in a relationship, you need to make time for that person. Same with friends and social time with teammates. A social life is important, as well as any other extracurricular activities. If you want to be successful, having your priorities written out is a must. Prioritizing your time is crucial in becoming the best all-around student-athlete you can possibly be.

Relationship Building: Once you've set your priorities, building relationships that are key to those priorities is crucial in constructing a support system around what you are trying to focus on and achieve as a student-athlete. Aside from your family, creating relationships with coaches, teammates, professors, and friends is the minimum. Over the years, you will figure out the people you can rely on, trust, and go to for help. By building each relationship, you will gain support in the important areas of life. Developing relationships (e.g., a favorite professor becomes a mentor) that create trust in people to seek advice from is extremely important in making educated decisions on important life, career, academic, and athletic choices.

Using Resources: Universities and colleges provide multiple resources for students, and you should take advantage of them. Again, these resources should align with your priorities and relationship-building efforts. The array of resources the university provides might include a tutor, librarian, mentor, career coach, psychologist, nutritionist, athletic trainer, or anyone else who is there to help you become the best student-athlete you can possibly imagine. The extra effort and time you devote to using these resources can make a huge impact on your college experience. You won't have all of these great "free" resources after you graduate, so why not take advantage of them now?

Mentors: An example of an ideal relationship (from a prior spoke (or leg) of the success wheel) is a mentorship relationship in which you connect to a key person who will help guide you through your decisions and life steps. Not everyone has a mentor, but we strongly advise you to work to find one. If you have more than one, even better. No two people have the same type of mentor and no mentor-mentee relationship is the same. Mentors are people who have experienced what you are going through and can offer advice or help for many situations. Mentors tend to be older than you, but someone who is just a few years older may be able to provide a more recent perspective on things. Depending on how the relationship works, age doesn't really matter. Find a mentor who cares about your personal development and long-term success.

Time Management: The previous elements all support the implementation of time management. Time management is the efficiency with which you use your time. It is important to any student in any context, but it is extremely crucial to a student-athlete. It sounds like such a simple aspect of life, but may be one of the hardest. Time management is a skill, and it can be acquired through experience. This is a skill that translates best into the working world, because it directly relates to priorities (i.e., if you know your priorities, you can allocate your time) and use of your valuable resource of time (i.e., the better your time management skills, the more efficient you can be with your efforts and the more activities you can fit into a busy schedule).

Organization: Organization may sound like a simple term (that usually gets overlooked), but it truly plays a large role in the success of a student-athlete. In the context of the wheel, once you know your priorities, relationships to build, resources available, and time plans, getting organized is a key next step. With how much goes on in one day, you must be organized in terms of where you need to be at certain times, and what is due and when. A calendar can be very useful, as well as utilizing technology for reminders and notes. Ultimately, organization helps you prioritize your activities and stay on top of what you need to achieve. A lack of organization will cause extra stress, missed deadlines, and possible tardiness. Being organized helps show responsibility and assertiveness, two important characteristics. And make sure you know what the difference is between time management and organization.

Motivation: Student-athletes must be motivated in the classroom, in the weight room, and at practice. Motivation stems from wanting to be successful, but the motivation must be for the right reasons. It comes from you, not your parents, your coach, or anyone else. The only person who can truly motivate you is yourself.

School/Sport Balance: As you build your plan for time, resources, mentors, networking, and other aspects, a balance between your dual objectives is important. Many coaches and administrators will argue about the relative importance of school and sport. However, the term "student-athlete" means that being a student takes priority over being an athlete. Today, we see a lot of "athlete-students." Don't be an athlete-student. Take pride in your education and understand your sport participation as a key aspect of the student experience.

However, regardless of what you think, stay balanced. Some readers may balance the two areas 50/50 and some may balance it 60/40 or 40/60. There is no "right" balance as long as you are aware of where your balance should be and where it actually is. Knowing that your high-level athletic career likely won't continue after you graduate, why wouldn't academics take priority?

Networking: Closely aligned with mentorship, networking is widely known to be one of the most important characteristics of success. More than ever in today's society, it is all about who you know, not necessarily what you know. As a student-athlete, you have more opportunities to network than any other student. You are automatically connected with alumni from your sport, as well as with coaches and administrators, plus their networks. Why not leverage those opportunities and network? Find out what they really do, how they got to where they are, and what you can learn from them about different career paths.

People are more likely to hire someone they know or share a common bond with, and the more people you know, the more connected you will be. If one individual cannot directly help you, that person may know someone who can. Build your network of contacts and use LinkedIn to network as well. Networking is extremely important because it allows you to develop relationships over an extended period of time. The longer you can build a relationship with someone, the more that individual will be willing to do something good for you.

From the collective experience of the authors, we know that much of the above narrative sounds trite. If you find that many pieces of advice sound repetitive and obvious, that's because "Trite is Right." After many years in the sports business, we believe there is no such thing as a network that is too big. One of us recently met an Olympic swimmer who will soon graduate from college. She was interested in looking into career opportunities in sport business. Her swimming network is extensive, but her network outside of swimming is small. We spoke about how to extend her connections with the same competitive fire she brought to the pool in her swimming career. Right after our discussion, a meeting with a team executive resulted in opening up another group of contacts. However large and influential you think your network is, it isn't as big as you will need. Digital networking tools are helpful, but face-to-face interactions pay the greatest dividends in advancing a career.

Career Focus, Macro and Micro: Having an idea of what you want to do after college is something you may not think about until your junior or senior year. At that point, it is often too late. Later in the book we will explain why you should be thinking about this in your sophomore year. You should develop a macro career focus in the field of study you desire, and this will help you pick a major, and create a broad career path.

Within your macro focus, you also require a micro focus, a specific part of the industry or field that you want to drill down on. This may change as your experiences help shape this focus. An example of a micro focus would be wanting to work in financial planning within the business field. Another example would be wanting to work in event operations, but focusing on customer service.

If you can see the end at the beginning, you aren't going to get off to a very good start. This one is all about multitasking. The most valuable athletes are those who can play the most positions or at least know what everyone's responsibilities are. Same goes for the professional world. If you have a marketing focus, learn finance. If you are thinking about player personnel, gain experience in sales. If you have a desire to work in a particular career, it is always important not to develop tunnel vision. Never get so micro that you can't keep your eye on the big picture. The 360-degree view is the best.

SECRET: RIDE YOUR SUCCESS WHEEL

Your success wheel will be different than that of your teammates, and your wheel is always customizable to the success you desire. This is one of those occasions where it really is about you. Consider your wheel your guide and road map to live by while in college. Most of the aspects in your wheel will apply to life as well, which is why it is even more important to develop your wheel early, to update it often and—most important—to follow it closely.

Bill Shumard, a former Division I Athletic Director, and now CEO of Special Olympics Southern California, provides a unique perspective on what parts of the success wheel he thinks are most important. He notes "having served as Director of Athletics at two NCAA Division 1 universities, I believe the student-athletes' 'success wheel' is indicative of the key components making up the life of a student-athlete." Shumard's perspective provided considerable input into the success wheel we present here. The following box provides his view on the three most important aspects (in his view) of the wheel of success.

BILL SHUMARD
(CEO of Special Olympics Southern California)

Mentors

As I look back upon my career that has spanned more than four decades in collegiate, professional, and amateur sports, my ability to select and emulate strong mentors has been a key ingredient to any success I may have enjoyed. Fred Miller was the Athletics Director at Long Beach State when I was an undergrad student working in the Sports Information Office. I admired Fred's leadership style and his ability to be the "face and voice" of the university's athletics program. He was clearly the one who first inspired me to pursue a career path to become an AD.

When I moved to the Los Angeles Dodgers, I was part of a front office team that was included among "America's Top 100 Companies" because of our strong ethics and impeccable business practices. I reported to Executive Vice-President Fred Claire, who was chiefly responsible for the Dodgers' uniquely successful organizational culture. I patterned many of the habits and disciplines I practice after Fred's leadership. When I moved to the collegiate level, I reported to Mike McGee, the AD at USC. Mike was a former football player and coach, with a doctoral degree in business & organizational leadership. Mike's sense of loyalty and unwavering financial acumen made a strong impression on me and patterned my own success as an AD.

When I became AD at my alma mater, Long Beach State, my president—Bob Maxson—had a strong background AND a keen interest in intercollegiate athletics and how it should be positioned/prioritized on a college campus. Dr. Maxson epitomized the power of encouragement, and brought a great sense of pride and tradition to a relatively young university. My leadership style is largely part-and-parcel of the leadership habits of Claire, McGee, and Maxson. I recognized each of them as a strong, admirable leader and would regularly pick their respective brains on a multitude of topics. I was fortunate that they took the time and thought enough of me to invest in my future. I will be eternally grateful.

Networking

A student-athlete has an incredible opportunity to meet and connect with a multitude of diverse people—including university administrators and faculty; coaches and support staff; boosters and volunteers; other student-athletes; the campus; and the community at large. While the student-athlete has many competing priorities during their time in college, connecting and establishing relationships with like-minded people at various stages of life and career is invaluable.

The student-athlete must begin to establish a reputation of integrity, trustworthiness, and loyalty to everyone in their respective universe. This will set the student-athlete apart from others and will lead to initial opportunities in establishing a career while building life-long relationships. I would also note that the student-athlete should establish themselves as a "giver" and not a "taker." In other words, always be willing to help others in need instead of just asking for favors and advantages. This is an important part of character development.

Time Management

It is a safe assumption that a student-athlete's weekly schedule, in the midst of a competitive season, is in the neighborhood of 70–80 hours a week. When you factor in class time, study hall, practice, physical training, training room, and travel, the student-athlete's time demands are incredible. When I was an

AD, I would tell our student-athletes that, if they were successful in managing their collegiate career and obtained a degree, time management of their actual career would be relatively easy in comparison. Being a collegiate student-athlete prepares one for a successful personal and professional life that can be rich and full. As one matures and moves through life after college—establishing a career; perhaps getting married and starting a family; and becoming a productive member of society—having mastered time management as a student-athlete in college will be a key ingredient in that success.

The success wheel as developed and outlined above is a useful tool for student-athletes. So, where do you start? Let us provide a few straightforward steps to follow.

Step 1: Create Your Own Success Wheel

Review the ten aspects of the success wheel explained above and create your own "wheel" with each aspect defined specifically for your situation and reality.

Step 2: Follow Your Success Wheel and Revisit It Frequently

It is one thing to just create your success wheel, but another thing to follow it. Revisit your wheel at least once a month and track your progress against each aspect of your wheel. Importantly, while tracking your progress, make sure you hold yourself accountable. It is easy to get caught up in everything going on around you and forget your wheel. Don't be that slacker!

Author Viewpoint—JAKE HIRSHMAN

I graduated with my undergraduate degree in three years while also being a student-athlete, and I couldn't have done it without my success wheel. Of course there are other aspects outside of the wheel that are important, but we thought these were the most important and overlapping.

I prioritized my academics over athletics because I knew my chances of going pro were slim, especially with the mix of injuries I had. I was driven to reach my goals and succeed in baseball, but it was more important to get good grades and gain experiences to build up my resume.

My relationship-building started in my sophomore year as I started to have classes for my major. I created relationships with my professors, coaches, teammates, and other administrators around campus. Looking back, this helped open doors for opportunities during the following year of school.

At the University of Redlands, I took advantage of the career development office because I was able to receive help on interview preparation for graduate schools. I was able to get my resume reviewed and other key skills sharpened.

Obtaining multiple mentors while I was in college was one of the best things I could have done. Bill Shumard, Fred Claire, Tony Miller, and John Lombardo are just a few of many who served as mentors for me throughout my time as a student-athlete. Their help, advice, and ability to seek out opportunities for me was invaluable in my success. Without them, I don't know where I would be today.

Time management for me was most important as I aimed to graduate in three years. Due to an injury, I had to continue my rehab and practice while I was taking twenty-three credits in the fall semester, and working three different internships all at the same time. Without quality time management and efficiency, there would have been no way I could have done all of that. As a sophomore, I even interned at the Inland Empire 66ers (A-league ball for the Angels) while I was in season. This was extremely difficult with practice times, but was attainable through supreme time management and a flexible coach.

With everything that I had on a daily schedule, organization was a skill that I developed and improved upon very quickly. Organization skills helped me with my time management, and paid off in the classroom. I kept a very detailed schedule of every day of every week to help me stay on top of everything.

Motivation was never an issue for me because I was never the best. I was always motivated to get better every day in every aspect of my life. All my life, I was told I couldn't do things or I wasn't good enough, and that served as fuel for me to prove people wrong. I wasn't the best athlete on the field, and I wasn't the smartest in every class, but through motivation and dedication, I always worked the hardest of anyone.

Well-balancing my academics and baseball was the single most important thing that helped me succeed in both. I was able to balance my time and put 100 percent effort into both responsibilities.

Networking has been my most valuable tool as I have started my career post graduate school. My early objective from networking was to find out everything possible about what people did in their jobs to provide a perspective on whether I would potentially be interested in what they did in the future. From talking to hundreds of people, I was able to rule out certain industries or jobs in order to narrow my career focus.

Networking has opened doors for me that nothing else could have. Every internship or job I have had was because I knew someone and had developed a relationship with that person. The more people you know and can impress, the more you can help put yourself in a position to get lucky at the right time.

Step 3: Be Very Strategic with Your Success Wheel

Many struggle with the difference between strategy and tactics. Tactics are individual acts and capabilities that, when used in a coherent long-term plan, become a strategy. Tactics are usually short-term with immediate results;

strategies create long-term systemic success. Be both strategic and tactical with each aspect of your success wheel.

To provide you with relevant advice on strategies and tactics around a success wheel, we sought the input of a successful student-athlete and interviewed Alexis Pinson, a collegiate volleyball player at Arizona State University and Ohio University. She graduated with her masters in sports administration degree during her last year of playing at Ohio and now works for the San Francisco 49ers as a sales and service coordinator. Alexis provides some great insight on how to ride your success wheel and succeed as a student-athlete.

ALEXIS PINSON
(former volleyball student-athlete at ASU and Ohio University)

1. What were your top three priorities as a student-athlete?

My first priority as a student-athlete was school. That was drilled into me since I was a kid just starting to play sports and it always remained my main focus. My parents always preached to me that sports are great but your body will only hold up for so long. You could get injured at any time and lose your athleticism but you can never lose your education. In fact, it was my emphasis on education that allowed me to graduate early from ASU and enter the MSA program at OU.

My second priority was of course volleyball. Volleyball was (and still is) one of my passions in life. If I wasn't in class or doing homework, I was either practicing, training, watching film, or doing something else related to volleyball. My roommates at ASU were some of my teammates as well, so they shared the same passion for the sport as me. They also never complained when I would fill our entire DVR with volleyball matches. It's probably one of the many reasons we got along so well.

My third priority was making time for my family and friends. One of the reasons that I decided to attend an undergrad school so close to my hometown was to be make it easy to still see my family as often as I could. After each of my home matches at ASU, a big group of people including my family, friends, teammates, and their families would all go out to dinner—whether we won or lost. These are some of my most cherished memories because it always put the matches into perspective. I was extremely lucky because my parents were able to carry on the tradition when I played at OU as they never missed a home game in Athens either. I was happy to prioritize my family when they would travel across the country several times over the span of a few months just to support me.

2. Did you have any resources that you used that helped you with your academics?

The one resource that I used the most when it came to my academics was the tutoring program we had at ASU. Our academic coaches would set us up with a tutor if we needed some extra help in a certain class. We could even just ask for help in studying for an exam. This was a resource that I found to be very valuable because not only were the tutors very knowledgeable in their respective fields, but many times they were familiar with a specific professor and provided you with special tips and pointers for those classes.

3. How important was networking for you, and how did you take advantage of being a student-athlete?

Networking was a crucial tool for me to get to where I'm at today, and being a student-athlete was the main channel that I networked through. I found that the easiest people to network with were former student-athletes themselves. There's a common understanding and respect between student-athletes that I discovered while networking. They know you can handle the challenges and stressors of that life and can translate that to being a successful employee. It's why employers always comment that student-athletes are great hires, and many of those employer-employee relationships are forged by networking with other current and former student-athletes.

4. What was the most important part of your success wheel and why?

The part of the wheel that contributed the most to my success as a student-athlete was motivation. Something (besides my alarm) had to get me up for 6 a.m. workouts every day. That same thing had to encourage me to study my notes again and again when all I wanted to do was sleep. Without motivation to get my degree and to make it to the NCAA tournament each year, I would've failed. That motivation to be able to say "I did the best I could" is what kept me going and led to my achievements.

5. What relationships did you build as a student-athlete that were most important to your success as both a student and an athlete?

The relationship that was most important to me as an athlete was my strength coach. This is usually a relationship that is underrated or gets overlooked, but it can be so important. Your strength coach is the one that will actually push you to do things that you didn't know you physically could do. Achieving those physical goals can do wonders for your mental state as an athlete. I was also fortunate enough to feel close enough to my strength coaches that I could come to them with other issues I was having outside of the gym and they'd always seem to find a way to channel those struggles into my workouts. Not only would I get a great workout, but most times I'd feel better as a person after I left the gym.

Also a word of advice when it comes to strength coaches—*do not anger them*. They can be a great resource and help you in so many ways but if you upset them, they can make your life a special kind of hell. I promise that if you put in a great deal of hard work, you'll help your teammates, your coaches, and most importantly—yourself. And everyone lives in harmony.

The relationship that was most important to me as a student was my academic coach. You should really listen to them when they suggest what classes would be best for you to take with your schedule. They know what they're doing. They are also a great resource when you feel like you need some extra help in a class. Don't be embarrassed to go to them—even with just the slightest issue. They're there to help you succeed.

6. At what point during school did you start to focus on your career and thinking about what you wanted to do in the future?

My future career was always on my mind since I started my collegiate education but it definitely became more focused probably a year or two before I graduated from ASU. I always knew that I wanted to work in sports but I just had to decide in which capacity. I had an idea that sports journalism and PR was something that interested me so I asked our team's SID if I could tag along and shadow them. I ended up really enjoying it but I didn't realize how much writing actually went into journalism and frankly, I don't enjoy writing enough to make it a focal point of my career. My advice would be to use those who are around you every day. If you think you may be interested in a position in the medical field, ask your athletic trainer if you can shadow them and learn from them. It will probably open your eyes and give you a firsthand look at what that job is really like. It can encourage and solidify your passions or, like me, make you realize that it's actually something that doesn't interest you that much.

7. Looking back at your time as a student-athlete, is there anything you would have done differently?

Looking back, I think the only thing that I would've done differently is to reach out and get to know more of my fellow student-athletes. They know exactly what you're going through living life as both a college student and athlete, so relating to them is a breeze. It's easy to get comfortable in your bubble and just hang out with your teammates, but I wish I would've taken the time to get to know more of my peers. Plus, they'll probably show up to your games and make you pretty cool posters.

Step 4: Prioritize within Your Success Wheel

In any strategic or tactical effort (and as emphasized in the Prioritize aspect of the success wheel), you have to make decisions about where to put your resources and focus your time. It is no different with the success wheel. In order to illustrate and provide an example, we interviewed Pim Thirati, a former student-athlete in golf from the University of Illinois. The following is an excerpt in which she offers her advice on what the most important part of her success wheel was.

PIM THIRATI
(former golf student-athlete at the University of Illinois)

The most important parts of my success wheel would be Relationship Building, Time Management, and Motivation. Being a student-athlete has definitely taught me all the aspects of the success wheel to a certain extent, but I would say these three aspects continued to be the most impactful after I have graduated.

Working closely in a team with coaches as well as the athletics department, the media, fans, and competitors has taught me how to interact and build relationships with other people, which are very crucial skills in life after college. Balancing between golf and school has taught me how to prioritize my time wisely. Working in sports can be hectic and, depending on your responsibilities, you could be working with various projects at once. Being able to manage my time is one thing I found very helpful for my career. Putting a substantial amount of time and effort into a sport you are passionate about requires a high intrinsic motivation. I believe this is something that sets student-athletes apart. I have invested in one sport for over ten years and as a result, I tend to be very self-driven and *self-motivated* in other aspects of my life as well.

My advice for current and future student-athletes is to try to not lose sight of other intangible skills you are learning outside of your sport. It is easy to get caught up in the wins and losses. In the end, I really don't remember the putts I missed. I remember the friends I've made and the grind we went through. The wins and losses WERE a big deal but looking back, they didn't define me and I'm glad I didn't let it take over my life. The end result WAS a big deal but the process is what shaped me.

CHAPTER SUMMARY

This chapter provides a tool you can adopt and implement to help guide and focus your efforts over the course of your time as a student-athlete. Maybe you looked at the picture of the success wheel and skipped the words. But we hope you read this chapter and started to wonder whether now is the time to build your own success wheel.

Secret 4

Acquire the Life Skills You Need to Succeed

THE SECRET IN A FEW WORDS

We all want to succeed in life. No surprise there. But in order to achieve success and accomplish notable goals, certain skills are needed. Sport teaches an abundance of life lessons many people are unable to learn in a classroom or anywhere else in life. These life lessons can occur for many reasons, but the majority of us learn the most from failure (which sport easily provides). Getting things wrong or failing always clarifies the need to acquire certain new skills in order to prevent repeating the same outcome. So, learn from your failures, and the real secret is to gain the life skills you need to succeed.

As a student-athlete, you have the opportunity to develop many life skills through your sport. and as you mature as an athlete, learning those skills will become easier but also more important. There is no doubt you'll need various tools to succeed at whatever goal you pursue, but recognizing what to learn is one of life's vitally important secrets.

LIFE SKILLS YOU NEED TO SUCCEED

Sport can help a young person develop key skills such as time management, competitive response, a true work ethic, goal setting, resiliency, and values clarification. The earlier you are able to recognize what these skills are and how to develop them, the more you can improve those skills. These "assets" are important not only for success as a student-athlete but also for future success as an individual and working professional. Not all skills are part of your natural human makeup. Some need to be developed from the ground up, and it helps to have a little guidance in which skills to think about the most. To open this chapter, we noted that learning from losing was a secret. But we want to be clear that losing is not a habit you want to repeat. So minimize your losses . . . but learn from them when they happen.

Dawn Buth, a former professional tennis player and student-athlete at the University of Florida, featured below, talks about which life skills were most important for her as a student-athlete, as a professional athlete, and as a working professional. She is currently Associate Director of Strategic Communication and Education at the NCAA's Sport Science Institute.

The first life skill Buth spoke about was a work ethic and how it was a key tool she learned as a student-athlete that has been foundational to her career development. We asked her to explain why a strong work ethic is so important. She offered the following explanation and supporting points.

> For me, work ethic has meant approaching everything I do with focus and commitment. It means having the self-awareness to understand my strengths and limitations, and the ability to maximize my capabilities within any given moment. It also means making short-term sacrifices and working through discomfort to accomplish long-term goals. When I retired from professional tennis, earning my graduate degree was an important priority for me.
>
> I accepted a position as the head coach at an institution that was my top academic choice and which had exceptional tuition benefits. The position, however, could only offer an annual salary of $15,000, so in addition to my full-time role and graduate studies I worked an additional twenty hours each week teaching private tennis lessons to support myself. During this time, I also had the opportunity to serve on the executive board of a nonprofit and participate in a once-in-a-lifetime internship opportunity. These experiences required making personal sacrifices and working long, physical hours, but they also opened doors of opportunity and provided some of the most incredible years of personal growth.

We also asked her to discuss the life skills that helped her the most in her professional life after a life in sport. First, she noted resiliency. For her, "resiliency is the most important life skill I learned as a student-athlete. We've all experienced setbacks, defeat or a lack of confidence and for me, resiliency meant experiencing these challenges and then finding a way to regroup, pick yourself up and try again."

She also highlighted time management as "the ability to manage multiple and competing priorities, [which] was always a part of my student-athlete experience and continues to be an important part of my professional experience. To this day, every morning when I get to work I take ten minutes to review my calendar and prioritize my workload for the day and week. Investing a small amount of time into planning on the front end goes a long way in efficiently and effectively managing time and priorities."

The ability to learn continually is another life skill Dawn reported as being of high importance. Specifically, she noted "the skill that has been most important and most fulfilling for me is the ability to learn and recognize that you can learn from every opportunity, every person and every situation."

In developing all of these key life skills, she noted three factors she believes are crucial: goal setting, value clarification, and utilization of resources. She explained:

> Goal setting and values clarification have been valuable tools in my athletic and professional life. Goal setting often involves making the implicit, explicit. It invites an athlete to articulate what they want to accomplish from their athletic pursuits and identify a pathway to accomplish it. There is a lot of interesting research about the power that comes from scripting and verbalizing your goals and every great coach and teacher in my life has challenged me to not only set goals for myself, but also write them down and say them out loud.
>
> Values clarification includes taking time to identify and narrow down your core values. These tools are simple but are an impactful driver for self-reflection, effective prioritization and intentional decision making . . . be both resourceful and ask for help.
>
> The ability to independently problem solve on one hand, and on the other hand be courageous in asking for help, cannot be understated in its importance to one's personal and professional development.

TIME MANAGEMENT

Oliver Luck, Executive Vice President of the NCAA, identified time management as the best life skill in his experiences. He described his view as follows:

> The best life skill that I was able to develop is time management and how to fit all of these different things into my day. Sometimes you can't because you run out of time. That's very helpful when you become an adult, when you're married, you've got kids, you've got a job. You have to squeeze a lot of things into a busy day. At work, you've got to look at a situation and figure out how you improve it.

RYAN SOLLAZZO (former student-athlete, football–D1,
Director of Sponsorships at Major League Baseball)

From a time-management standpoint, map things out. I would write down my goals, and set deadlines. I would set midpoint deadlines, and then try to map out how many days it would take me to get to the midpoint deadline. By beating that deadline, I would ultimately bring the final deadline 4 or 5 days earlier. If I couldn't do it, then I knew I had 4 or 5 days extra to meet that deadline. Being able to map out a strategy, have a vision for the strategy, and then have a plan on how you want to execute it is extremely important.

TEAMWORK

Kristen Brown, a former basketball student-athlete at Northern Illinois University who is now Associate Athletic Director–Administration at the University of Maryland, emphasizes teamwork as a key life skill. She noted "teamwork is crucial to learn as a student-athlete because you deal with so many different personalities on a team. Learning how to interact, and work well together with people from different walks of life, different ages, different backgrounds are certainly skills I use every day. Communication is very important in building relationships, and helps me out every day in my job."

MANAGING AND HANDLING PERSONALITIES

Nick Manno, a former student-athlete baseball player at Mount Union who went on to work for various teams in Major League Baseball, provided a very interesting life skill which he called "learning how to manage personalities" and noted it was very important to him during his tenure as a student-athlete. He explained further that

any team culture and atmosphere will have introverts, extroverts, and others who are outgoing and those who don't take criticism well. There will be those you deal with that you like and those you don't. The reality is whether you are on a team or working in an organization, you are going to have to deal with different personalities.

You are going to have to manage those personalities accordingly. You are not going to get along with everyone you work with or play with, but understanding that not everyone is going to be like you, and not everyone is going to think like you is important. At the end of the day, you need a common goal and have to find out where you fit. My advice for managing personalities is to be yourself, know where you fit, and know where you fall. Be your own person, and try not to fall into the traps of others . . . Try to put yourself in their shoes and situation to better understand their perspective.

As a leader, you need to be able to manage any situation, and have the discipline to be able to still do the best you can even when you are not 100%. Athletes are the same as professionals. You don't always want to get up and go to work, but we have to be professionals.

DEALING WITH ADVERSITY

Manno stated his belief that the ability to deal with adversity is "the biggest life lesson that can be turned into a skill, whether it's a team concept or something you are not doing in your own job or own career, allow yourself to be reflective and figure out what you can do better in those situations. Self-evaluation is crucial; Learn how to be self-reflective and understand where you need to improve."

ACCOUNTABILITY

Former volleyball student-athlete at Arizona State University Alexis Pinson suggested that accountability was a key life skill. "Being a part of team in college really taught me the value of being reliable and knowing that my teammates could count on me as an athlete and as a person. This has certainly carried over to my professional life. I take great pride in knowing that my bosses and coworkers see me as an accountable person and I know that that is a skill that I honed as a student-athlete."

Nick Manno also touched on accountability, saying, "You have to be accountable to yourself, because you cannot get better without holding yourself accountable. Don't blame someone else for your shortcomings. You have to be able to learn from every situation, and understand that if I make a mistake, why did I make that mistake and can I learn from it?"

Ryan Sollazzo added that accountability for a student-athlete also means "being able to be coached and being able to take constructive criticisms is very important in being successful. A challenge for a lot of people is the ability to turn a negative into a positive opportunity."

Sollazzo tells a story showing how important it is to develop life skills outside of sport.

> My redshirt sophomore year, I blew my knee out in spring practice. At that time, I thought it was the worst thing that could ever happen because as an athlete your whole life really revolved around sports. Looking back, it was probably the best thing that happened. While I was always very focused on academics, that actually gave me an opportunity to get experience and figure out what I wanted to do for a career.

Since I was still on scholarship, I still had to contribute in some sort of way. I was unable to do that on the field, so the new stadium plan presented an opportunity to be the spokesperson from the student athlete standpoint. I got to travel with our head coach, our AD, our President of the school. I didn't get this experience because I was a star player, but more because I was available, with the team, and willing to help.

Sollazzo also suggested using summers wisely. He "always took summer classes." Impressively, Sollazzo followed his plan and graduated with a 4.0 GPA, went on to do graduate work, and is now well into a successful and rewarding professional career.

COMPETITIVENESS

Garrett Shinoskie, former football student-athlete at Capitol University, listed a few more skills that we agree are important: "My advice is to apply the exact same skills that made you successful in sports: patience, hard work, pride, determination, being coachable, etc. Life is competitive and to be successful you must have the same mentality you had as an athlete."

Former Duke University wrestler Immanuel Kerr-Brown warned against falling into the trap of "competing not to lose rather than to win." He explained that when you're in this state of mind, "you walk out into competition hoping not to embarrass yourself, and then you start to wonder what everyone else thinks about you because you just can't seem to win." Kerr-Brown suggested taking the same positive approach to your academic, professional, and other nonsport goals as well. He suggests identifying your "AOC's" [areas of concern] and addressing them as quickly as you can.

Kerr-Brown offered one additional and important skill for student-athletes. He suggested strongly that student-athletes view teammates and classmates as "motivation" and not competitors on and off the field. He describes the issue: "The problem with comparing yourself to your teammates without this critical approach leads to you thinking, 'They are just so much better than me,' which ultimately leads to 'I stink.' You do not want those thoughts to cross your mind. Anything you do that places you in a negative mindset is detrimental to your success. That applies to you athletically, personally, and professionally. Negativity gets you nowhere."

PATIENCE AND COACHABILITY

Patience and coachability go together in this section because you cannot be coachable without being patient. Many things in life are about the process. In fact, almost everything is about a process. Patience is key during the process toward a goal. Not everything can happen at the snap of your fingers. As many say, good things come to those who wait. Whether your patience is tested in the classroom or on the field, you'll learn a lot by waiting for what's to come. For example, if you are a freshman who just walked into an extremely competitive program and you need to redshirt or ride the pine for the year, you must be patient. Many student-athletes would think about transferring once they don't get what they want, but wouldn't you want the challenge? Have the patience to keep getting better each day, knowing your time will come to shine. It may be the next year or your senior year, but when your time comes, you will look back and say it was all worth the wait.

And being coachable is one of the most important life skills. Life is full of learning, and the ability to be coachable, on or off the field, immensely enhances your ability to learn. No one wants to coach someone who isn't coachable, and no one wants to help someone who isn't coachable. Being coachable is easier for some than for others, but there's a reason you have two eyes, two ears, and one mouth. Observe and listen more than you talk. Soak up the information like a sponge and be flexible and open to learning new ways whatever the task may be. At the end of the day, being coachable will get you much farther, and people will be willing to help you.

CHAPTER SUMMARY

This chapter presents a series of life skills, suggested by people who have "been there" and "done that." Prioritize your list of missing skills and address the most important or most needed ones first.

The highlighted traits in this chapter are:

1. Managing and handling personalities
2. Time management
3. Resiliency
4. Work ethic
5. Dealing with adversity
6. Teamwork
7. Accountability
8. Competitiveness
9. Patience
10. Coachability and the ability to learn

It may sound hard. Some of these skills require personal reflection and then the discipline to change human behavior. Now go get it done. As Yoda told Luke Skywalker, "Do or do not. There is no try."

Secret 5 Be Balanced in Everything

Authors' Viewpoint

This may be the shortest "box" in the book. All of us strongly agree, and so did all the former student-athletes we asked, that Secret 5 (aka "the balance secret") is essential, really essential, to the future success of any student-athlete in the "other 99 percent" bucket. And by balance, we don't mean balancing academics with athletics, or balancing studying with training. We mean balance in all respects. Each aspect of your life, from sleep to partying, to relationships to a private meeting with your coaches, to television watching and video gaming, to your choices on commuting or how you spend your weekends . . . all of them require balance. Yes, we need you to dissect your entire existence and make it more efficient and more productive.

THE SECRET IN A FEW WORDS

Balance, balance, balance. Balance is a word you MUST put into your top-of-mind vocabulary. All the time, in all things. Given your two MASSIVE commitments to academics and athletics—and with the growing requirements around each from just the first four secrets—you need to really consider every activity and your use of time. Deciding to join a club to make friends, for instance, will remove a couple of hours a week from your other pursuits. You need to gauge the importance and value of each activity to your goals, your mental health, your academic success, and your athletic performance. Of course, we do understand (and agree!) that you have to find enjoyment in life, but these decisions MUST be taken very seriously. As many athletes have learned, you can't always excel in all three areas of the student-athlete experience. Academics, athletics, and your social life are the three things you most need to balance. Our advice to you is that it is only possible to excel in two of the three, and academics is always one of them, so choose wisely and balance well.

BE BALANCED IN EVERYTHING

Secret 5 is about balance in all things. In everything. It is about reviewing all of your activities, pastimes, studies, and athletics, looking at them holistically, and determining the best way to use the most important resource a student-athlete has: time. Efficient time and effective time. In order to provide clear direction, we have organized this secret by the various activities of your student-athlete life and will provide you with direction in making these decisions.

Much of what you decide here may impact the plan you constructed after reading Secret 1. We encourage you to update your plan after reading this chapter and consider its direction.

To introduce our discussion of balance, we ask readers to imagine you're a gymnast on a balance beam. You can do many things on the beam, but lose your balance (and it can happen easily) and you fall off.

BALANCE IN ACADEMICS

OK, so you've learned a lot about balancing academics in Secrets 1 and 2, but there is more here to consider:

1. *Focus on your most challenging class first.* Just as athletes always work on their weakness (e.g., a decathlete who is amongst the best runners but a weak thrower puts the majority of his efforts into his throwing), so should you. That class you are worried about (perhaps statistics or accounting?) should be your priority and where you put any extra time. When you plan out your life each semester (see Secret 1) and allocate study time, review your courses closely and put extra time into those courses you are worried about or those courses you know you won't like (and will have a hard time studying for). Trust us, your GPA will thank you! And, if you ever apply for grad school many years down the road, you'll enhance your chances!

2. *Study often and early.* You are an athlete. Do you stay up all night practicing the night before the big game or key qualifying race? Never! So, why do that with your studying? Sure, you can push at the end, but work out a study plan that peaks as an exam

approaches but allows you to go into that exam rested and ready, and—very important for any student-athlete—does not negatively affect your physical training. Most athletes can think back to times where they had to stop training around a major exam. It's not good for mental health, not good for sport performance, and usually not good for grades.

3. *Access key academic resources before you need them.* This is very simple, very intuitive, and very logical, yet few do it. If you're graduating in May 2023, don't wait until April 2023 to talk to your advisor about a job or to set up a meeting with the career management office. Same for getting an internship or dealing with a class you might be failing. Get help (from a professor, an advisor, student services, or others) early. Universities are full of services and professionals to help student-athletes, but only if you seek them out.

BALANCE IN ATHLETICS

After academics, athletics is the second major part of your dual-focused life and a part that requires close attention to balance. A few suggestions from our collective experience:

1. *Train in the off-season.* Yes, this may seem like overkill, but many of the "other 99 percent" tend to slack off, just a little, in the off-season as they progress through college and find other interests, fall in love, get a great summer job, and so on. If you can focus on your fitness and the foundations in the off-season (regardless of your sport), you won't experience as much of a "shock" when you're back on campus. You'll also have less stress and anxiety about losing your spot or scholarship. Many student-athletes choose to stay on campus each summer to advance their academics, access awesome training facilities, work with their coaches, and enjoy their college towns. If this is an option for you, consider attending summer sessions. Having time to take a few classes and get ahead academically while also maintaining a training routine can be a tremendous benefit in moving you toward a great next season and lightening the academic load during the year.

2. *Choose a practicum or internship outside of your team.* It is both a waste of an opportunity to build your resume and experiences outside of your team and a potential drag on time if you work for your coach or manager for the team to which your scholarship is linked. You'll end up working much more, losing balance, and

doing so for a position that will not advance your resume as much as an external position will.

3. *Take advantage of injury time or being red-shirted.* This may seem counterintuitive, as you are desperate not to lose your place on the team and want to show your loyalty and support even if you are not playing. Be strategic here. Be present and do your part but keep it to a minimum and use this time to get a practicum or internship done, join a club, connect with alumni, travel, work part-time, do an independent study with a leading professor, etc.

BALANCE IN FAMILY AND FRIENDS TIME

Balancing family and friends with all your other time commitments is especially challenging in your first year of college, and perhaps somewhat after that. Your family (parents, siblings, cousins, and all the rest) and friends (high school pals) have been a large part of your life, and now you've moved away. In the two semesters of school, you'll have precious few quiet nights and about twenty-six weekends to do "stuff." Those weekends are special for work, training, planning, volunteering, socializing, and studying. They are key. You'll want—especially at first—to head home often, to connect with friends, to go to events with them, and to uphold traditions you all had from high school. The same with your parents: you'll want to go home, they'll want you to come home, and there'll be various family events. As hard as it is, you need to make some tough decisions. Here are our top priority recommendations.

1. *Be picky.* You'll have so many opportunities and desires to go home. Many. Family events. Last-minute party invites from friends. And more. Before the semester starts, set your boundaries. One trip home per semester (even if you live close) plus Thanksgiving is a good rule. Or even less. Then pick the date and stick to it. You can make it up to your friends over holidays. But you must help your friends understand that because you are a student-athlete the demands on your time are way more than they ever were in high school.

2. *Have your parents (or grandparents or guardian) visit you or have them meet you at your competitions.* Your parents are the easiest to convince here. Your college likely has special weekends. Take advantage of these. Surprise them and book a hotel room for them and ask them to come to a game or event. They'll want to. That way you can balance their visit with school and practice. You can also have your family and friends meet you on a road trip. You'll end up with support from those you care about during the competition/match/game and they also will probably enjoy seeing you do what you love, play your sport.

3. *Put time in your schedule to call home.* This is a big one and an often unmeasured time crunch. Particularly if you are homesick. Instead of getting a great night's sleep, you stay up talking until 2 a.m. or later with old friends. So, before the year starts, set a time (say 9 to 10 p.m. on Sunday) for calls home. Try to keep them short (fifteen minutes?) so you can call three or four family members or friends each week. Mix it up. Then complement the calls with social media connections to keep in contact.

BALANCE IN SOCIAL TIME

This is a big one. Perhaps the biggest one. College life comes full of amazing opportunities to party, socialize, travel, play, chat, and more. Social life is a huge part of college and something you want to enjoy and take advantage of. But, it can also be the reason why you struggle academically, athletically, or both.

In fact, many students who are not student-athletes flunk out or struggle because they do too much socializing. This can be drinking, partying, playing too many video games, or just chatting nights away with friends. There is no parental supervision and life is easy and great. We have all struggled with this and have learned the hard way in many cases. So, our three priority recommendations here are:

1. *Figure out what you are addicted to and avoid it.* Maybe it's video games that you love or maybe it's binge watching Netflix and snacking on junk food. Figure out your vice, acknowledge it, and either work it into your schedule in small chunks or avoid it altogether. For some people, it's an all or nothing proposition. If you find yourself doing anything that has a negative impact (sleeping through classes because you were up too late, gaining weight because you are drinking and eating too much pizza) on the priorities you have for yourself to achieve success, you need to get a handle on it immediately. Whatever your vice is, TV or partying , figure it out early and cut it out of your life.

2. *Put quotas on partying.* Partying not only takes away that particular night but also takes a lot out of you the next day. For a lot of student-athletes, 5 a.m. or 6 a.m. practice times put a damper on partying during the week, but with the demanding schedule you keep, you also need to put the brakes on for the weekends to catch up on sleep and rejuvenate yourself. Set a quota (once a month, once a week, etc.) for your partying and stick to it. Don't be persuaded otherwise.

3. *Choose a great living situation.* This is important. If you're in a residence hall, fine, but if you're not, choosing an appropriate

place to live is key. Live with teammates (who are serious students) or with classmates (who are serious students) and not with partiers, or in a place known as a party house, or even in an apartment building or on a street where late-night noise and partying are common. You will not last long as a student-athlete in such an environment.

BALANCE IN EMOTIONS

Emotions run high, and those who need to stay spiritually connected (whether through religion or not) to keep their emotions level must make time to do so. Not everyone needs this component in their life, but some may, and it may help others who don't currently have it.

Relationships are a big part of life. And, we're talking about romantic ones. Lovers. Sexual partners. Boyfriends. Girlfriends. One-night stands. There are many viewpoints on relationships, but the reality is that most college students engage in various relationships throughout their four years.

And unless you entered college with a supportive partner who understands your situation and gives you the time to focus on sport and school, we recommend thinking long and hard about whether a potential partner has your best interests in mind, and whether your student-athlete experience will benefit as a result of a relationship. There is plenty of time to find a partner after college. Don't think you need to be in a rush to find someone.

A few specifics from us here:

1. *Stay single or date but do so sparingly.* A new partner typically will want a lot of your time—and you'll want to give it, too, which is hard to do while living the time-constrained life of a student-athlete. Then, if the relationship endures, stress will arise either from your declining performance (school and/or sport) or from your partner who feels like you don't want to spend enough time together.

    Dating can be great, and less of a time commitment. But, date sparingly and be clear that it is for fun and not for any long-term commitment. We know that is easier said than done, but just be aware of what you are or aren't getting yourself into along with everything else that is going on in your life. Check your priority list one more time, and act accordingly.

2. *If you have a long-term partner or meet a very supportive one, establish and communicate very clear ground rules to avoid problems.* If you stray from #1 on this list because you find someone you think is perfect or your high school sweetheart has moved to town, then consider using this simple tactic: Have a

very serious talk, explain what your goals are that you need their support for the next few years. Let them know you want that person in your life and expect the relationship to last but you only have a few hours each week to devote to it. This is a very hard discussion because no one likes being told they will be "fitted" into someone else's schedule. This talk may even end your relationship. But failing to have this discussion with someone you care about can lead to disastrous results.

3. *Connect spiritually if that is part of you.* Over the course of a semester, year, or years, a lot will happen, and a lot will be thrown your way. Keeping your emotions in balance is extremely important throughout your experience, and if staying connected spiritually or religiously helps ground you, then continue to do so and don't slack. Make it a routine for yourself if you know it is a big part of your life.

BALANCE IN DOWNTIME

Downtime is important for anyone's mental health. Chilling with friends. Lying on the couch watching your favorite team, movie, or concert. Playing your favorite video game. All are part of your downtime, and downtime is valuable. But you have to manage it. If you are practicing the time management strategies already provided in this book, you have this nailed already. Some simple steps.

1. *Set a maximum time for any activity.* If you love watching football on Sunday, pick one game (not three) and plan study and training and other commitments around that game. Even better, don't turn on the game until the paper that is due is complete, your assigned readings are done, you have gone out for a run or done whatever it is that is important to achieve that day.

2. *Cut out "useless" downtime.* Quite simply, things like aimless web surfing, staring at your Twitter feed, checking out the latest Snap Chat features, television watching without a purpose, and other mindless activities need to go. These are not only unproductive but often leave you feeling stressed and more tired. This takes discipline.

3. *Try to double-dip downtime.* Use your downtime wisely—stretch during television or movie watching, play an online game with a friend from home, invite your mom and dad to a golf day, etc. By double-dipping, you achieve two or more things at once and save yourself time that you can use for other things later.

MATT VANSANDT (former track student-athlete,
Director of Championships at Big South Conference)

Make school your 9-to-5 job. Being efficient and focused during your day will allow you to enjoy a work-life balance. When I was at school, I made it my 9-to-5 job. While you could be napping, playing video games, or going out with friends, you can be working efficiently to prepare yourself for a routine you may have when you get that first job. In college, you have so much free time, that your transition to work is difficult because you are by yourself for the most part, and you have this bulk of time during the day to get work done, and if you don't get your work done, you won't be successful.

BALANCE IN ANNUAL PLANNING

When you plan your year, think balance. There is really one general strategy here: you need to have balance over the twelve months for each of the four years of your student-athlete career. Periods of push (academic and athletic), periods of downtime/friends/family, periods of push—academic only, periods of push—athletic only, periods of work experience and life experience, and be sure you don't develop periods you can't handle. Some suggested tactics.

1. *In peak competitive season, cut back on everything else except school.* Do not plan weekends or visits home, cut out extracurricular work, parties, etc. This is your time to shine athletically and keep everything rolling academically.

2. *At exam time, only staying fit matters.* Yes, for the period of exam week and before it, school is number one with just enough time set aside to stay in shape for sport. As in #1, remove everything else from your. Be insanely focused!

3. *Use summers and winter breaks very strategically.* One of the great things about the academic calendar is that you receive periods of time out of school. This is when you can really catch up with friends and family, get work experience, do career planning, be social and more, while concurrently maintaining your fitness and sporting form and staying healthy via sleep and nutrition. Do NOT use these breaks as "benders" where you go on a party tour. Sure, you might kick back a bit more than during the tight academic year, but you have so much stuff to do when academic responsibilities are low and athletic competition is not happening.

BALANCE IN EXPERIENTIAL CHOICES VERSUS FINANCIAL CHOICES

Student-athletes sometimes make decisions based on very small amounts of money. We've seen some turn down an internship with a blue chip organization so they could go home and work another year at their old (and non-career-forwarding) job. And the reason was mainly $'s. Which, in the long term, makes no sense. A career-forwarding internship (which may cost you a few thousand dollars as compared to your former job) has the ability to set you on your way to making hundreds of thousands of dollars more. Ask any professional in their thirties or forties if $5,000 more would change their lives and the answer will be "no." They wouldn't mind it, but it really is not a big factor. So, our tactics here:

1. *Make important life decisions based primarily on what moves you toward your goals instead of on cost.* As we noted above, a few thousand dollars now versus the opportunity to make much, much more later is something to remember. Think about your earning potential over time, not today's rate of pay.

2. *Prioritize experiential opportunities with career upside.* Yes, you know the term "opportunity cost." This is key to think about when you have options for practicums, internships, projects, summer jobs, work-study terms, and other work experience. Ask yourself, "Where will this lead me?" or "Could this organization hire me long term in a full-time role?" or "What are full-time salaries like in this industry and this job?" or "Which gets me to where I want to be (see Secret 1) faster?"

3. *Find a way to make things work financially in the short term.* This may sound obvious, but you don't need a fancy apartment for a summer internship or a cool car when you get your first job. Get a roommate. Stay in a cheap apartment on the subway line. Sell your car and bike to work. Do whatever it takes to get started and get the experiences you need. Money, mortgages, and stuff you "want" will come later.

CHAPTER SUMMARY: ADVICE FROM NINE PEERS

We felt the best way to summarize this chapter would be to provide a Top 12 list of advice on balance from nine peers—fellow student-athletes. We asked a large number for their input, reviewed the list closely, and selected these as the most helpful.

1. "You still have to balance your academics with your athletics because you do have obligations to your team. I get that, but ultimately, you have to stay focused on what's most important. Those three things: athletics, academics, social life. What is most important of the three is your academics. You either believe that or you don't. If you believe it, then you're going to act on it. If you don't believe it, you are going to have a really hard time getting through it. You probably won't get through it because

you're not giving it the commitment that it deserves. What happens with many young men and women is that they realize this, but not until they're maybe a Junior or Senior. At some point, the lightbulb is going to come on and it needs to come on as early as possible."—*Oliver Luck*

2. "My first day in college, our head coach told us that there are three aspects to college when you're a student athlete; baseball, school, and your social life, and you only really have time to be great at two of those. I tried my hardest to balance all three of those and it took dedication, time management, and a great work ethic that has transitioned well into my career. Any sustained success in life requires these traits, and seeing these things transition to success in college showed me that doing the same in my career would have similar results."—*Kevin Hurd*

3. "It's important to figure out your daily schedule. Figure out when all of your things can take place during the week and don't procrastinate, don't push things off. Look day-by-day or look week-by-week to figure out when you have time to enjoy your friends and have fun, and know when you really need to buckle down."—*Oliver Luck*

4. "You have to be very disciplined. That entails learning to say no. 'Sorry guys, I'd love to. Maybe I can catch up with you guys later or something. I've got 3 hours of studying I have to do. I got a test I have to prepare for. I got to write a paper.' The earlier that lesson can be learned, the better for a student-athlete because there are more time demands for a student-athlete than there ever were before."—*Oliver Luck*

5. "If you can be disciplined in anything that you do—and I'll just define discipline as doing the right thing when no one is watching—when it's just you, if you can maintain that discipline and that routine, that will help serve you long term. For athletes, being disciplined, having a routine that's consistent, that will ensure a lot of success because your time management skills are going to be put into that routine. Your fitness, your training, it's going to be a part of your routine, it's a part of your schedule, it's a daily thing, it's a habit, it's a positive habit. It's a continual learning curve. For student-athletes, I would say, 'Hey, you can be disciplined and you can have a routine that includes these elements and if you're disciplined about maintaining that, you'll be successful, and you can apply that to every area of your life whether you're a player, a coach, or a professional, or whatever role you have.' The thing that is difficult is managing boundaries

and managing other people's expectations, because you can't manage their expectations. But, you can manage your own boundaries."—*Jeff Rodin*

6. "Redshirting isn't something that anyone really wants to do. Truly, it's a reality check for some and for some, it's a way to get better. It's basically a year of working out. Whether that's in the weight room, on the field, or whatever it may be; dieting; in the classroom, it's a year for you to get better. It helped me get a little stronger, get a little experience with our team and with our coaching staff and helped me fit in."—*JR Reynolds*

7. "If you are a player that gets redshirted, take advantage of it, don't shut yourself off. I've seen more kids that redshirt that waste the extra year than utilize that year. When you have a year that you can step aside from competition and focus on the process, it can sometimes be a blessing. I think you even see that with players who get injured. They are forced to focus on the process, and they come back a way better player because they are able to step back and see a different perspective on things. When you are always in competition mode, you can become very narrow minded, and you can lose sight of the process sometimes."—*Rob Smith*

8. "Social life, in my opinion, is very, very important. I don't necessarily mean like going to parties, socials, or the bars. I'm talking about getting to know your peers, whether that's on a team, in the classroom, or in your dorm. So many people come from a variety of backgrounds, different life experiences, different nationalities, everything. In college, learning about other people is vitally important for your growth, and understanding different points of views and perspectives. Being able to understand everyone's point of view, talk to people, and show a genuine interest in their background I think is extremely important particularly as it translates into sales, and interacting with people professionally. Without that experience, I would have a hard time getting into sales from the very beginning. In my opinion, having that social life is just as important as academics, as long as you can balance it, and get the grades you need to get to accomplish what you want to."—*Brooks Neal*

9. "Quite honestly, I still struggle with balance. It's easier at certain times of the year and at certain times of the season. There are certain times where that's all that you do, and you have to understand that, and the people close to you have to understand that. You'll end up spending more time with your team or with

your job than you will with any other relationship. Understanding that as a collegiate athlete, it's very different than high school sports. Being a student-athlete forces you to manage your time almost to the point where it's done for you. It can be difficult when someone transitions out of that lifestyle because you now have a lot of free time and it's not managed for you. Therefore, it's really important to have that understanding and application of time management, and when it's time to do certain things, whether it's training, studying, sleeping, you have to do it at that time. Otherwise, it's not going to get done."—*Jeff Rodin*

10.   "You have to manage your own life. There is no one to hold your hand anymore and schedule everything and map everything out for you. Understanding how to create balance in your life and recognizing that the balance amongst your various interests will change over time. A lot of athletes are very focused, driven, and goal-oriented, and that's good because they achieve their goals and they understand it takes steps to get there. There is a bigger picture sometimes that people miss out on, so how you figure out how to navigate that path is important."—*Chris Dawson*

11.   "You have to find a balance with friends. There are so many perspectives that you can gain from all the different people that you can meet on a college campus. If your career path isn't in sport, then you really have to branch out."—*Kelsey Cermak*

12.   "It is extremely important to have balance while you are in school as a student-athlete. There has to be some balance between the athletic side, preparation, getting ready for games, being successful, and being part of a team. There also has to be a balance with your academics. You've got to hit the books; you've got to make the time that you put into it count. You've got to have some level of social life too. Interactions with people are something that we all need. If they get out of balance, if any of those three things become dominant, I don't think that's going to lead you where you desire to go."—*Steve Cobb*

This chapter draws upon the experiences of the authors and the input of more than a dozen interviewees to provide some direction to student-athletes about balance and keeping your lives, objectives, and time in synch with your priorities and goals. However you read this chapter, we hope you take away from it the critical importance of balance in all you consider to how your four to five years will unfold. Seek balance. Find your balance. Be Balanced.

Secret 6 Make Smart Decisions on the Other Stuff

THE SECRET IN A FEW WORDS

Secret 6 flows from Secret 5 but really puts the attention on the "other stuff" and not the academic and athletic elements. It is ONLY about the "stuff" outside of athletics and academics. It focuses on making smart decisions—the nonsport and nonacademic decisions that you have made or will make. This secret is straightforward and clear in its meaning: you must make smart decisions about nonsport and nonacademic matters because they will affect your success as a student and as an athlete. These decisions include anything and everything from how you use social media to how you pursue relationships, the time you spend with family or friends, your weekend behavior, your choice of transportation, and so much more.

MAKE SMART DECISIONS ON THE OTHER STUFF

The first five secrets were largely related to your athletic and academic lives: how to balance them, what to focus on, how to plan, how to develop life skills, support options, and resources. But, as was clearly described in Secret 5 (balance), these two pursuits, the primary foci of the average student-athlete, do not exist in a vacuum. Neither do you. As Secret 5 told us, your relationships, family life, friends, downtime, and so much more will all directly or indirectly influence your success as a student and as an athlete.

To shed some light on these other decisions, we reached out to Christa Mann, currently in management at Major League Soccer and a former collegiate and professional athlete, who outlined four particular areas of the "other stuff" that she would recommend any student-athlete consider.

First, she suggested seeking out a study abroad program to acquire international experience, to form a more global view of the world, to make new friends, and to facilitate nontraditional learning. She described her overseas experience as hugely important to her future career success and said this about her supportive coach: "If I could give anyone advice, it would be to find a coach who believes in you as an athlete but more so believes in what your dreams are away from the field."

Mann further emphasized how she was able to maintain her athletic fitness and readiness while taking advantage of her time abroad. "When I studied abroad, I went to Spain. I lived with a host family. After school I would run to the park and play pick up soccer and then run home. I still did my fitness every day, I still got a lot of touches on the ball."

In short, with a bit of effort, you can maintain your athletic preparedness while achieving some of the "other stuff" needed for success after college. "For me it was like striking that balance getting the study abroad experience traveling the world but also realizing that soccer was a major component in my life."

Second, Mann discussed the importance of building professional relationships. This advice builds on what we provided in Secret 5 about personal relationships. A key aspect of her advice to student-athletes was to take on leadership positions in college, such as joining a student club. She remembered: "I found myself in leadership roles during my junior year where I had to be the stand-up person, [so] I can't make mistakes or I can't be in the wrong places at the wrong time." She emphasized the importance of these leadership traits later in life.

So, find opportunities to build these skills and lead.

Third, she advised student-athletes to "make tons of friends. I think everyone should date, and understand the type of person they are and the type of person they'd like to be with." Mann told the story of a contact from a previous job who had "recommended two other women who were moving into the city who didn't know anyone either but were friends. The three of us live together now and we have a blast."

Finally, she discussed the tool of social media as a key "other stuff" component for student-athletes to consider. She suggested that "when it comes to social media, you should just be a part of the right conversation about social media. It's an opportunity to build your brand, to build who you are, to show your ambition, to show your preparation, and potentially get you where you want to go." When asked to explain, she noted that, in today's age, "your first impression to anyone is always going to be on social media . . . [which is an opportunity] to show you can be a student-athlete and this is what the life of a student-athlete is like."

Let's take a minute here and further discuss how you can use social media and how to be smart with it. We reached out to a few recent student-athletes to get some support for our points. Importantly, social media is not all positive. In fact, there is a high level of risk if you post inappropriate content or items that could be viewed negatively by your school, your coach, or your sponsor. Kelsey Cermak, a former student-athlete at Iowa University and now Assistant Director of Championships and Alliances at the NCAA, advised that "you have to be careful and not take any [compromising] pictures because you are under a microscope as a student-athlete."

We won't say don't post any photos or graphics but we would strongly suggest you think carefully about each photo before you click "send." Avoid overly intimate photos, avoid ones of you drinking or partying or looking out of control.

Hallie Olson, a former student-athlete and now Manager of Corporate Development at the Chicago Bulls, recommended, "You need to keep everything clean. You need to not have any beers, or anything incriminating on your feed or on Facebook. I would stay private on all of my social media channels like Instagram and Twitter."

Another key point with social media (like any communication efforts) is to consider who your specific target market is for each and every communication you send regardless of channel. Olson said she "would recommend that you know your audience, and know future employers are looking at your social media channels. Nobody wants to see you in front of a beer pyramid or saying anything controversial. Those things need to be private and it's really tough, but it needs to happen."

Matt Engleka, a former student-athlete at Ohio University and owner of LEJ Agency, provided this important advice:

> Now [today], as an athlete, you are living in such a fishbowl that people are looking to capture an athlete out of character and that's something extremely difficult to deal with when you're nineteen years of age. When Bryce Harper was growing up, the one thing he always did was carry a water bottle everywhere he went out in public. Why? Nobody can put anything else in your hand at that time. There's no question about what he was drinking. It's a bottle of water. The second you've got something else in your hand, someone is going to take a picture of it and then it's all over the place.

RYAN SOLLAZZO
(Director of Sponsorships at Major League Baseball)

I think people, nowadays, coming out of college need to be very careful and very sensitive with technology. I don't have any social media, but people in our world do look at that stuff and you need to be smart with what's out there. You have to understand that a lot can be taken out of context whether it is social media or emails, and sometimes it's best to just pick up the phone and actually talk to people.

Dan Butterly, Senior Associate Commissioner of the Mountain West Conference, pushed for a strong emphasis on "networking" as a key priority for student-athletes. He recommended that you identify whether networking is an area of weakness early on and if so, fix it. As an athlete and a student, you have social networks established around you by the university, and as people seek you out to support you (especially as an athlete) there is visibility benefit.

We asked Butterly to give some advice if you are in this situation. He said:

> If you're introverted, you have to associate with people who are, maybe, in your same career field or go to a speaker's series where you can learn more and meet people that are in your same wheelhouse. Challenge yourself to completely go out of your comfort level because that's the type of job that you're going to go into. That's the type of situation you are going to place yourself into.
>
> If you're introverted, you're not going to go into a development position or a sales position. It's going to be very difficult and very challenging for you in that career. There are other ways for you to network, though, with like-minded people who are going to be in your career field.
>
> Extroverts, obviously, have a lot easier time going to a mixer or going to a function that's not necessarily in their wheelhouse, but they just like meeting people. They like being out and about and having a drink and getting to know people. You just have to try and associate yourself with people that are going to be in your career path and get in a comfort zone and establish key relationships as best you can.

This is very important advice from a seasoned senior leader in collegiate sports in the United States. We recommend you follow it.

In addition to the four areas outlined by Mann and the point made by Butterly, you need to know about a few other decisions related to "other stuff" that a student-athlete needs to be ready for. We'll try to be very tactical here . . . to clearly illustrate how you need to consider each and every decision and how you need to really protect your time, as your primary resource.

1.   *Work part-time or not?* This is often a very difficult decision but shouldn't be. Obviously, there may be cases where a student-athlete needs the money to make ends meet, but normally working part-time would be to earn extra cash for nonessential things. So, if possible, try to decline to work part-time. The answer is "no." Sure, it will cost you a few amenities, but as we outlined in Secret 5, the amount you would be likely to earn will have very little impact on your life down the road.

2.   *Join a student club or not?* This decision is more difficult, as there are considerable potential upsides to joining the right student club at the right time. A key point is looking at the decision from a career perspective. Not all student clubs are created equal. Some are for fun and enjoyment, while others provide true networking, learning, and skill development for a career. For example, joining and spending time on the "analytics club" would make a great line on a math major's resume, provide beneficial learning opportunities, and probably catch a recruiter's attention.

3.   *Do an extra concentration (major, minor, etc.)?* This is something to talk about with your advisor, but we highly recommend it . . . provided the major, minor, or concentration will really help your hoped-for career. So, if you're studying chemistry, a minor in religion may not add great value. Or, maybe it will. We suggest taking classes of high interest to you, but be cognizant of your goals. Something that will help you get a job, advanced degree, or fellowship. From our experience, and you might find this surprising, when students take a set of more challenging courses within a specialization they are passionate about and plan to make their career in, they do better (in terms of both grades and enjoyment) than by taking a series of electives that they don't really care about but pick because they seem "easy." Yes, you are better off building your resume than cherry-picking easy electives.

4.   *Go on a date?* Here's a very tactical decision that you should take seriously. Dating is often stressful, takes time, and costs money. Many student-athletes see it as part of their heightened visibility that people may want to date them just for being an athlete. Skip dating if you have no interest or feel it will place you in an awkward setting. Don't go because you think it is expected of you and especially if you have no interest in the person or in dating in general (see Secret 5). Dating is not all bad, but dating

someone on a regular basis creates obligations and brings a wide range of emotional highs and lows that you must manage.

5. *Take a leadership role with a student organization or even with your sport team?* This is a very difficult decision and one where we'd advise you to proceed with caution, serious caution. There is a significant career upside (including leadership experience to list on your resume and a chance to lead groups and test your own strategic approaches), but there is a huge risk of overcommitting your time, especially if you become captain of your own sport team where you are already highly implicated. One of the authors took the role as captain of the swim team in her final year of competition and had her most disappointing year athletically but gained the benefit of being a team captain, which helped multiple times later on. At least five times in job interviews, the topic of having been captain of a university swim team came up in a positive way from the interviewers.

6. *Go to a party, event, luncheon, or meeting?* Much like going on that date, you need to critically review these decisions and opt out unless the benefit is clear and you want to attend and fully participate. Financial advisor Warren Buffet is famous for saying "when you're in the room, be in the room." What this means is that if you plan to go to a class, talk, or any event because you "should be there" but expect to sit at the back, not pay attention, not get involved, or play on your phone or check emails, then do NOT go. Either leverage the opportunity to the max or skip it. Simple.

7. *Hang out in the lounge/living room and watch television?* Oh, it seems so appealing. Long day, tons of homework ahead, friends, and a comfy couch. But that couch will suck you in and you'll miss your studying, your workout, your important call home, or you'll delay them all and lose sleep, damage your health, and impair your performance the next day. The tactic here is quite simple but hard to do. Use the "lounge time" as a carrot. Once you finish your work, get your exercise in, and do your key personal stuff, reward yourself with some relaxing time.

8. *How to choose my close friends?* As generally noted in Secret 5, this is a challenging decision as well. UNC Coach Anson Dorrance gave some great advice based on what he sees with his women's soccer team at North Carolina. He noted that "it is absolutely critical student-athletes develop close relationships with people around them and make sure the people they pick are positive. The cliché we use and share with the girls we train is you are

basically with the six people that you will hang out with the most. So choose wisely. Hopefully you have chosen people who have academic ambitions, because if you have them in your circle of friends, you are ultimately going to have academic ambitions."

9. *Go to class?* The famous question, and the answer is very clear—Yes. Without exception. Not only will it help you pass, get a higher GPA, and improve learning, but it will show your professors and your classmates (all of whom become important allies in your career down the road) that you are trustworthy, focused, serious, and someone they may want to hire one day. Put class in your schedule and stick with it. No exceptions.

OLIVER LUCK
(Executive VP of Regulatory Affairs at NCAA)

Go to class and take notes. If you go to class and if you take notes, you will pass. Think of class the way you think of practice. You wouldn't think of missing practice. Coach would be all over you, and you would probably get demoted. No athlete thinks of missing practice; so, take class the same way and when you're in class, take notes. Take down what the professor is talking about. You are spending the time in class, so you might as well be productive and benefit from it. The sooner you learn that, the better off you're going to be.

---

10. *How to choose the people I hang out with?* This piece of advice is similar to #8 above but different in certain respects. This is more about "association"—your choice of the people you associate with, and whose character or image might come to be associated with you. Are you known to hang out with fellow students in your program who are not athletes or do you avoid nonathletes? Are your friends on the team academically serious or are they partiers? Again, think it through. What clubs are you in? Think of the perceptual difference from being in the "analytics club" or the "accounting society" versus a "beer drinking club." People notice, and it affects your image. Serious athlete. Focused student. That's the brand you want. That is what you want people to think about when they think of you.

We could go on and on with this list but we're pretty certain you get the point. Every activity is a decision. Make each decision wisely and selfishly.

CHAPTER SUMMARY

Making smart decisions on the "other stuff" will not only help you during your student-athlete experience, it will create good decision-making skills and a sound foundation for later in life. We all make decisions every day on hundreds of things (whether you think about it or not), and by making smart decisions on a continual basis, we train ourselves to make prepared, quality decisions.

You won't make the right decision every time, but as long as you can make smart and prepared decisions, you will finish the journey well off.

Everyone makes mistakes in life (we are human, after all), but make the smart decisions at the right time by just taking an extra minute to think about "the other stuff."

Secret 7 — Seek Support Everywhere

There are a lot of examples in the world where one needs to find out how to do something hard and goes to a friend for advice. And in many instances, help and support can be just the start to a lifelong relationship. Life, of course, isn't always easy or simple, but there are many people around you who are actually paid to provide advice or facilitate solutions to challenges NCAA student-athletes face during their time in college. So here's the secret: Find those people and cultivate them as resources for the times when you aren't sure how to fix a difficult or stressful situation. Said another way: start building a network of "friends" (as soon as you can) who want to help you succeed.

SEEK SUPPORT EVERYWHERE

This secret draws particularly from a few of the specific aspects/tactics noted in Secret 3 about the success wheel (e.g., time management, using resources, networking, mentors, etc.). Dr. Kevin Hall, a former student-athlete who is now a physical therapist, outlines his experiences with this secret in the following passage.

KEVIN HALL (former student-athlete at Wichita State University, Doctor of Physical Therapy at the Mayo Clinic, Scottsdale)

The biggest lesson I learned in those five years [of college] was that people are your greatest resource. College sports programs are designed with an immense amount of personnel dedicated to helping the athlete succeed on and off the playing field. Coaches, trainers, academic advisors, teammates, even the people who check on class attendance—all played a role in my success.

I spent hours talking with advisors to create a class schedule that allowed me to finish the credits I needed for school while ensuring I made it to practice and games. I utilized study hall rooms for quiet places before tests and to print out study materials. And I sought out advice of coaches, teammates, and family when I struggled to find balance in my career.

Most importantly, what I did was create relationships. Relationships that helped me shape my game, opened up job opportunities, and made me appreciate the many resources I had. Letters of recommendation don't write themselves, and I was fortunate to have the endorsement of faculty and medical professionals because of relationships I forged years prior.

My former coach, Gene Stephenson, used to say: "You're only spoiled if you've been given a lot and you don't take care of it." While he was referring to our program's reputation, the same can be said for using the resources at hand.

To realize great dreams or goals, one must always have a solid support system and the intelligence to utilize the resources around them.

As high-performance, competitive athletes, the Hawaiian expression "Mo' bettah" makes a lot of sense. I want more of the good thing. Coaches and business leaders sometimes express the same sentiment by saying, "We need to get better faster than our competitors."

But what does that expression really mean? The two key words in the sentence seem to be racing toward a collision like a linebacker and a running back hitting the line of scrimmage at the same time. Or two field hockey players racing to control a ball in the midfield. We're destined to see a moment of "better" and "faster" beating "okay" and "slower."

The concept certainly fits the lines from the Bob Dylan song quoted above where you face a dilemma and we just want to say to someone, "Tell me quick 'cause I gotta run." But whom should you ask and what should you be asking them? More importantly, will they be "invested" in you enough to immediately start helping you get stronger, smarter, and more successful?

By this point, most of you who are NCAA student-athletes reading this book have settled into a routine of understanding the main players in your intercollegiate life. You have a head coach, a position coach, the head athletic trainer, a strength coach, teachers, and possibly the resident advisor on your dorm floor or the individual responsible for your housing (owner, landlord, property manager). These people are the primary folks issuing orders that you feel obligated to follow.

Coaches and trainers want certain physical achievements. Learn the playbook. Make this move here. Develop these muscles. Rehab this nagging injury. Work harder at your game.

Meanwhile, teachers want papers written or group projects finished. They hint about midterms, pop quizzes, and finals. Work harder at your books. Back at your "crib," there are rules about noise, trash, and parking. "Y'all better keep it down up there or we're going to call the cops."

In each of the above instances, someone is setting rules or establishing guidelines leaving little for interpretation. When Coach calls for a sixty-yard run, it doesn't do much good to think about negotiating the distance or the speed.

What this means is that many student-athletes get into the habit of expecting someone else to tell them what to do. There is always someone to set rules, create the culture, and dictate all of your actions.

For many, the number of people the student-athlete trusts for solving problems is a very small circle. In their sport it may be a veteran (or smarter) teammate. At school it may be a classmate or tutor.

This limits how a student-athlete thinks about problem solving (which is one of the most important traits that employers look for in hiring new employees). In fact, one interviewer we know is famous in job interviews for asking a hypothetical question for which there is no right answer. One of his questions runs along these lines: You are sitting in a rowboat in the middle of the Pacific Ocean right over the famous Marianas Trench. You drop a cannonball over the edge of the boat. How long will it take for the cannonball to reach the bottom?

For many of us, the question is just stupid and our first response is, "How the heck should I know?" But there are clues in the question that can allow someone used to solving problems to create an answer. Some of the ways in which someone might respond could include:

- Well, it would be good to know how much the cannonball weighs and whether the water temperature matters (wanting more facts).

- Well, if the trench is famous, it must be pretty deep, so I'll guess that it's at least five miles deep (showing some knowledge and a willingness to make some assumptions).

- Was there a reason I was dropping cannonballs in the middle of the ocean? (trying to determine what the interviewer is really seeking)

- I don't want to guess at something without the facts, so let me ask you if I can give that answer to you later today (buying time to find a solution).

What the interviewer is looking for is how a candidate starts to reason out a solution. What the student-athlete can do is create the perception (even without knowing anything about the Pacific Ocean or Newtonian physics influencing the laws of gravity in liquid) that they are up to the challenge and have resources available to them for problem solving.

But where would you start if you got asked that interview question? You'd be pretty certain none of your teammates know anything about dropping cannonballs in some faraway ocean. You certainly wouldn't want to ask your coach, English professor, or landlord. They'd give you that funny look and suggest you need to get your priorities straight.

Right. But this is where your support network comes in. This is when you know there are people who can help right away.

In many cases like this, there are a variety of stumbling blocks, depending on which member of your support network you ask. Some of your "network" resources might respond like this:

- I dunno, dude, that's a pretty tough/stupid question (True meaning: I can't help).

- Look that up on Google or Wikipedia (True meaning: Here's a clue but I can't give you more than that and you're on your own to solve the problem).

- Go ask _____, they're really good with weird stuff like that (True meaning: Let me deflect helping you and get you to work with someone else who may or may not have time for you).

- Go ask at the library. That's why they're there (True meaning: Let me deflect helping you but point you toward a support staff that doesn't know you).

- I'd like to help you but you need to come back during office hours (True meaning: I can't help you now and if I'm lucky you'll go to someone else to solve the problem).

Like the cannonball scenario above, there are other matters that might elicit the same responses.

- Who can help me create a good resume?

- Where do I go to try to get an internship during our out-of-season training window?

- Who can help me pick out the right interview outfit?

- I'm feeling really down about the amount of playing time I'm getting and my "significant other" seems mad at me.

- I wonder if I'm eating enough (or too much) or getting the right amount of sleep?

- I've had a death in the family and I feel really messed up about it.

- I'm falling behind with my schoolwork and if it gets worse, it will affect my eligibility (or scholarship).

- How do I get my finances under control so I can afford stuff?

- How do I get a job I'll like when I graduate?

- How do I get a job in my field when I graduate?

- How do I make more time to get involved with non-Athletics activities?

- Should I think about going to grad school right away or work for a few years?

- How do I get a job?

These are only a few of the questions a student-athlete might ask during four or five years at an NCAA institution, and the inability to get the right support can have crippling ramifications not only for enjoyment of one's sport but also for lifelong success. Additionally, small matters often become big ones or cause other small matters to multiply.

It reminds us of the legendary English proverb, possibly a reference to King Richard's defeat in battle in 1485:

> For want of a nail the shoe was lost.
> For want of a shoe the horse was lost.
> For want of a horse the rider was lost.
> For want of a rider the message was lost.
> For want of a message the battle was lost.
> For want of a battle the kingdom was lost.
> And all for the want of a horseshoe nail.

In the story above (which William Shakespeare alluded to a hundred years later in his play *Richard III*), the loss of the smallest item (the horseshoe nail that fitted the shoe to the horse's hoof) caused all kinds of mayhem including the loss of the rider, message, battle, and kingdom.

You may not think your postcollegiate career is as important as a kingdom, but the reality is that little losses (no bigger than a nail) can cause things to unravel and ultimately create situations far worse than you ever imagined. The kingdom you imagined for yourself when you were heavily recruited to play at your current university could possibly be slipping away as you realize you won't be starting this year and certainly won't be turning pro.

Said another way: getting advice about how to address the missing nail (or even larger matters) is really important—and a key skill set to develop on your own.

So what to do? In the movie *Ghostbusters* (and we're talking about the original one from 1984), the famous phrase was, "Who ya gonna call?" And the shouted response was "Ghostbusters!"

On the TV show *Who Wants to Be a Millionaire,* the contestants almost always reach a question for which they need help and can use one of their "lifelines," which have included "50/50" (the computer eliminates two of the three wrong answers), "Ask the Audience," or "Phone a Friend."

Brett Fischer, physical therapist for the Arizona Cardinals, suggested alumni are one of the options for that phone call.

> For student-athletes, there are so many alumni to take advantage of. Athletes have an opportunity to get to know them, and find out what made them successful. Some may have played sports when they were in school, some may have not. Regardless, they're successful. I think a lot of the athletes think their sport is never going to end. I don't care who these people are. They are just fans. They're just alumni.
>
> Well, they're successful alumni and they got there somehow. It's important for the college athlete to look at those people as positive resources for advice, for wisdom, for internships, everything. They're a great resource. It's something in college you've got to take advantage of.

In these examples above, there was a ready resource. Got a house with ghosts? Call these guys! Can't remember whether helium is heavier than oxygen? Call a friend. But which friend? And what is the college equivalent? Know of an alum who is really connected? Pick up the phone.

At most schools, the following people are probably a great place to start:

- An administrative mentor you've developed (possibly the associate athletic director for your sport) or a graduate assistant who played your sport and is spending one or two years assisting your team while getting an advanced degree

- The senior academic support staff individual (often connected to the provost's office) who is responsible for selecting tutors for the Athletic Learning Community

- The faculty athletic representative (FAR), who traditionally serves as the link between the university's faculty and all student-athletes and is also usually involved with your school's athletic conference and the NCAA

- The career counselor your Athletic Department may have established for helping student-athletes with matters involving post-collegiate careers; this individual often creates career fairs for athletes, brings in motivational or inspirational speakers, and sometimes is involved with the Student Athlete Advisory Committee (SAAC)

- The career counselor or internship coordinator in your specific college (not in the Athletic Department), if your university has different schools like business, education, music, etc.

- Your faculty advisor

- The leadership council for your SAAC (which generally requires one representative from each sport played at your school), consisting of fellow students recognized by their peers as leaders, who generally meet weekly or biweekly to discuss matters involving student-athletes like yourself—and like you, they are dealing with time demands placed on them by coaches and teachers

- Your athletic director

- The chancellor or president of your university or college

At this point, having read the list above, many of you might be thinking, "As if I could just call up the university president or the athletic director and ask them a question. The people who wrote this book are so out of touch."

For us, this is the *gotcha* moment because we seriously believe you can reach out to people that you believe are *waaaay* beyond caring about your success. And we think you'll be surprised to find how many of those top executives or distant "adults" really do enjoy helping college students solve problems. In fact, one of the reasons they chose to work in higher education instead of on Wall Street or Main Street was because they truly enjoy the educational imperative of helping and serving others.

The secret here is finding people near you who really do care about your success . . . people who enjoy helping others.

John Nowicki describes how he used relationships directly related to his status as a student-athlete to, first, gain internships and then to help him launch his career.

JOHN NOWICKI (former lacrosse student-athlete, Account Manager at International Speed Corporation)

The one relationship that stands out to me was a university professor, who also served as a consultant for the University of Detroit Mercy (UDM) athletic department and the Miami University athletic department. Over the course of four years as a student-athlete at UDM, I developed a strong relationship with this professor by meeting with him regularly to discuss coursework, athletic performance, and post-college plans.

During the early part of my senior year, I received an offer to visit Miami University with him to interview for a summerlong internship within their athletic department. Over the course of my internship, I took advantage of every opportunity to meet with staff members from different departments, coaches, and administrators. Through this process, I developed two crucial relationships with staff members with the hockey program and on the university development staff, which led to my next two career moves—the Central Collegiate Hockey Association (CCHA) & Ohio University's Sports Administration Program.

The staff members with the hockey program assisted me with an introduction to administrators at the league office, the CCHA, which was based back in Michigan near my home. The staff members with the university development staff introduced me to the idea of getting my MBA and Masters in Sports Administration at Ohio University, which has a strong reputation for launching the career of sports business professionals across a variety of disciplines in sales, marketing, communication, and management.

Through the process of completing the internship with the CCHA and attending Ohio University, I was able to apply similar relationship-based networking practices in the sports business, ultimately leading to my acceptance of a full-time role in the industry. The common theme through each of those roles was taking full advantage of the relationships that surrounded me while I was in each organization, which ultimately would lead to my next opportunity.

For all the student-athletes out there, my challenge to you is reflect upon the relationships currently surrounding you. Coaching staffs, athletic department members, university professors and staffs, and teammates' families, that may be able to provide the introduction that launches your career.

The questions for you are: Do you know who the right people to call are, and are you spending enough time thinking about what your full potential is? Student-athletes who hope to turn professional in their sport always know that "full potential" means getting drafted, signing a contract, and making a pro team (or making the cut on the pro tour). But for you, one of the other 99 percent who don't know what might happen after your college sports days are finished, "full potential" could mean almost anything.

Or think of it this way: Some people are good at sports or talking in public or answering questions in class. That's fine. You can be good at all of that, but you need to be one of those people who gets really good at asking for the right help at the right time.

HILLARY (BACH) NELSON
(former softball student-athlete at Arizona State University, Partnerships Manager at Positive Coaching Alliance)

I think that your support network is crucial. The first day on campus, I introduced myself to my academic counselor and I let her know that I wanted to be an Academic All-American. That was number one, and number two was I needed a calculus tutor. Math was not my strong suit, but I knew I needed help and I knew I was going to have to take calculus in order to get my business degree. The best advice I ever got was to never be afraid to ask for help. There are so many opportunities out there, and we have to encourage those athletes to take advantage of the opportunities.

Don't forget to give yourself credit for the hard work you put in to get this far. There were late nights or early mornings that I missed school dances or I spent Friday nights at the ballpark instead of the movies with my friends. I had sunburns and scars, whatever it was in my career, I earned those. I have to remind myself that I earned this opportunity because it can be easy when you get to a big campus to be intimidated. You're not the big man on campus anymore. As a student-athlete, be grateful and enjoy it and understand that you're there for a reason. They recruited you there for a reason, and they need you to keep working hard and to sustain that excellence that you've shown up to this point. You can't just show up anymore. That's not what got you there. You got to keep running the same pace and keep fighting for your goals.

I really got involved in my college. For example, they had a writing center where you could meet with a writing tutor and they would give you corrections on your paper. All of that makes you work because you have to set your own deadlines before the actual deadline so you have time to get in there and make another revision and go back for a second revision. Secondly, team trainers were extremely important to utilize. Having an understanding that you're putting your body through a lot more than you're probably used to coming out of high school is important. Go the extra mile or get up the extra hour to stretch or do rehab or whatever you need to do to make sure your body is maintaining the optimal efficiency.

I think our boosters are underutilized by student athletes. They're there because they want you to be successful. They're there because they care about your program. They care about you. They're cheering you on every game. They're following you. Talk to them. They're successful human beings. They all have a story. They all have a job. That was a great resource for me when I was a student-athlete.

Administrators on campus. Those people are there for your success. They really dedicated their professional careers to helping you live the best four years of your life.

Your professors are a big part of your support network, especially those teaching subjects that directly relate to your major. If they've been doing it for a while, hopefully they know a lot of successful people in the industry you're hoping to work for. Ask them for ideas. Ask them for contacts. Don't be afraid to walk up and introduce yourself on the first day of school because you want to have that first positive interaction before you have to go to them with a missed class letter or problem or a conflict down the road.

CHAPTER SUMMARY

You may not think "Seeking Support Everywhere" is much of a secret, but our collective years on college campuses have shown us that too few student-athletes actually ever master the system of solving problems and *getting better faster than their competitors* (which includes everyone around them who wants or needs to get a job when they graduate). No question, there are a lot of people on your campus and a lot of students with problems to solve.

So let's repeat that concept: Getting a job after graduation means that you are in competition with just about everyone on your campus who has the same challenge. Ending up with a successful outcome is a function, then, of the following:

- Knowing whom to ask for help (where they are, how to get to them)
- Knowing what to ask and how to ask it
- Building a large network of "friends" and support staff who actually find great enjoyment in seeing your long-term success
- Understanding that attention to the little details (the horseshoe nails) is really important to the big picture
- Remembering that postcompetition career success is not a sudden thing; it is a developed thing

As management expert Malcolm Gladwell wrote in his book *Outliers,* no one makes it "big" on their own. Everyone needs help and those who learn whom to ask for guidance and assistance and how to ask for those things end up receiving advantages that lead to their individual success.

Start working now on getting "mo' bettah."

Secret 8 Your Major Really Matters

MATTIE WHITE
(Associate Athletic Director for Academic Services
and the Excellence Academy at Indiana University)

You should major in something where you can develop a set of transferrable skills for taking into any career. Your career may not have to do with your major right away or five years down the road, but you want to develop transferable skills that can apply to any career.

The three keys to picking your major are:

1. Determine what you are passionate about. If you do what you love, the money or fame will come. You will likely be more successful if you are passionate about your work.

2. Evaluate your skill set and know where your strengths really are. Know what you are good at and what you can improve at.

3. Trust the process. Picking the major is just the first step. There is a lot of hard work to follow, and you just have to stick with it.

Keep this in mind as you read this chapter: "High school prepares you for college and college prepares you for life."

THE SECRET IN A FEW WORDS

For many student-athletes who have never thought about anything more than playing their sport, the concept of getting a job when they "grow up" is pretty daunting. There's an inner voice that says adults have jobs but college students have fun. While we won't dispute that perception, the academic major that you pick plays a huge role in how you think about yourself and what you think you'll do after your playing days end. Pick the wrong major and you might not have very many choices for jobs. If you are indifferent about your future, you might end up lost for some period of time. So, like it or not, your major and your post-collegiate aspirations define you and will likely shape your future.

YOUR MAJOR REALLY MATTERS

Every university and college is different . . . just as every student-athlete is different. But strangely enough, there are a number of similarities with both groups. Every university or college is intent on providing its student-athletes with degrees (from any number of majors), and all student-athletes who imagine graduating see themselves strolling across a stage . . . and receiving a diploma stating they have developed some level of knowledge in a particular topic area.

For movie buffs, the most famous graduate in cinema history may be the Scarecrow in *The Wizard of Oz* who, after the Wizard gives him a diploma, is suddenly "intelligent" and begins spouting a geometry equation. Before handing the Scarecrow his diploma, the Great Oz declaims that every living creature has a brain but people who graduate from college can actually think deep thoughts.

Perhaps the Wizard was right. Perhaps if student-athletes earn degrees and walk across various stages, they will be able to construct thoughts and utilize a highly developed sense of reason for solving complex problems. But . . . and this is a big but . . . will they be able to get a job they want?

So let's back up and talk to a career counselor who works with student-athletes every day.

Mark Trumbo is the Life Skills Coordinator in the Stevenson Educational Center for Student-Athlete Development at Syracuse University. He recently reflected that students have long been asked the question, "What do you want to major in?"

He believes that might be the wrong question to ask those student-athletes, because now more than ever, students want to feel a part of something bigger than themselves. They want to connect more with an organization's mission, ideals, and culture.

"Identifying a major shouldn't be a mindless activity of comparing features and benefits," says Trumbo. "A student-athlete's passion and skills, put together, will provide a guide to answering the bigger question . . . which is . . . what problem do I want to solve?"

Trumbo's belief is grounded in the conviction that a student-athlete's first class in college should be figuring out his or her career.

"For too long, students have been trained mentally to believe the point of college is to do well in college," says Trumbo. "This, frankly, is a detrimental mindset for any student. Changing or choosing a major that is the path of least resistance for your respective sport cheapens the value of an education. The process, to me, needs to work in reverse. What cause do I want to fight for? Where can I build a legacy that impacts human lives? Is there a problem where I can be part of the solution?"

How does Trumbo sum it up? He says student-athletes have to identify their passion and develop the necessary skills to work in that field. Then they need to find the educational platform that checks those boxes and leads them to like-minded employers.

Put another way, we think a student-athlete's selection of a major plays a huge role in how employers see a recently graduated student-athlete. And not only do employers study potential new hires but they bring certain perceptions with them.

All of us know there is bias in the world and it comes in many different forms. Some schools are thought to be better than other schools. Some revenue sports are thought of as more important than nonrevenue ones. Some cities are considered cooler than their country cousins. The list goes on.

You will be able to fill in hundreds of other ways that people create bias (both good and bad), but the one category you want to consider (and this is both hard to imagine as a freshman . . . and hard to handle as an abstract concept) is the perceptions of employers.

Think of it this way: for you to get a job, someone has to hire you. And that person doing the hiring is going to call on a number of considerations to calculate risk (in hiring you). Here are a few of the things employers and human resource personnel might review:

- The university or college you attended
- Your major (your primary area of study)
- Your GPA (if you provide it)
- The sport you played
- The success you had while playing (i.e., did you go to a bowl game or Final Four, become an NCAA All-American, earn All-Conference accolades, make the All-Academic team?)
- Your region of the country you are from or country of origin
- Whether you know anyone at that company (particularly any senior executives)
- Your personality and how you dress (if they see you in person)
- Your social network habits (as available to them by way of casual or in-depth research of what you have revealed on social networks)
- Your references

For only a few of the above items . . . at this point . . . can you personally control the answer. Perhaps the most important one is your major and the second is your GPA . . . which does not have to be revealed.

The words you choose or the phrases your university uses to define your primary area of study—your degree and your major—are interesting. There are the "mythical" inscriptions that will be written on your diploma. For example, the diploma language, written in some fancy calligraphy, might indicate Bachelor of Science, Public Communications. But what you might say in a verbal interview is that you were a broadcast journalism major with a minor in finance. The parchment your parents get framed might simply say "Engineering," where you would fill in a bit more of the story by saying you majored in civil engineering with a focus on structural design.

You get the point. What you say about what you studied is important.

This handful of words, the expression of your accomplishment, the description of how you spent the majority of your academic time . . . are significant and will undoubtedly shape an interviewer's perceptions. And— BIAS ALERT—some majors or collections of words sound more impressive to certain employers than others.

When you start at your university or college, you might not think much about it because much of your youthful energy will go into impressing a coaching staff and earning the maximum amount of playing time possible. Those coaches study you (in one way or another) every day at practice and during games. Your "diploma" with them (think of it as your varsity letter) is shaped by a variety of optics and measurements:

- Are you punctual for meetings and practices?
- Are you committed to team and voluntary workouts?
- Are you respected by your teammates?
- Do you produce the expected competition results under pressure?
- Are you reliable and consistent?
- Do you cause headaches, issues, or problems?
- Are you a positive influence on others?
- Are you a winner?

Each day, those observations get made and often by the same people. In fact, most athletes get graded on a game-by-game basis and the results are often shared around well before the next game.

But on the academic side of the ledger, there is very limited daily grading because classes and faculty continually change, and even within a lecture hall, it is rare that a professor studies a student with the same intensity as a coach. Faculty members want all of their students to do well, but there is no scoreboard at the end of each class. In many cases, it's just meaningful material presented and notes taken. In some classes there will be discussion, but the professor may remain indifferent to whether you participate or beneficially influence others.

What this means is that after four or five years of careful scrutiny by your sport coaches, teammates, athletic trainers, strength coaches, and the local (or national) media, you may find that, beyond end-of-term grades, there was very little accounting done by your professors and instructors about you, the soon-to-be professional. Yes, they measured you with grades, but then they moved on to the next class. You were left with a GPA, some knowledge and, for many, a gnawing sensation (maybe a growling) in your stomach that what you learned may not help you get the job you think you want.

Selecting a major or articulating your career aspirations is really important. And choosing a major that really interests you is far more important than grabbing an easy major.

Let's say that again: ***Choosing a major that really interests you is far more important than grabbing an easy major.*** And you know that if we placed it in italics and then made it boldface, it must be important.

So let's make this chapter operational for you.

1. Make sure you have a target (your major) that might lead to a job you could want. For most athletes, sport is a passion, so don't rule out a career where sport is the business or a big part of the business. And don't rule out interests in music, movies, advertising, special events, marketing, video gaming, animals, and many other areas that can also lend themselves to a career. Work doesn't have to be a drag.

2. Make sure the major you pick is something that really interests you (not your parents, coach, or academic support staff). You are the one who will have to go to work after you graduate.

3. Make sure that if it's too late to change your major, you start aggressively determining if you can add a "minor" that you really like . . . or what the job opportunities are for people graduating with your major. Many people say it's never too late . . . but sometimes it is . . . for one thing. But not for another.

4. Go to every career fair your athletic department or university offers. Go meet with people who actually have jobs available and are looking for future employees. They can tell you what they are looking for. In addition, don't be afraid to talk to professionals in your athletic department and any of the sport organizations that support them (such as broadcasting companies, sports marketing agencies, legal firms, health care suppliers, equipment manufacturers).

5.   While many people don't want to stay in school any longer than possible, understand that if you can achieve at least a 3.0 GPA as an undergraduate, you can keep the door open for going back to graduate school and majoring in a subject area you might really like.

6.   Use the academic resources available to you before or after practice (your academic support staff and life skills coordinator) and within your college or current major to get known by the faculty and emerge as someone others want to help.

At the end of the day, your major and your grades will help you get into graduate school if that is part of your plan. We say this because a 2015 NCAA study (see the chart below) indicates that a high percentage of student-athletes think about going to graduate school after they are done competing. Stop and think, because although you may not consider this as an option right after college, you may reconsider a couple of years down the road. And let's face it, just being a student-athlete isn't going to get you into graduate school.

IT IS AT LEAST SOMEWHAT LIKELY THAT I WILL GO TO GRADUATE SCHOOL AT SOME POINT AFTER COLLEGE

	Division 1	Division 2	Division 3
Baseball	54%	55%	54%
Men's Basketball	54%	56%	63%
Football FBS|FCS	61%/57%	62%	58%
Men's Other	59%	62%	65%
Women's Basketball	72%	70%	76%
Women's Other	73%	72%	75%

NCAA Research. (January 2016). *Results from the 2015 GOALS Study of the Student-Athlete Experience.* Retrieved on May 22, 2017.[1]

Based on the collective experiences of the authors, the last point in the list of six recommendations is—we believe—particularly important. Researchers have frequently commented that many of the most successful people were the ones who created meaningful relationships with a few key faculty members. Sometimes those experiences took place right after class and sometimes they happened during office hours or informally on a weekend or over a coffee. The mini-secret (now revealed for the first time in this chapter) is that getting a few faculty members to care about your personal success and the development of your postcollege life is key.

Best of all, you (the student) get to pick those faculty members you really like. Invest some energy in getting to know them, because they are an incredible resource for talking about your dreams, plans, crazy schemes, ideas, goals, and hopes.

If you've ever seen the movie *Back to the Future* (with Michael J. Fox), you'll know that high schooler Marty McFly (Fox) spends a lot of time with eccentric scientist Doc Brown . . . who has conveniently invented a device that allows time travel. Setting aside the quirky physics of the space-time continuum, what's interesting is seeing McFly engaging his curiosity and meeting with the equivalent of a professor outside of class. Marty gets a lot of advice/wisdom, and as the movie suggests, "hanging out" with Doc is life-changing.

You might not believe us, but (apart from the time travel) the same thing could happen to you.

CHAPTER SUMMARY

We hear too often from students who don't like their major or, in some cases, don't even know how they got their major. People along the way told them what courses to take to stay eligible. That's a shame, because picking a major is one of the most sure-fire ways to influence how you see yourself and how you imagine the rest of your life unfolding.

Yes, we understand not all college graduates get jobs in the field of their majors. And we know that some majors don't lend themselves to exciting jobs. But failing to pick a major you are passionate about isn't the way to go.

As the late Stephen Covey (author of the seminal book *The 7 Habits of Highly Effective People*) advised, "Start with the End in Mind," which is to say, "start with a clear understanding of your destination." But then Covey added, you are your own creator. You get to design what you become. You create your own weather because "whether it rains or shines" you determine your own outcome.

You might not like "owning" your future, but start by identifying a major. That action will become a major strength (or foundation) and yes, we get that you might not yet know what you want for the future.

So ask for help and advice from professors, "Doc Browns," and life skills counselors early and often.

And keep in mind that you can't always get what you want, but if you persevere, you stand a good chance of getting what you need!

Secret 9 Take Nothing for Granted

THE SECRET IN A FEW WORDS

Injuries can happen at any moment in your athletic career, and, in the worst cases, end it in a heartbeat. No amount of fitness and skill can guarantee you an injury-free athletic career. The only thing you can do to prepare for such an unfortunate outcome is put yourself in a good position on the off chance this does happen. In the meantime, you should prepare for anything and always have a plan just in case. Think positively about everything but remember life will throw you curveballs, and you don't want to get frozen at the plate and strike out looking. At least be able to foul off the pitch and give yourself another opportunity.

TAKE NOTHING FOR GRANTED

A lot of times we get carried away in the moment, and we never allow ourselves to take a step out of the figurative batter's box to realize how fortunate we are and appreciate what we get to do every day. As a student-athlete, you are fortunate to hang out with a small group of athletes who get to compete for their school in a sport they love. You get an opportunity many kids wish for. Our advice for you is simply this:

1. Take a step back to realize where you are and what you are doing.

2. Recognize how fortunate you are to play your sport collegiately.

3. Keep things in perspective . . . have you ever thought about the people who have career-ending injuries and what their lives are like?

4. Appreciate the little things, because you won't realize you'll miss them until they are gone.

5. Finally, play every day like it's your last. We know this is clichéd, but it is really true. You never know when something will be taken away from you in the blink of an eye.

Believe it or not, a minor injury, or even a career-ending injury, can teach you more than you could ever imagine. We wouldn't wish this on anyone, but if it does happen, you need to have a positive perspective and mindset.

The stories presented here illustrate how student-athletes who experienced physical injuries learned the importance of developing perspective on their situations. We hope their stories about confronting and overcoming unexpected setbacks will provide you with models worth learning from. The key lesson from these stories is that things change, stuff happens, and plans go out the window. You must be able to adapt all of the secrets we've shared in the first part of the book to whatever comes.

GRACIE FRIZZELL (former women's basketball student-athlete at Ole Miss, physical therapy graduate student at Arkansas)

I was in the seventh grade the very first time I picked up a basketball. By the time I was a senior [high school], I was extremely driven to pursue my dream of playing basketball in the Southeastern Conference. The greatest high in my athletic career was the day I signed a National Letter of Intent to play at the University of Mississippi. I thought I would lead my team to a state championship that year, however fate decided to intervene in December of 2010. I ruptured my anterior cruciate ligament (or as most people would say, their ACL) while going up for a simple lay up in practice, and when I found out the news, I thought my life, and "more importantly" my basketball career, was over. So many thoughts ran through my head as to how I would come back from an ACL injury and be able to compete at such a high level as the SEC. After surgery, which was in January of 2011, I faced many emotions that were mentally draining for me, athletically and personally.

As an athlete, I had a loss of identity. . . . I did not understand why this would happen to me so young in my career or what I would do without a ball in my hands. And then reality hit me with the fact that I had nothing besides basketball to lean on. Yes, I was a good student, but it was not something that I put my focus towards in my young life. I had no true friends that I could lean on that weren't involved in athletics.

This injury proved to me I needed a balance in my life that I was lacking. I had a choice to make. I could either throw myself a "pity party," give up, and never get better, or I could find some gumption about myself and attack my experience head on. As a competitor I made the choice to attack physical therapy head on, rehabbing every day as cautiously, yet aggressively as I could, and taking one day at a time.

I was in the best shape of my life when I reported to Ole Miss as a freshman, and the coaches were impressed with where I was in my recovery process. My confidence in my skills, speed, and strength was at an all-time high, until one afternoon something went horribly wrong. I felt a sign of instability in my knee when playing one on one, and I experienced the same gut-wrenching feeling that something was terribly wrong.

I had an MRI soon after the incident, and met with the doctors that same afternoon. When the doctor walked in and told me that my "newly" placed graft was torn again, I honestly think I went into a state of shock. I had worked so hard for six months for a moment to shine in the SEC, and I felt like it all went down the drain. After a long conversation with my Ole Miss coach, we talked about how I would redshirt my freshman year and continue to rehab so I could fulfill my dreams of playing college basketball.

What I thought was a career-ending injury turned into one of the biggest blessings in my life. I grew mentally, physically, emotionally and spiritually from my experience. I knew that I had a way to gain empathy towards others who are not only going through an athletics injury but any injury or disorder that they are facing. I am now in pursuit of becoming a physical therapist, and I am frequently overcome with joy for being able to give others the empowering feeling of overcoming obstacles in their life. I found my purpose in life through what I thought was a tough time because of college athletics.

Shauna Happel, a former soccer player at the University of Northern Iowa, also dealt with injuries in her career, and her experiences define this secret.

SHAUNA HAPPEL (former soccer student-athlete at the University of Northern Iowa)

As athletes, injuries are simply part of the sport that we love. Our passion, commitment, and dedication are what drive us to give everything that we have in order to compete. Day in and day out we continually work to achieve success. There isn't a day that goes by that we don't think about our sport and reminisce about the moments that we spend with our teammates. Oftentimes athletes take all of this for granted. We live in the moment and take each day as it comes.

The scary thing is we never know what practice tomorrow may bring. Some days we can't wait to get out on the field and then there are other days where we dread the mere idea of what physically exhausting tasks we may encounter. Whether it be negative or positive our thoughts and our heart are always with the sport and we couldn't imagine life without it. However, with the blink of an eye all of this can change and leave us in a blur of confusion and emptiness. Our sport can be taken away from us at any moment and the culprit can be described in one word: injury.

I can't remember hardly ever having to sit out of a practice or game. I could probably count on one hand the number of times that happened in fifteen years of competitive sports. However, as my final season of high school soccer was coming to a close my athletic career would take a turn for the worse and be greatly altered. I was diagnosed with a stress fracture in my right shin. I worked through the injury as I headed to Northern Iowa University on a soccer scholarship. Fast forward to my freshman year, and I acquired another injury.

I suffered a spiral fracture to my fibula (on the same leg that I had the stress fracture). To make matters even worse, the doctor said I was going to need surgery to repair it. I could not believe what I was hearing. Here I am on my first day of the spring soccer season and I find out I am going to be out for the entire season. I went into my sophomore year dragging my shin pain with me. I kept playing throughout the season as the pain continued to get stronger and more frequent. It got to the point where I was wearing a boot during the day and took it off to play and practice. Fast forward to the next season, and I found out that during the first week of preseason I tore the labrum in my left hip. It turned out I needed surgery to repair it, and an even longer rehab process than anything else I had done before.

Being sidelined with a season-ending injury meant that I was going to be watching my team play and practice from behind the confines of the sideline. I never could have imagined how hard this task would be and the toll that it would take on me mentally and emotionally. I already knew the physical toll that this injury had taken on me, but I could have never predicted the effects that this injury would have on me in other aspects of my life.

I felt like I had been on a mental and emotional roller coaster for the previous few months. Even though it has been really tough to get through this, my driving force has been positivity and to be grateful for everything that I have and have been able to experience. One of the hardest things to come to grips with was that I was not going to be able to play soccer for an entire season with my teammates.

When people think of an injured athlete they don't really think about much more than the fact that they are injured. Most people don't even consider what the athlete is going through mentally and emotionally. The biggest part of getting over an injury isn't the physical aspect like most people would assume. How an athlete deals with the injury mentally plays a huge role in the athlete's recovery process.

My advice to athletes who are sidelined for the season is to keep a positive mindset and be grateful for the opportunities that they have had. Instead of dwelling on their current situation they should focus their thoughts on getting better and what they can look forward to when they make a full recovery and are back playing. Don't let the sideline be a barrier that separates you from your team; instead view it as a motivator. The sideline is like a finish line that, once crossed, indicates the completion of the rehab process. Each day work hard to make strides in your recovery and make your way closer to crossing the finish line. There is no greater feeling than accomplishing your goal and crossing back onto the playing field with your teammates.

Scott White, a former NCAA Division I baseball player at Ohio University, also experienced injuries in his career that quickly taught him to never take anything for granted.

SCOTT WHITE (former baseball student-athlete at Ohio University, Jacksonville Area Account Director at Superfit Foods)

I tore my labrum, rehabbed it, played through it, and played with a lot of pain. I only had one year left, which made me realize my playing career wasn't going past college with my injuries because I then had a torn UCL [ulnar collateral ligament] at the same time I found out. My whole right arm was basically useless. It made me realize that baseball wasn't in my future and I wasn't even in a major that I wanted to be in.

There had been some days I was playing as a sophomore and I would think, "I've got two more years and possibly more . . . ," and the possibility of being injured in a split second can happen at any time. The thought of not being able to play again doesn't really cross your mind. It really hit me the day after my Tommy John surgery when I woke up in the hospital in my sling. I had a huge scar and my elbow was the size of a balloon, all swollen and everything. I was in so much pain and I thought, this could be it, the last time I play.

There is a mindset you acquire. Being injured helped me acquire that mindset to not take everything for granted. It is hard to put yourself in that mindset if you haven't been through an injury or some kind of big setback. I would suggest taking an extended period of time away from the game to make yourself realize how much you miss it, or stop doing something you love to do and see what that feeling is like.

So, based on what we've learned from these comments, what should you do if an injury or an unexpected absence forces you away from the game? We've come up with a list of three key and simple suggestions.

1. Play every day like it's your last.

SCOTT WHITE (former student-athlete at Ohio University)

I always tell current players now to soak up everything. Enjoy practice, enjoy training, and enjoy the little things, because you don't appreciate them while you are doing them, but when you look back it, you will. Make the most of your opportunities because you never know when your last time will be; sports are unpredictable."

---

2. Be prepared for the worst and always have a Plan B.

SCOTT WHITE (former student-athlete at Ohio University)

Never look too far into your successes and never focus too hard on your failures. Let them motivate you a little, but don't dwell on them too much. Find a support system, whether it is your coaches, teammates, or other support staff, to help you deal with those failures. It is also much sweeter when you can share those successes with your support system too; they aren't just there for you when you fail.

3.   Always have an alternative image of yourself that does not depend on sport.

Even if you are one of the top prospects in the world, you still need to have a game plan for yourself outside of playing your sport, because you just never know what the next chapter of your book involves. There are literally thousands of examples of athletes at every level who had a brilliant career full of potential (and probably wealth) stopped because of injury, personal challenges, or other setbacks.

CHAPTER SUMMARY

Our favorite quote from one of our former coaches is, "Yesterday is in the past, tomorrow is not promised, so control the only thing you can, today." This applies not only to sports, but to life. You never know what is going to happen tomorrow, so treat each day like it's your last. It sounds clichéd, but it's true. As many athletes who were injured during their careers will tell you, "You don't know what you have 'til it's gone." Or as Boy Scouts might advise: Be Prepared.

Secret *10* Manage Your Highs and Lows

THE SECRET IN A FEW WORDS

This secret is about managing your success and/or nonsuccess on the field and in the classroom. Both pursuits—academic and athletic—will produce good days and bad days, great results and disappointing results. It is important that you manage both.

As an athlete, you are used to having a coach explain expectations, demonstrate desired behaviors, and then provide feedback on your performance, based on which you make adjustments. Unfortunately, your coach can't always be by your side as you navigate your athletic, academic, and personal life in college. There will be support staff in place to explain expectations such as the grades needed for academic success and to retain eligibility, but rarely will there be someone around who educates you about the highs and lows you could face as a student-athlete.

Without knowing what might be coming your way, you can find both the triumphs and the disappointments overwhelming. This secret shares with you many of the possible highs and lows you could face as a student-athlete and coaches you through some approaches for managing them. Not only will this information help you breeze through whatever comes your way as a student-athlete, but the strategies will also prepare you for your professional and personal life after college.

MANAGE YOUR HIGHS AND LOWS

Highs and lows are part of life. Maximizing the benefit of the highs and avoiding or rebounding from the lows are key to a balanced life. Big wins and small losses. You've heard the sayings and the slogans. Kelsey Cermak, a former student-athlete and now an assistant director with the NCAA, notes that "you always have to be prepared for success and failure. You can never get too high off of a win, and you can never get too low after a loss."

Rob Smith, NCAA Division I baseball coach, has the following advice for first-year students:

> My biggest advice for freshmen is to understand and be open minded to learning how to handle failure and adversity. It's not that you aren't good enough, it's that you may get swallowed up by the process, physically and mentally. It's a shock for many freshmen to have to balance all that you have to, especially at the Division I level.
>
> I think the ones that handle it all the best are the ones that come in with the least amount of expectations. When freshmen come in with too high a level of expectations, failure can really set them back too much. When the walk-on guy is just excited to have the opportunity, he rapidly adapts and that is because of the lack of expectations. Have realistic expectations so that you can exceed and succeed.

Smith emphasizes the need to manage your expectations. Be realistic in your goals, plan for the long term, and do not get derailed by one bad result or test score.

"THAT LOW": WHEN YOU REALIZE YOU MAY NOT BE GOING PRO OR THAT YOU'RE LOSING YOUR SPOT

A potentially life-altering "low" can be realizing (perhaps gradually, when reality finally sinks in; or perhaps suddenly, when reality hits for the first time) that you are not going to go pro.

Eddie Gill, a former NBA player and student-athlete and now a successful businessman, told us about a "low" like this he went through.

> For me, coming out of college as a senior and going into the draft was one of my down moments. I kind of built some steam up going into my senior year, and throughout my senior year, there were some projections of middle first-round and middle second-round. I fell completely out of the draft and was not drafted at all.
>
> That was a harsh reality for me that I had to come to grips with and realize that it's going to be a harder path, and that I could only control what I could control. That's the game of life, some things aren't fair. You can do everything "right" and it doesn't happen for you, which is okay.

You have to continue to pick yourself up and get back after it. Throughout my professional playing career, I had a variety of ups and downs where I thought I was at a place and was like "I'm here. I'll be good for X amount of years." Then boom, something else happens and you're somewhere else playing again. It happened a lot, but I've always tried to remain self-confident and sure of myself and continued to keep pressing on.

Another former student-athlete, Hillary Nelson, described her reactions when her playing time was drastically cut and her role on the team lessened.

The toughest year of my life was my junior year. I was a pitcher, had a new pitching coach, and my playing time was cut by 80 percent. I was in a rough roommate situation. I was having a hard time at home, and then my mom passed away. It was the sudden death of my mom in April that really just put me over the edge.

For me, that year really put things in perspective. It helped me take my internal focus, where I had been so focused on Hillary Nelson and how I was going to be successful. It helped me see life through an external focus on how I was going to make the world better, how I was going to make my team better, and how I was going to make the game of softball better.

In response to the "toughest year of her life," Nelson said there were three keys to her getting through this mental minefield. First, she set high goals (academically and professionally) to challenge herself off the field of play.

Second, she said she really relied on the resources provided to her and the people around her. "Surround yourself with winners," she advises, and she also stresses "never being afraid to ask for help if you need it."

Third, she tried to work harder that she thought possible and test the limits of her work ethic. "If you want to succeed more than you want to sleep, you'll find a way to make it happen."

Hillary also noted the importance of learning from failures (on the field, in the classroom, or in your personal life). She noted: "If you don't have failure, you don't learn to appreciate success. Specifically, my failures, in those bad times, those hard times, made the best times seem so much greater."

WHAT ARE THE HIGHS AND LOWS TO EXPECT?

The life of a student-athlete is already a whirlwind as you balance your academic, athletic, and personal lives. As a student-athlete, however, you will experience highs and lows athletically, beyond the successes and failures that all students face.

A first element of this "secret" is to know where these highs and lows might come from so you can be prepared to maximize the highs and mitigate (reduce) the impact of the lows.

As a student-athlete in college, you can expect that your coaches, professors, fellow students, and maybe even the media will take notice of your victories and losses on the field (or on the court, in the gym, on the ice, in the pool, etc.). Your successes and failures outside your sport will get less attention but are no less significant for your overall success. It is important to be aware of potential challenges that could come your way. In some cases, you can work to avoid pitfalls such as academic problems, but in other cases there is absolutely nothing you could have done differently to avoid a troublesome situation.

- *Academic Highs:* Achievements such as scoring an A on a challenging statistics exam, receiving an acceptance letter to graduate school or medical school, completing all the requirements for your degree, and making the Dean's List or honor roll should not be filed away or kept quiet. Embrace the success. Call your parents. Celebrate with your friends. Have a wall in your room where you post the results. Share the good news on social media.

- *Academic Lows:* Depending on your goals and plan, you'll know when you've failed. If your goal is to get your computer engineering degree, then a C+ in a challenging math course may not count as a "low"; but if you're hoping to go to law school one day, then a C+ could affect that goal if your overall GPA is borderline. Failing a test, scoring well below your needed level of achievement, falling off the Dean's List or honor roll are all examples. Your response to these "lows" needs to be VERY proactive. Assess the situation, figure out what went wrong, and come up with a solution. Do you need a tutor? Do you need more study time? Do you need more sleep to be alert in class? Ask the hard questions and make changes to solve the problems you identify.

- *Athletic Highs:* These are big, and given your spot in the "other 99 percent" for whom this will be the highest level of sports achievement, you should cherish these accomplishments. They can be as "small" as a terrific workout, making all morning practices one week (or month), hitting your nutrition goals, or getting positive feedback from your coach. Or they can be major, like a victory over a key opponent, a conference championship, or qualifying for a bowl game. These are moments you will never forget and are ones to treasure and celebrate, as that will help as you transition to life postgraduation and without high-performance sport.

- *Athletic Lows:* Again, like the academic highs and lows, these can be minor (e.g., sleeping through practice, loss of playing time, a minor injury, making a bad play at a key moment) or major (e.g., getting cut from the team, a major loss, not qualifying for postseason, losing your scholarship, a major injury). The same response as to an academic low is necessary here: conduct a deep analysis of the situation, identify the problem(s)/issue(s), and fix them (right away and with a clear plan).

- *Personal/Social Highs and Lows:* These have been discussed previously, but we're noting this area again as these personal and social accomplishments and challenges need to be addressed and celebrated (or mourned) along with academic and athletic extremes.

WHAT IS THE SECRET TO MANAGING YOUR ATHLETIC SUCCESS HIGHS?

Athletic success is defined differently by each individual. For some student-athletes, success is winning national or conference championships, while for others personal skill improvement, personal bests, or even a spot on the team might be the measure of success. Whatever the definition of success is, managing it requires diligent attention. The following list provides you with a sample of approaches that you can adopt to help you manage your athletic success (i.e., the "highs"!):

- *Enjoy your success:* It is OK to be proud of yourself and share your accomplishments. You have worked hard for what you have achieved.

- *Be respectful of teammates:* Teammates may be struggling to hit their own athletic goals, so be respectful when celebrating your individual achievements. This is especially true if you are "passing" teammates with a throw, lift, or point total, or by earning a starter role or breaking their record.

- *Understand your school's media protocol:* Many institutions have a protocol in place for student-athletes interacting with media (i.e., all media inquiries must go through the media relations staff member for your sport). If your achievement results in media attention, be sure you're aware of the procedure for how media should be contacting you and follow established expectations.

- *Know how to handle media:* Talking with media and sharing on your own social media affect how you and the institution are perceived. Be humble, be appreciative to those who support you, and consider how what you say or write could be perceived by both teammates and competitors.

- *Move forward:* Accomplishing goals and achieving success are awesome, but then what? Athletes can flounder and lose focus if other goals are not in the pipeline. After recognizing success, it's time to attack the next goal! This also goes for continuing to celebrate an achievement for too long. After a day or two, your teammates will get tired of hearing about what you did, so move on for everyone's sake, including your own.

SEEK OUT THOSE ACADEMIC "HIGHS"!

You may feel like an athlete-student, but remember that you are a student-athlete. That means that academics deserve at least as much attention as your sport. The "highs" for either need to feel equally important for you. We get that the media doesn't really care about your B+ on the scary accounting exam or the all-nighter you and your group did to get that major project done on time—but you do, your groupmates do, your family does, and so you need to call out those "highs" as well. The "Enjoy It" and "Move Forward" tactics above should be adopted for the academic highs as well as the athletic ones.

Many student-athletes encounter academic problems that often have nothing to do with intellectual ability. Typically, your academic problems occur because you have not committed to academics the way you have to your sport. A lot of time goes into athletic goal setting, but how much time do you spend on academic goal setting? You need to balance this.

Where do you find the motivation to achieve academic highs? Well, of course, we all know that staying eligible to play is the bare minimum in academic achievement, but for many, achieving that goal is a high that deserves to be celebrated. If you aim for more than staying eligible and earning passing grades, then you need to commit to academics just like athletics. The benefits of making the Dean's List or receiving an academic award will be noticed later when it's time for a job interview, grad school application, or scholarship consideration.

A very simple and useful plan is to take the same approach to academic goals as you do to your athletic goals. For example, think of the approach you use for your strength and conditioning workouts: you attack them. You probably have goals related to increasing your speed, strength, and stamina and know that unless you show up to strength and conditioning sessions ready to give 100 percent, you will not reach your goals.

You probably have a detailed plan of exercise, times, and goals to follow for each workout. Those goals translate into improved athletic performance in your sport or else you probably would not have them. Take exactly the same approach to your academic goals. Think about mandatory study hall. If you approached studying the way you do your strength and conditioning workouts, you would be setting goals for yourself related to what you need to accomplish in your study sessions each week and overall for the term. Additionally, you would recognize the direct link between achieving these study goals and your improved academic performance. It really is that simple: a change in your perspective almost guarantees improved performance in the classroom.

Approaching academics the same way as athletics will also help you deal with academic problems or frustrations. College is challenging for most, and not every class is going to be one that you are in love with. Just like when your coach makes a change you are not very excited about and you suck it up and keep on moving along, you can do the same thing academically.

Another idea that worked for some of the authors in their time as student-athletes is to approach any academic concept or class that you are struggling in just as you would attack a challenge in your sport: get the help you need, buckle down, and throw yourself into figuring out how to overcome the obstacle. If you are having trouble with a blocking technique on the field, you spend extra time practicing it. The same principle applies to academics: if you are having trouble with something, it will require extra practice. But you can get through it!

It is true that academic success is unlikely to catch the attention of local media, but think about how good you feel when you put in the work to study for an exam and then have that pay off with a high grade. What about all the people who care about you? I suspect many of them would be as excited to hear you earned an A on a test as they would be to hear you scored a goal.

Author Viewpoint—DR. HEATHER LAWRENCE

As a student-athlete diver at the University of Florida, I experienced my share of both highs and lows. In my four years I accomplished a variety of academic and athletic goals such as winning an individual Southeastern Conference title, setting school records, being recognized as an Academic and Athletic All-American, and even being inducted into the Student Hall of Fame for my academic college. Reading this list, you may think that college was smooth as can be for me, but the reality is that it was not.

I also had my share of struggles while at Florida. The biggest challenge was during my junior year when all of a sudden, right before the championship season, I became unable to get myself to do even the simplest of dives. These were movements that my body had been doing since I was ten years old and there seemed to be no explanation as to why it was happening. Mental blocks are not new in the world of athletics, but I was not ready for it to happen to me and I clearly was not prepared for how to handle it when it did. The level of frustration directed toward me by teammates and coaches about my inability to perform escalated as time went on and I didn't just snap out of it. At one diving meet, I even just had to jump off the diving board and take "0's" from the judges. Understandably, that was not received well by anyone, including me.

Initially, I tried working with mental health professionals on campus, submitted myself to hypnosis, and also talked with medical staff, but nothing seemed to be helping me.

Along with the head diving coach, I finally did my own research into sport psychologists who might have expertise in working with athletes with similar issues. As a result, we identified a sport psychologist in Miami, Florida, who had experience with divers and thankfully he was willing to work with me. With the support of the Director of Athletics and medical staff, I packed up the car and headed to Miami to work on myself. This took me out of school, conditioning, and practice (or at least the minimal practice I was getting) for a week.

The experience in Miami was worth the sacrifice as I was able to overcome the mental block by working with the expertise of the sport psychologist. Some days he was even up on the 10m platform with me helping me work through all that was causing the performance problems for me.

At other times, it was more about helping me realize that diving was not the only part of my identity and that the pressure I was putting on myself was disproportionate to the real amount of me that was a "diver." Basically, I was way out of balance. I was training too much, putting too much pressure on myself to excel, and had my self-worth entirely wrapped up into how I competed and practiced.

Although it took some time, I did completely overcome the mental block I experienced and went on to an undefeated senior year of dual meets serving as team captain, became an SEC Champion, was an NCAA All-American in two events, and most importantly, had fun again being a diver. Looking back at this tough time in my life, I know that putting in the work and being willing to sacrifice to get better taught me how to handle other types of adversity. Whether it was having a fussy newborn at home and going into severe sleep deprivation, being incredibly overworked professionally, or just feeling out of control with all life has thrown at me—I know that all of the various roles I fill as a person do not define who I am. So, the perspective I learned through having a mental block as a diver continues to be a valuable experience for me in my personal and professional life.

DEALING WITH THE HIGHS AND LOWS

Next, we'd like to share some general principles that apply to dealing with the various highs and lows we've outlined.

1.   Keep a Level Head

     Take a moment to pause and think before you react to whatever is happening. As you know, everything you do could be blasted out on social media immediately. Perception is reality, so whether the situation is good or bad, work hard to ensure your reaction reflects how you want others to see you. This goes for in-person interactions with friends as well as more formal media interactions.

2.   Know, and Use, Your Resources

The good news is that you are surrounded by coaches and administrators who care a lot about you. The bad news is that everyone is busy and it is up to you to reach out and get the help you need to navigate the circumstances you find yourself in. Focus on asking the appropriate person for assistance and the sooner the better. Rarely do bad situations get better on their own, so reaching out as soon as you have a feeling about something not going your way could save you a lot of headaches down the road.

3.   Keep Perspective

A college campus can make any situation seem better or worse and definitely bigger than it really is. Remember that the situation will pass and you will get through it, so making a conscious decision on how you will handle it is important. Whether it is a success or a failure, one situation does not define who you are as a person, as an athlete, or as a student.

EXAMPLES OF USING THE STRATEGIES

Here are examples of a triumph and a disappointment to illustrate how to activate these strategies.

Example: Dealing with a Triumph

As your final semester of college begins, you are nominated for both Conference and NCAA postgraduate scholarships. In your four years, you have not been an individual champion athlete beyond some dual meets, and your team has qualified for NCAAs but never placed in the top ten nationally. However, you have dedicated yourself to being a team leader and supporting your teammates, being engaged in community service on- and off-campus, and achieving a GPA of 3.8 in a rigorous major. Additionally, you have already been admitted to grad school and plan on starting after a summer of traveling abroad.

Shortly after the nominations, you learn you have been awarded $20,000 in postgraduate scholarship money from the NCAA. How do you handle this success?

1.   Keep a Level Head

You are the same person before this award as you are after this award. It could be tempting to feel superior to teammates as they struggle to decide what to do after college and you already have a plan in place as well as no financial stress now because of the scholarships. Continue to be the team leader you always have been, and now even more student-athletes may start to look up to you as they learn of your awards.

Mentor and guide those younger than you to help them achieve just as you have.

2.   Know, and Use, Your Resources

What could you possibly need help with after winning a postgraduate scholarship? The answer is, a lot. After being on an athletics scholarship, you may know very little about how to access the award money via your institution or how it affects other financial aid or even taxes. There are probably expectations for academic performance to retain your scholarships, so find the individuals in the athletics department who can point you in the right direction to begin to understand graduate school and how scholarships are awarded.

3.   Keep Perspective

Find out who put together the nominations that led to your being awarded the scholarship and thank them by writing a handwritten thank-you note and stopping by their office. Other handwritten thank-you notes should go to your parents or guardians, your coaches, the athletic director, and any other people on campus who supported your success. Then, realize that you have a long road ahead in a challenging graduate program. Enjoy your summer and return to campus ready to give back to the athletic program (i.e., volunteer) that has provided you this amazing opportunity.

Example: Dealing with a Disappointment

Despite your best physical preparation, you suffered a season-ending ACL injury only halfway through your sophomore year as a field hockey player. It is a big blow to the team overall since you have been the conference player of the week twice already as well as being the team-leading scorer for the season thus far.

1.   Keep a Level Head

You are the same person before this injury and after this injury. It could be tempting to feel sorry for yourself (and you can for a few days before it's time to get back to work), but that does not move you any closer to recovery. During your rehab, you have an opportunity to take on a new role supporting your teammates and a chance to lead by example by how you approach your rehab. Since your teammates are likely feeling a bit bummed about your injury too, you can help the coaching staff get them back on track by understanding how good other players are and spending time individually with some key players, encouraging them to really step up their playing to fill the void.

2.   Know, and Use, Your Resources

You will be spending a lot of time with athletic trainers and the sports medicine staff. Recognize how hard they are working on your behalf to help you heal. Head into every early-morning rehab session with a great attitude and ready to do whatever they ask of you. They know how to get you playing again as quickly as possible, so it only ends up hurting you if you don't use them as your resources.

3.   Keep Perspective

Although you end up missing the rest of one season, you still have two more seasons to play and will come back stronger than ever. Plus, you hopefully have at least seventy more years of living to do after college and you want that knee to be as strong as it can be for all of the life adventures that await you. Your recovery period is also a great time to excel academically. If you end up with a little extra time because you aren't traveling with the team, put it to good use and work to earn the highest possible grades you can that term.

. . . .

Sometimes life hits you from all sides (athletic, academic, personal) at the same time. You might even be in the middle of an athletic success and an academic challenge at the same time. There is no playbook to get you through every possible scenario you might face, but you can get through anything that is thrown at you and come out on the other side of the situation feeling proud of how you handled it and knowing you were strong enough to tackle the challenge and beat it.

As a student-athlete, there will be times you feel like you are on top of the world, and there will be times you feel like nothing more could go wrong. How did you handle the highs and lows, along with stress? What advice would you give to a student-athlete on how to deal with stress? How much do the "highs and lows" relate to life, and have you pulled from past experiences as an athlete to help you in the work world?

DEALING WITH FAILURE: PERSPECTIVE OF DREW SAYLOR
(former student-athlete, Minor League Manager with the Los Angeles Dodgers)

Learning how to deal with failure and how it motivates you, and how it should inherently inspire you to work harder, is one of the most important lessons you can learn. I think, for a multitude of reasons, having failure is vital to the improvement process because when you fail, you get a chance to rework the equation, then you test it again. If you're truly a lifelong learner, you're always going to be finding ways to push yourself to the extreme. You're going to fail.

Once you fail, it's an opportunity to go back and rework the equation and try again. At the end of the day, it is imperative that student-athletes find a way to maintain that process because that's what makes them valid.

As a student-athlete, wins, losses, and personal statistics, that's kind of what you live and die by. Inherently, we're all committed as people. We don't like to lose. I think that, being able to look at it from a scientific standpoint, going, "OK, well this is my process, this caused failure. How can I fix it?" I think that understanding similarly, Urban Meyer talks about, "the outcome is the event plus your response." When you look at that equation, your event, you really don't get a chance to choose your event—the event basically chooses you. The outcome, you don't really have much say in that because you go out and you compete and the outcome is really a product of your process. The only thing that you can control is your response. How do you deal with what goes on? Is your response to shut down and say screw it and drop your wrench and walk off the worksite? Is your response to sit there and have an uncontrolled rage outburst that actually hurts your teammates and the environment that you're in? Or is your response to press onward? Is your response to continue to work harder to find a different process to change the outcome?

In addition to Saylor's lessons on dealing with failure, Nick Manno had a piece of wisdom to add as well.

NICK MANNO
(former baseball student-athlete, Pro Scout with the Seattle Mariners)

When you play baseball, failure is a big part of it. You can't have a fear of failure. I think that applies to scouting. Scouting is not unlike playing. You are going to be wrong a lot. Learning to deal with failure and adversity is something you definitely take with you as you go on any other walk of life. You have to understand that process is really important. In the professional world, if you have a process, a plan, and you stick with those, you will be successful more times than not. If you don't have a plan or process and you fail, you have nowhere to turn.

CHAPTER SUMMARY

Life isn't easy, life isn't fair, and when life kicks you down, you have to get back up. You may be on top of the world one day and on the bottom of the ocean floor the next, but you have to learn how to manage your successes and failures.

As the great Johnny Cash once said, "You build on failure. You use it as a stepping stone. Close the door on the past. You don't try to forget the mistakes, but you don't dwell on them. You don't let it have any of your energy, or any of your time."

When you fail in life, just get right back up and try again. And when you succeed in life, cherish it, and keep wanting more. Stay humble, don't forget who you are, and keep things in perspective.

Part 2 The Transition

Now that you have succeeded as a student-athlete and prepared yourself for the end of your playing career, consider the transition you are about to make. The next ten secrets will guide you in the process of your transition out of sport and into the next chapter of your life, your book. The previous ten secrets will help you succeed and ultimately prepare you for the transition that everyone struggles with one way or another. The worst part about it, is that it happens to everyone, whether you go pro or not. It's only a matter of time.

So . . . no matter whether you are a high school senior, college freshman, or college senior, just know that these next ten secrets will truly help you in your future.

Secret *11* Face Reality in Sports and Life

THE SECRET IN A FEW WORDS

Most young people between the ages of seventeen and twenty-four want to live life to its fullest. To get busy living. To live like an immortal. In fact, many twenty-year-olds behave as if they are *immortal. They believe they will be young forever. But there is risk in not facing reality. We all age and even the greatest athletes eventually slow down. They lose a step.*

So think about these truths. A college degree may suggest you are educated. Playing a sport in college confirms you are physically talented. Wearing a team uniform or team-supplied apparel implies you are privileged.

But those perceptions are often misleading. If you skipped classes or cheated, or if you ended up in a major you didn't care about, you may not be as educated as you'll soon wish you were. If you think you're unlikely to turn pro in sports, you'll soon know for certain if you weren't talented enough to go pro. If you are relying on a varsity jacket for recognition and special treatment around campus, you will soon learn the emperor's new clothing doesn't mean much a month after graduation.

Those are realities and they come to all of us at different times as we get a handle on how the larger world works. This chapter is for the realists. This chapter makes sure you are looking at the truth about your skills as an athlete and the life rushing toward you.

FACE REALITY IN SPORTS AND LIFE

It's one thing to seek reality or know it when you see it . . . but it's another thing to face reality when you are uncertain. Many people hope that even though the truth (or the reality of a situation) may be unwelcome, a little luck or self-persuasion will still produce an outcome that isn't all bad. That innocence, naïveté, or positive thinking is okay up to a point, but there comes a time for all of us when the truth can't be denied or ignored.

To provide you with some perspective on facing the reality of sports and life, we interviewed four former professional athletes and a professional basketball coach who have all been successful. We asked all five to give us their views of the reality facing a student-athlete postgraduation.

Eddie Gill, former NBA player and student-athlete at Weber State, said:

> Let's just say you do play professionally, and now you are a part
> of the 1 percent that do go and play professionally. Let's say
> you're one of the very few that get to play for ten years, because
> in most sports, the average careers are three to four years long.
> By the time you get out of the game, you're around thirty-two
> years old, and you may have fifty more years of life. What are
> you doing with it? I think being a freshman student-athlete, you
> should start developing the thought of, "What do I want to do
> with my life?" If you're able to utilize those four years to really
> train yourself for what you would like to do, or any passion you
> might have developed, that's going to turn into success.

Dawn Buth, Associate Director of the Sport Science Institute at the NCAA, noted:

> I feel it's essential that college athletes approach their academic
> experience with the expectation that professional athletics will
> likely not be a part of their long-term career development. Even
> if an athlete finds they are in that 1 percent, injuries, performance,
> and sustainability can be unpredictable variables—investing in
> your collegiate career can maximize your opportunities and pay
> long-term professional dividends. I encourage student-athletes to
> take ownership of their career development, exposing themselves
> to a variety of academic and life experiences during their collegiate
> careers. Be a sponge, explore the world around you, learn about
> yourself, and discover the classes, topics, and career paths that
> resonate with you and will help inform your academic choices.

Seth Etherton, former MLB pitcher and student-athlete at USC, responded:

> Education is first. There aren't many who can make a good
> salary in minor league baseball, let alone making it to the pros.

Having an understanding for the grind that minor leaguers have to go through is important. People are unrealistic on what the professional baseball life is like. I would advise student-athletes to understand your talents. Each organization drafts new guys at your position each year. Guys who were done with the game struggled the most with not having a plan for when they were done playing. Just like student-athletes, you need to be aware of when the end is coming and having your plan in place.

Matt Engleka, former student-athlete at Ohio University and owner of LEJ Agency, said:

You're going to know fairly early if going pro is a potential reality. It's not about the people within your inner circle that are telling you that. It's when you get the confirmation from outside that you're good enough, that you're recognized at that next level. I think there is a lot of false sense of possibility of going professional from today's athletes simply because everybody is "the big fish in a small pond." You have to ask yourself, "How long do I think I can pursue a professional career?" Every year, there are thousands of you out there doing the exact same thing. What makes you stand out that's going to make you that much better than the others? I think that it's hard to accept, but if the question was posed to prospective college athletes, "What if your athletic career ends in your freshman year?" would you be ok with where you're going?

Rod Baker, Assistant Coach for the Philadelphia 76ers, comments:

The sooner you realize that the game cannot become a job, the better off you will be. The smart ones realize that it may not continue for long. In the pro's, there is someone that is after your job every year, just like there are freshmen after your roster spot or starting position every year. You have to continue to prove yourself every day. Student-athletes have to be realistic. There are some who will go pro and some who won't. As a coach, I never wanted to steal anyone's dream, but I would tell my guys that they needed to have something else to do. Have some other skills, and get your degree, because even if you do go pro, it isn't going to last forever. Most won't be able to live off the money made as a pro, so you are still going to have to go get another job. I would always tell my players that you need to create as many marketable skills for yourself as possible once the basketball goes away.

Some student-athletes ignore a variety of slowly accumulating or fast-moving warning signals and never master nonsport skills like facing the facts and owning the truth. Let's look at warning signs that are pretty common:

Language	Outcome
I can function on four hours of sleep.	Illness, injury, depression
I don't read the assignments. I just skim them.	Poor grades on tests, low GPA
Burgers and pizza. The diet of champions!	Overweight, less playing time
My prof doesn't take attendance so I skip a lot.	Poor grades, no benefit of the doubt
My natural skills have always been good enough.	Outworked and outplayed
I'll play pro for a few years and be set for life.	For real?

Granted, college is a place to make mistakes and learn from them, but college also ends rather abruptly . . . from flunking out, dropping out, or graduating. We want every reader of this book to graduate and find a successful pathway through the rest of life. But like the board games *Monopoly, Life,* or *Chutes and Ladders,* there are days when negative realities take place. It's when you land on the wrong square and slide backwards. You suddenly face a brand new reality. I was ahead . . . or I was making progress and . . . BANG . . . now I'm behind.

The same probably holds for video games like *Halo, League of Legends, Grand Theft Auto, World of Warcraft, Overwatch, Diablo, Call of Duty: Black Ops,* and *Super Mario,* even *Tetris.* Some days you level up quickly and some days the computer or the other online players are just that much better.

Many of us learn early on to make excuses to explain our bad luck. Or failure. If we can shift the blame for our failing reality onto someone else, then the reality isn't really our own fault. It begins with someone else. If my parents had only been smarter. . . If my family had only been wealthier . . . If I'd only been given a second chance . . . If I'd only gone to a better school . . .

The "If only" game works for a while but, like many other escape vehicles, it runs out of gas quickly. At some point we have to "own up" to the present reality. We have to face facts and then make new decisions on how to survive and thrive.

We caught up with Drew Saylor, who played baseball at Kent State and briefly played in baseball's minor leagues. Drew is a great example of that NCAA student-athlete who put most of his energy into making it as a pro and then had to learn about the reality of jumping from good college player to an athlete trying to make it as a full-time professional player.

"The biggest challenge for me was understanding the difference between the college game and the pro game," said Drew when we caught up with him.

I didn't know who I was. On the baseball field, I was just kind of told, arbitrarily, to do these things and I was just physically better than most of my peers and that's how I got drafted.

As you get into professional baseball, the ability for you to be able to comprehend, apply, filter, delete and add information is imperative and I look at that, in the same context, as if you're getting an actual, real job. You do all of this studying. You do all this other stuff. You think you are ahead.

What the studying should do for you in college is it should make you think. It should make you sit there and challenge the things that go on. In a workplace environment, your thinking should make you sit there and become serious.

I think from a student-athlete perspective; my main goal was to be drafted. I knew that was one of my biggest challenges. That was my goal. Once I was drafted, I found the first few months I'd suddenly lost my drive. I lost my motivation, I lost my "Why?"

Once you achieve that goal and that's the only thing you ever thought about, you eat, breathe, and sleep that same sentiment, there are tons of points where once you get it, you say "OK, well that's it. I'm done. What am I going to do now?"

I see the same thing in a lot of players that go into the minor leagues, but also in the major leagues where it's all about just getting that first contract. Let me get paid. Let me make my first $10 million and then all of the sudden, you start to see the lack of production.

You see their lack of effort. You see their lack of preparation. I really do think it's because they've finally achieved that goal, and they lost their direction, they lost their rudder. They are kind of just drifting wherever the wind takes them.

In your journey, it's all about finding that "Why?" Finding that direction. Finding that ability to be motivated on a day-in and day-out basis. We need to be journey-focused, not destination-focused. I think, at least for me, it is imperative that student-athletes are nimble [and thinking about the long haul].

I think having a backup plan is imperative. I always thought that I was going to teach in some way, shape or form. I really enjoyed the interpersonal relationships, and I loved my interaction with people. I think it's also because I grew up in a household where my father taught and coached for forty years.

It's something that I've always been drawn to, something I just innately learned as my life has continued to evolve. I think a lot of times people just have this one goal in mind, and then if they don't get it, their lives are completely in ruins.

More than anything else, find out what you are passionate about. Whatever it is. Continue to understand that whatever you do in life, you're going to have to work for it, you're going to have to press for it. The same stuff that you do in school, you are going to have to do that 100-fold to be successful in life.

I think that a lot of student athletes get into this notion that, "I'm going to go play and nothing else." Players have to have the mentality going into college that they're going to have to work extremely hard. The amount of time they put into your weightlifting, study tables, etc. That's how life is, and I think a lot of student athletes think, "Well, I'm working so hard to try to achieve this goal, and then once I'm done with this goal, then it's going to get easier."

Life doesn't happen that way.

I kind of relate it a little bit to having kids. You have a baby and you have to carry out all this stuff for the baby. Then you're like, "Oh, I can't wait for him to be a toddler because when they're a toddler, I'm not going to have to live around all of this stuff." Then all of the sudden they become a toddler and you say, "OK, well at least I'm not lugging around all these different blankets and stuff, now I just sit there and I have to carry toys."

Then they have all of this stuff, toys. "I can't wait until they become older, then they'll be able to able to move and do things on their own," you know so on and so forth. They get a license and a car. At the end of the day, you're trading in things. You're not eliminating things. There's going to be different phases you go through that are going to require the same amount of effort out of you regardless of whatever it may be. It's just the responsibilities kind of modify.

Effort and responsibility are two great words Drew Saylor used to finished his interview. Facing reality in sports and life is largely about keeping your effort levels up when a situation gets tough, but it's also about taking responsibility for the outcome you still want.

Most student-athletes dream of pro sports careers because of the perceived lifestyle advantages that will come with playing at the elite level. They'll enjoy big contracts throwing off loads of money. Big houses. Big hotel rooms on the road. Limos. Private yachts. Servants. Agents. Accountants. Mad parties. Attractive fans. They covet the lifestyle they've seen in *Entourage*. They will be Vincent Chase (or the female equivalent) and life will be filled with people telling them how good looking they are.

Well, to quote Cher in the old movie *Moonstruck* (where she slaps Nicolas Cage in the face), we need to tell you to "Snap out of it." The *Entourage* lifestyle exists for maybe a few thousand people in the world, and odds are great you will not be one of them.

One of our favorite stories (and part urban legend), is told by super-agent David Falk about a young rookie joining the Chicago Bulls when Michael Jordan was the star of the team. On the first day of practice, the rookie showed up early to make a good first impression. Jordan was already there with a full sweat going.

So the next day, the rookie arrives an hour early convinced he will get there ahead of Jordan and show famous No. 23 his commitment. To his surprise, Jordan is already there. So the next day, the rookie gets up in the dark and leaves for the gym before the sun is even up. He gets to the gym as the janitor is opening the doors. He knows he has beaten Jordan because he was the first one there when the building got opened.

You know, of course, how the story ends. The ultracompetitive Jordan is already inside the building shooting around. It is at this point the rookie realizes how bad he will have to want it if he wants to run with the best.

BRIAN SANDERS
(former baseball student-athlete, Senior Vice President of
Stadium Operations for the Los Angeles Angels of Anaheim)

You have to have the passion and drive to keep going in your sport. At some point you have to be realistic that it can't last forever. As a student-athlete you have to know you put in all of the effort, know you've put in hard work and effort when is right time for you to say it's over and take the needed time to refocus. Having a good perspective and outlook on what it is you're going to do after the fact. Taking those experiences from sport and whatever drove you as a student athlete you've got to use in the next phase.

To reiterate this idea:

DREW SAYLOR
(Minor League Manager at Los Angeles Dodgers)

We need to be journey focused, not destination focused.

Facing reality takes many shapes, but here are a few key thoughts:

- Own your own reality. Don't live someone else's.
- Don't put off owning the facts. They'll only get worse. Said another way: Things may look bad (at times), but addressing problems

sooner rather than later almost always limits the damage. Putting off confronting reality usually makes things worse.

- Generally speaking, you will know your own reality better than anyone else. Yes, there are things beyond your control (e.g., whether you will start or play; how someone else feels about you), but you are generally the only one really paying attention (all the time) to you. Know yourself.

- Denying the truth and putting blame on others will not protect you forever. Eventually, the harsh truth comes out. Translation: Lying, denying, and crying (on command to get out of trouble) are troublesome habits and the sooner you get beyond those traits, the better off you will be.

- Being a student-athlete can be as good or as bad as you make it. But one major reality is that if you are a student-athlete, others will hold you to higher standards, possibly cut you less slack, and believe that you are more fortunate than they are. Accept that reality and understand that your reality is shaped by the perceptions others have of you.

- Make sure that you know that many people on your campus are prepared to help you face your realities, be they mental health, career development, personal development, physical health, academic, or aspirational (such as going to grad school, getting internships, or studying abroad). One of your best realities is that many people want to help you.

Lastly, to provide you with some perspective from those student-athletes who didn't go pro, one former student-athlete who is now an associate athletic director summarized her story for you.

KRISTEN BROWN
(former basketball student-athlete, Associate Athletic Director–
Administration at the University of Maryland)

I was a basketball student-athlete at Northern Illinois University. Where my story actually starts is my senior year in high school when I tore my ACL. That was an injury I never really 100 percent recovered from. It was an injury that probably led to other injuries. I ended up having a really injury-prone career at NIU. After having three surgeries in three years on the same knee, I ultimately decided to call it a career. I interned with my coaching staff my entire senior year as a part of my scholarship to stay in the game and be around my team."

You always want to go out on your own terms knowing you had that four or five-year career and reached your full potential as a player. It's something everyone wants for their ego and pride. I didn't get to go out on my own terms but for those who have a serious injury, you have to ask yourself if you really want to still push yourself and play? At some point, you have to think of the long term and the one sentence my doctor said that got to me was "Kristen, I know you are an active kid, you're competitive, but I know there's going to be a time you want to do things with your kids that you are not going to be able to do if you have another knee surgery." You have to live another fifty to sixty years after you are done playing.

CHAPTER SUMMARY

We have all heard friends or family talking about someone who lives in a fantasy world. They generally are writing that person off because he or she can't see what everyone else sees.

As a student-athlete you have to deal with a lot of challenges and juggle a lot of balls simultaneously. Schoolwork, playing time, practices, weight training, eating properly, preparing for life after college—the list is practically endless. You also have to manage expectations (your own and those of others) and draw certain conclusions. In short, you have to see yourself as you really are.

Learning to be honest with yourself may sound like a TV cliché, but there is significant power in developing the ability to call "bull crap" on yourself. When you look in the mirror, the truth will always be evident in your eyes.

So get comfortable facing the facts and get busy with living. It's okay to have doubts and to not be sure about which way to go. But face reality. If you've hit an iceberg, you have to give the orders to evacuate quickly.

If you've broken a rule, don't assume you can hide that truth forever. It may not be pleasant in the short term, but dealing with the truth early on is more beneficial to who you really want to become. Put in the effort but also take responsibility for your own outcome. Don't blame others for your life's trajectory. You get to create your story and how it progresses.

AND . . . If you still don't believe in the reality of going pro, take a look at Appendix A, where we have provided data from the NCAA studies to put the pro "thing" into perspective. Notably, Appendix A makes clear that the NCAA is the best pathway to going pro in North America but that student-athletes vastly overestimate their chances of "making it," with great variability across sports. Interestingly, the reports also note that making the jump from high school to the NCAA is comparable in difficulty to going from the NCAA to major pro.

Secret *12* Mentally Move On as a Senior

THE SECRET IN A FEW WORDS

One of the hardest parts about your transition into postcollege life is mentally moving on from your sport. In today's world of sport specialization at a young age, many of you have played your sport since you were five years old. At the latest, you probably started by age twelve.

Regardless of when you started, you have devoted a lot of years, time, and dedicated effort to becoming the best athlete you can be. The amount of time you put into being a student-athlete might even trump the amount of time you have put into anything else in your life up to this point. You have put hours into your training every day, hours into the gym, and hours into all the other aspects of getting recruited and chosen to play at your institution. As you play and compete, you try not to think about the day it will be all over. Unfortunately, that day comes for everyone, and how you deal with it mentally is important in your transition.

Our secret is that you have to mentally move on as a senior. Many student-athletes hold on to their dream until the last possible second and struggle with being mentally prepared for when that time expires. Chase your dreams to the fullest, but be mentally prepared for when the time comes that you won't be going pro.

MENTALLY MOVE ON AS A SENIOR

Wally Ritchie is a former Major League Baseball player who had a thirteen-year career in the pros and spent time with us reflecting on his ability to mentally move on from his career as a professional athlete. Imagine how much harder it would be to separate from your sport if you played pro after college. Wally provides some advice on how to mentally prepare for that transition.

WALLY RITCHIE (former Major League Baseball pitcher)

When you're playing, you don't think about the end of your career.

Athletes are not one dimensional. The transition from after your playing career affects many facets of your life, including education and career, mental well-being, relationships, finances, health and wellness. These areas are all important parts of life outside of sports, but you need to manage your education and careers along with your mental well-being to successfully navigate this transition in all spheres of life.

Whenever an athlete's playing days come to an end, transitioning to the next phase of life can be a difficult process. Whether you're a senior in college, or, in my case, a thirteen-year veteran of professional baseball, it's difficult to leave behind a sport in which you've invested so much time and effort/heart and soul and it's been such a big part of your life. Very few athletes choose to walk away from their sport. The choice is often made for them, which makes it much more difficult to separate and leaves many ill-prepared for what lies ahead.

Education and career decisions are one piece an athlete can put in place before their playing career ends. Prepare an educational and career plan with help from academic and career advisors while you're still playing. Find something that you enjoy and provides a challenge. I didn't have a plan in place when my career ended, so not only did I have to figure out what to do with my life, but I also faced the mental and emotional challenges that come with not competing anymore. No one prepared me for the realization that what I'd worked for my whole life was now gone. One day I was a professional athlete, someone that others looked up to, and the next, I was done. The mental transition remains the toughest part because it's hard to explain to others if they haven't been through it and it's not tangible. Finding a way to stay involved in the game and fill the void made it a somewhat smoother transition for me. But, don't expect it to be easy.

One of the things that many athletes deal with when they look back at their playing career is regret. Regret can cost you unnecessary time and energy and it gets you nowhere. I know from experience that running through scenarios of how you could have done things differently and how that would have changed the outcome of your career is fruitless and frustrating.

The solution? Do everything you can to succeed in your sport while you're playing. Prepare yourself mentally and physically for your sport. Practice to improve each day and be ready to excel during the games. Push yourself and leave it all on the field during every single game, so when you are done, you can look at yourself in the mirror and your teammates and say "I did everything I could."

Life after being a student-athlete is a difficult shift, but with a realization (usually early in the senior year) that it will happen, early preparation, an awareness of the challenges, and a willingness to reach out for help, student-athletes can more easily navigate the transition.[1]

James Biddick, a former athlete and career management expert, provides similar insight.

JAMES BIDDICK (former field hockey athlete in New Zealand, Assistant Director of Graduate Career Management at Ohio University Sport Management)

There is a scene in the movie *Moneyball* where a baseball scout cautions a teenage Billy Beane (played by Brad Pitt) that "we're all told at some point in time that we can no longer play the children's game. We . . . don't know when that's gonna be. Some of us are told at eighteen, some of us are told at forty, but we're all told." This is true for every athlete, but particularly pertinent for the student-athlete.

How does one simply "move on"? How does a student-athlete begin to mentally move on from something that has occupied such a large part of their life—not only in terms of time through early morning trainings and long travel; but for many student-athletes, their sport is also a huge part of their identify and social grouping.

Having been a former student-athlete and played to a high level in multiple sports, particularly field hockey, I know the mental adjustment from playing to no longer competing can be a challenging one. There are a number of different ways to help with the mental transition and it is hoped that the following paragraphs provide some understanding, as well as guidance, when faced with the inevitable task of moving on mentally from the "children's game."

There are those student-athletes who, as a result of the high demands placed on their time, body, and mind during college, are thankful to see the end of their college sporting career and are more than ready to embark upon the next chapter in their life. This specific group of student-athletes will never again feel the desire to pick up a bat, lace up a cleat, or put on a helmet. For them it is a welcomed transition, and from a psychological standpoint, they may experience greater happiness the day after their final game.

But what about those student-athletes less eager to leave the sporting spotlight upon graduation? One obvious and very common way to help with the adjustment is to remain involved with the sport through coaching. Although no longer on the field, there are many mental benefits gained from coaching that are similar to those felt by the student-athlete, such as being part of a team, as well as being around like-minded people who speak the same lingo and who inherently understand one another. Coaching also provides the former student-athlete with the satisfaction of "giving back" to the game they still care so much about, and the opportunity to act as a mentor for younger athletes (similar to the role played by seniors toward freshmen).

Another option that is less formal than coaching is social sporting leagues and general forms of physical fitness. Athletes who particularly enjoyed the training aspect of their sport, and still feel a desire to compete, continue with their fitness endeavors, through such communities as CrossFit. Social sporting leagues or CrossFit-type activities mimic many of the mental benefits experienced by student-athletes—comradery, physical enhancement, and perhaps the most important of them all—the challenge of competition.

Whichever path a student-athlete decides to take postgraduation, it is important to consider how no longer playing the game will impact their psyche, as well as what practical steps can be taken to support the mental transition.

Biddick's advice above is specifically for those who play four or five years and graduate with a degree. However, as we know well, there are different ways for a student-athlete's career to end:

1. End of eligibility/graduation (the aforementioned "traditional" path where the student completes four years of eligibility and earns a degree)

2. Injury (as described in numerous chapters so far, a major injury can quickly, if not instantly, end the athletic career of the student-athlete)

3. Being cut or released from team

4. Voluntarily choosing to stop

5. Not getting drafted or picked up as a free agent, or missing an Olympic team spot

All five career-end scenarios require different ways for the retiring student-athlete to mentally move on from her or his sport. One can be much better prepared for graduation than for either a career-ending injury or being cut. These two unexpected and sudden routes are much harder to move on from because there are a lot of "what if's" or "if only's" that many athletes think about and endlessly assess. If you voluntarily choose to stop competing, it is more likely you have already moved on, and it's easier to make your transition mentally on your terms. If you don't get selected in the draft or picked up as a free agent, you just have to accept the reality of the situation. If you miss the Olympic roster spot, maybe it just wasn't meant to be, but perhaps waiting another four years isn't going to work either. Is it time to move on?

Previous "secrets" in this book have covered the reality of your career finishing at the end of your eligibility. We have also shared the secret that preparation for this transition needs to start in your sophomore year. You've also been advised to be prepared for an injury to end your career at any moment in time, and how difficult that can be.

Getting cut or released from a team happens to student-athletes who don't improve or whose place is taken by a more talented younger player or who don't fit into their coach's plan anymore. In these cases, their scholarship is often revoked, and other decisions about staying at the university result.

In other cases, a coaching change or an institution's decision to cut a program for various reasons can affect your athletic career. These cases are out of your control, but nothing says they can't happen.

There are many ways you can deal with the end of your athletic career, and each is affected—as noted above—by the way in which your career ends. We summarize three approaches here.

1. Going cold turkey (i.e., hard stop, full change to your new life, move on from your sport completely). This is the most challenging and possibly the most depressing.

2. Ongoing involvement as a nonathlete (e.g., fan, volunteer).

3. Continuing to work in your sport in a professional capacity (e.g., professional employment in ticket sales, sponsorship, analytics, officiating, administration, coaching, training).

Most student-athletes are able to move on successfully if they have other passions to pursue. A career focus or other interests and activities can occupy the time the sport previously took up. This draws on a number of our secrets.

Kevin Brice, a former Division III baseball player at Pomona College, works for the Los Angeles Angels as a quantitative analysis assistant. He reflects on his transition period and how he had to move on from playing the sport he loves. He was fortunate to find a job quickly, but the transition period for him was sudden and rapid. His experience provides valuable insight on the challenges that graduating student-athletes "changing status" encounter.

KEVIN BRICE
(former student-athlete in baseball at Pomona College,
Quantitative Analysis Assistant for the Los Angeles Angels)

I found out I got a job two days before graduation, just after the season had ended, and I started the next week. The quick transition didn't allow me to think about it all that much, and I didn't have time to contemplate anything. The transition from playing to working got smoothed over by the fact that I am working for the Angels, and I am around my sport of baseball. Having that job set up after graduation is key in smoothing that transition out. . . . I would advise any athletes to try and stay around their sport to help with that transition.

Coming from a school like Pomona College, where academics are the priority, most of the guys have the reality that they are done playing after school. I think I realized I wasn't going pro after my first summer ball season after my freshman year of college. I was a good college baseball player, but didn't have the tools for the next level.

When I realized that, I decompressed a little bit and just tried to have as much fun as possible playing the game. Once I accepted that, and it is hard for a lot of guys to accept it before it's too late, I just wanted to enjoy playing the game, and enjoy being around my teammates. I wanted to make sure I had a plan B, and was prepared for the end of my collegiate career.

Elizabeth Woerle is a former Division I soccer player who had a successful collegiate athletic career and played professionally overseas after graduation. She attended graduate school at Ohio University and works in the athletic department at the University of South Carolina. Like Kevin Brice, she had a successful transition from her senior year, heading to Europe to play soccer professionally for two years before returning to the United States for graduate school and to begin her career. She has this advice for senior student-athletes.

ELIZABETH WOERLE
(former collegiate and professional soccer player,
Stewardship Coordinator for University of South Carolina Athletics)

I think the best thing you can do is to continue to play if you have the chance. You can get a "real job" the rest of your life, but you can't always play sports [at a high performance level]. If you have the opportunity, your body allows it, do it. Second, enjoy every bit of your college career and invest as much as you can of yourself into it. If it hurts when your career ends and you have to hang the boots up, that means you truly invested yourself and you were committed.

If you can walk away and brush your hands off, then I would question your commitment and passion for the sport you were playing. Anything in life that we love and invest in, whether that be a sport, job, or relationship, if we lose it, it stings and it causes a bit of heartbreak. It's not bad that it meant a lot to you. It is important to grieve and recognize these emotions.

Sport can always be a part of your life one way or another. Lastly, my biggest piece of advice would be to not wish it away. Put your everything into every time you step on the field because that way you won't look back and think I wish I would have, could have, should have.

CHAPTER SUMMARY

No student-athlete wants to think about that last practice, meet, game, tournament, or competition, nor do you want to think about the day after your playing career ends. When it's accompanied by being told that you aren't going to make it pro, it stings even more.

But now you know that you should think about "the end" and plan for it (starting in the sophomore year)! That kind of thinking will go a long way toward preparing you for your senior year and life after.

Secret *13* Identify Who You Are

THE SECRET IN A FEW WORDS

Having an "identity crisis" is to be expected at some point during the transition out of sport and into the next chapter of your life. All those hours you have put into sport from the time you were a child now need to be focused on something else. As a student-athlete, you are always told to be in the present, enjoy the moment, soak it all in. Yes, you should do that. However, when you have been identified as a tennis player, football player, swimmer, or any other elite athlete for over a decade, you can feel lost when you no longer have that identity to those around you and to yourself. Right or wrong, it's common for your purpose in life to be associated with your identity. But you are not your sport. You are so much more than what you have done on the court or field the past few years. As you transition from your athlete identity to the next chapter of your life, it is time to reorganize your identity and adjust your goals to serve your new purpose.

IDENTIFY WHO YOU ARE

When we interviewed Jeff Rodin, Director of Community Outreach and Development for the Arizona Diamondbacks, he talked about the identity aspect of your transition, drawing from his experience as an athlete and a coach. Rodin stated,

> You must also ask yourself, "What's my purpose? Did I already fulfill my purpose? What's the point?" Knowing that your identity is not a student-athlete, or coach, it's much broader than that and that's why I think the things outside of the game—the people you

surround yourself with, the things you do, the things you believe, the things that you spend time doing—perspective is huge. If people don't have that perspective and you don't have someone help remind you where you came from and to not forget who you are, what is your identity? If your identity is the game, or your identity is your job, at some point that is going to stop.

Everyone has a different identity and a different experience after transitioning from sport to life. Because of this, we interviewed six former student-athletes to provide guidance on how to find your identity.

JONI LOCKRIDGE (former softball student-athlete, former Director of Digital Strategy at the PGA)

How did you handle the transition from sports into life, and how did your identity change?

My graduation from college sports into life required that I shift from a physically driven team structure where I had developed and polished my skills over fifteen years, to a knowledge-driven organization . . . where I didn't know anything.

Looking back, I'm not sure I realized that I was facing a transition until I had to force myself up the steep side of the learning curve. But just like running hills, we all learn that it becomes easier once you embrace the burn. I recognized that the same skill sets that helped me achieve my athletic goals can also help me achieve my professional ambitions. It was not, however, a clean process:

I felt an overwhelming sense of *disappointment.* This isn't why I spent the last twenty years of my life in school. I *questioned* everything. It wasn't until I began taking control in answering some of the questions about myself that I started seeing breakthroughs.

I recognized that the more uncomfortable I was in the task, the more I learned, and the more satisfied I felt in the end. The logical next step was to find more responsibilities that made me uncomfortable and challenged me. From there, I found a sense of quiet confidence in my own skin and really started to get to know myself.

What advice would you have for future student-athletes on how to handle their change in identity?

The shift from athletics to work forces former student-athletes into a new social category—one that humbles us, but that spans our adult lives. My advice: be open to new perspectives and be ready to modify your approach, but do not abandon what makes up your core identity. Your fundamental values and your culture should remain true. Your moral compass should not shift from North to South. You may find that your identity becomes more layered and more complex, but it's an evolution over time, not a revolution overnight.

Athletes come with a set of guiding principles that give us an advantage. We know how to work with people through wins and losses. Follow your instincts, and work as hard on yourself as you work on those TPS Reports (Oh, and watch *Office Space* if you didn't catch that reference).

What were the two hardest aspects of your identity shift, and did you see the same things happen to your friends and teammates as they went through it too?

The hardest aspect of the transition was defining the strange, foreign ecosystem around me.

If you think about a traditional sports team structure, each competitor has a clear idea of other roles, personalities, strengths and weaknesses. A traditional work structure is more fluid. There is rarely a scoreboard or a shot clock. Positions aren't as clearly defined, and there are often three to four competitions going on at the same time. Training is loose, and more resembles that time your friend showed you how to drive a stick shift, than the hundreds of times your coach broke down your swing in painstaking detail.

My former teammates and I all dealt with this in our own ways. Most of us became a chameleon of sorts, changing colors to blend in or stand out . . . then returning to our natural state as soon as we were able to catch up with one another. A few changed their identity overnight in order to fit in quickly. I believe these individuals struggled the most.

Which brings up the second aspect: don't give up. Carry forward your athletic goal of developing the best version of yourself. Every. Single. Day.

Brooks Neal, Director of Corporate Partnerships and former lacrosse student-athlete at Syracuse University, also talked about his identity upon graduation.

> For me, losing my identity was very, very challenging from the sense that you spend your whole life kind of working towards one thing. I grew up wanting to play football and lacrosse at Syracuse because I grew up outside of Syracuse, NY, and lacrosse is huge in the region. Ever since I can remember, it's all I really wanted to do. I made it. I got there and accomplished my goals . . . and it was exciting. Then it's all over in the blink of an eye. Lacrosse is a spring sport and I had everything going for me heading into the NCAA tournament with graduation right around the corner. But, we lost in the first round of the NCAA Tournament and my athletic career came to a screeching halt. It felt like the world came crashing down on me and it was hard to cope with.

Dawn Buth, Associate Director of the Sport Science Institute at the NCAA, talked about her experience of having the opportunity to play professionally as well. She provided her perspective on values during her transition.

> My transition from athlete to working professional was one of the most difficult identity challenges I have faced. I devoted hundreds and thousands of hours to the sport that I loved, then suddenly, skills that once seemed critical to my success no longer seemed useful or to have the same type of value. Early in my administrative career, one of my supervisors offered an important insight, "I don't care how hard you work, I care about results." As an athlete whose upbringing and athletic philosophy revolved heavily around the concept of process and work ethic, this statement generated a profound paradigm-shift. While it did not change my approach to work ethic or the degree to which I valued it, this statement taught me an important lesson about perspective: Not everyone values the same things, and to have the most impact, I needed to be proactive in understanding and considering the values of others. This began an important period of self-discovery in which the skills I developed as an athlete grew and evolved to help serve me in a new way.

Christa Mann, Manager of Communications at the MLS, highlighted self-evaluation during her transition after playing overseas in Iceland.

> It was definitely a situation where you are going through a lot of self-evaluation and you're trying to assess who you are and what you are. The hardest thing is seeing yourself as more than an athlete. Prior to going to Iceland, I saw myself as someone with a multitude of skills who just happens to play soccer and be pretty good at it. After Iceland it was like I was only a soccer player. When I stopped playing, I didn't know what I was supposed to be and was questioning if I had I prepared myself.

Hillary Nelson, former softball student-athlete at Arizona State University and now Partnerships Manager at Positive Coaching Alliance, spoke about what she saw with her teammates and other student-athletes in relation to their identities. "The biggest mistake I see in athletes and all sports is when they fall for that mischaracterization that their identity is in their sport, meaning that they are only as valuable as their abilities as an athlete, and I had a friend tell me once 'I don't know what I would do without softball. I'll never do anything as well as I hit that ball.'"

Nelson's transition may have been easier than most after playing professionally, because she states, "My transition was much easier because I used sports to launch my career. I leveraged the contacts I made during my playing career into references for my first job. The world doesn't care about how much you know, but who you know and how hard you're willing to work." One could assume that getting a job right away and working hard toward different goals can provide you an identity instead of searching for one.

Hallie Olson, a former student-athlete at Ohio University, tells her story of how her identity changed once she started working for the Chicago Bulls.

> I was a swimmer my whole life, and that was something that I identified with. I was never the most talented by any means, but my work ethic was there enough to where I could try and set myself apart from folks. Come college, as much as people say they're a student before an athlete, it's really hard. I would say that I was probably an athlete over a student. I definitely put a lot more focus on athletics. That's what was always driving me and running through my mind. I certainly cared about what was going to be happening with my career down the road, but that just seemed so far off that it seemed more important for me to focus on sports. From an identity standpoint, it was a challenge to transition into life because once I was done with school, I thought, "OK, well who am I now?," I don't really have any sort of identity anymore. You're identified sometimes when you have your job, like when you introduce yourself at a networking event it's, "I'm Hallie, I work for the Chicago Bulls." It used to be, "I'm Hallie, I'm on the swim team," when I was hanging out with people at school. There was certainly a void that I felt, and I did feel a little bit lost because you lose all of that time that you spent doing things involved in your athletics. The year after I graduated, I didn't know what do I do with all this time? That whole year was just funky. I think back, I feel like I didn't have a direction. I feel like I wanted to work in sports but I didn't really know what capacity, I was really trying to find myself.
>
> It's just fine-tuning how you're describing yourself and also thinking of yourself. You are a brand. At the peak of what your brand used to be, your entire brand used to be athletics, and now it's not anymore. It will always be a part of you, but it's just not something that is at the forefront anymore. Now it's just developing what's the next chapter? What is the next chapter of your life? What are you looking to achieve? Once I started feeling successful somewhere else, when I got a job, or when I was doing things in Ohio where I felt like I was making an impact, that's when I started feeling like I don't have this crisis, I'm not going through this brand-identity crisis anymore.

Hopefully you can relate to some of these stories, and realize that you aren't alone in this. Most student-athletes, and many non-student-athletes, go through this stage of trying to find their identity as they transition out of college. Knowing that your identity is always evolving and changing, you have to understand it isn't a quick fix. You can't just snap your fingers and make one appear. You can't go to McDonald's and order a new identity, either.

Now that you have read about finding your identity and have received advice from those who have gone through that process already, it is important to know that many student-athletes are easily depressed during this search for an identity.

It is common for any human to deal with depression and anxiety when making a major change in life. In the case of making a big decision, for example, such as getting married or buying a house, many people go through a period of "cognitive dissonance" or regret about making that momentous decision. It is normal and common.

This is no different, if not more profound, in the case of the graduating senior student-athlete. In fact, "about 30 percent of the 195,000 respondents to a recent American College Health Association (ACHA) survey reported having felt depressed in the last 12 months and 50 percent reported feeling overwhelming anxiety during the same period."

Often athletes claim it takes at least three years after their playing career is over before they play their sport again for fun, especially after competing at a high level. Most sports played at the intercollegiate pace cannot be repeated in a different recreational setting. Therefore, the competitive drive athletes love is hard to find in their specific sport again.

To illustrate that depression after college is very real, comments from three interviewees are included here.

Jamilah Ali, a former gymnastics student-athlete at Bowling Green State University, recalled:

> When I graduated from college, everything changed. I was instantly depressed not knowing what would come next. Everyone my whole life knew me as the gymnast and when people would ask how my gymnastics was going, my heart broke more and more. Gymnastics was the one thing I always prided myself on, since I had worked so hard to be successful in my sport. The depression just seemed to get worse and worse as the summer went on and life did not go the way I wanted.
>
> I ended up becoming a club gymnastics coach and some days would tear up during coaching just thinking about how that was never going to be me again. I was so depressed because I never mentally prepared for life after gymnastics and felt I would never be as good at anything else. I ended up seeing a psychologist for

about a month to really help me realize that I was so much more than just an amazing athlete.

So my advice to the younger athletes is for them to find another passion besides their sport while still playing. And not to be scared about opening up about how hard it is no longer being a college athlete, and to start talking about life after athletics before it happens.

Connor Hancock, a former student-athlete at the University of Redlands, and now Assistant Manager of Digital Sales Administration at NBC Universal Media, talked about his experience as he transitioned out of playing baseball.

I was not in a good place after I decided to stop pursuing my dream. Like a lot of athletes, I went all in on my sport. All I did in college was go to class, hang out with friends, do schoolwork, and play baseball. The hardest part for me after baseball was over was that I felt that I had lost my identity. The majority of my time, effort, and emotions were tied into this one thing for nineteen years but all of the sudden I did not have it anymore.

When you feel like you have lost your identity, it really makes you reflect and question the decisions you have made leading you up to whatever moment you are at in your life. I went through many different stages of emotions and it was an extremely hard time for me. After looking back on my college experience, there are things I would have done differently in both school and baseball. The bad thing is that I cannot change any of that. The good thing is that you can learn from someone who has lived it. So my advice for you is to reach out to those who have learned those lessons in order to avoid some issues or know how to deal with them as they appear.

Kristen Brown, a former basketball student-athlete at Northern Illinois University, added the following from the perspective of an administrator:

Some student-athletes can be depressed during that transition phase if they can't see the big picture or don't have any long-term plans. I could see the big picture and the long term because basketball wasn't everything for me, it didn't define me. I loved the game. I'm passionate about it. But if I didn't have it in my life, I was okay.

I had a good perspective on it. I think I was aided by the fact that I was still involved in my program and I was still around my team. When it is a clean break and they are not involved, not traveling, not interacting with their team, depression can occur because you they go from all those things to nothing.

As you can see, sport provides emotions and confidence that few other activities can when performance goals are achieved and awards are won. Thus, when a career ends via the student-athlete choosing to stop playing, being cut, getting injured, or running out of eligibility, the act itself can easily lead to depression. One way or another, "sport career termination induces dramatic changes in athletes' personal, social and occupational lives. This can, in turn, potentially affect individuals cognitively, emotionally and behaviorally."[1]

In some of these scenarios, depression arrives as student-athletes lose a core part of their identity and must redefine themselves. As we have stated, depression is something that 30 percent of graduating student-athletes deal with. You aren't alone. But don't ignore it—address it, and learn how to avoid it or deal with it.

If you have any symptoms of depression or concerns about mental health, get professional help immediately. Your institution will have mental health services available to you, just like any other student, in an anonymous, confidential manner. Additionally, some athletic departments offer further support to student-athletes. Be sure to become aware of the resources you have available to you.

Here's what we advise:

1. Include time in your plan/schedule for friends (old or new) who are not your teammates.

2. Find at least one interest/passion outside of your career choices and your sport (music, language, gaming group, etc.) that you can manage.

3. Book at least two weeks a year in which you are free from sport and academics to focus your thoughts and expand your view of the world. Travel. Spend time with your family or friends.

4. Talk to a sports psychologist or talk to your mentor(s) about any issues you may be having. Talking it out helps more than anything else.

5. Spend more time involved in activities outside and with other people.

6. Make sure you have a diet plan that works for you, and eat healthy as it pertains to your lifestyle.

7. Continue to exercise regularly, as it will keep up your confidence and health.

8. Develop a plan for stress management, as unexpected events will occur throughout life and create stress.

9. Assess your strengths, build upon them, and then use them to your advantage.

10. Remind yourself about the positives that lie ahead and leverage your positive attitude about your future.

CHAPTER SUMMARY

As you transition out of being an athlete and into the next chapter of your life, you must consider these four major actions:

1. Self-reflect and think more about who you really are.

2. Look in the mirror and ask yourself what you want your identity to be.

3. Figure out what your next move is and identify with that.

4. You be you. Don't try to be someone you aren't.

Your identity is always changing and adapting to life. Remember who you were as an athlete because it will always be a part of you, but find that next thing to take the place of being an athlete.

As simplistic as it sounds, if you get depressed for feeling lost, just talk to someone. The more you talk to people and try to figure out who you are, the more you will learn about yourself. With that said, it takes many former athletes a long time to move on from their sport, so patience is the key. In a world where everyone wants instant gratification, you may have to wait just a little bit to truly find yourself and your new identity.

Secret 14 Find Your Other Passions in Life

THE SECRET IN A FEW WORDS

The majority of student-athletes don't participate in their sport after they transition to life-after-college. Either the competition just isn't the same or they are burnt out or it's impractical (e.g., who goes out just to throw around a javelin for fun with friends?). Finding new passions will help you enjoy life moving forward. This secret is to "find your other passions in life" because if you aren't passionate about what you are doing, you aren't likely to succeed at it because you won't want to.

DANNY WHITE
(Director of Student-Athlete Development at Virginia Tech)

It is really hard to learn about yourself when you aren't experiencing things. Different experiences will help you determine what you do and don't like.

FIND YOUR OTHER PASSIONS IN LIFE

Every student-athlete comes from a different background, plays a different sport, and has different success in athletics and academics. However, to remain balanced (Secret 5) in the postgraduation years, it is important to have other passions—at least one—beyond sport and school. Try new things, develop different interests, and then figure out what you care about.

This is a pretty open-ended secret. We get that. But it is not to be underestimated. A passion for something is rare. Don't misconstrue watching something on television regularly (your favorite TV show) as a passion. A passion should be something you can do forever, that you can get better at, and that can draw you to other social groups. It could be history, playing the guitar, or woodworking.

And this does not need to wait for graduation. Some quick tactics you can start anytime. In fact, start today. These are randomly presented, and some are vague while others are specific. Just some ideas to draw from, in no particular order!

- Take an interesting elective on a topic you might really like.

- Join a student club that is unrelated to your major or your sport (and that you might be interested in).

- Develop a new social network around a topic you find interesting.

- Join a club or some other social competitive group.

- Attend a guest lecture on campus.

- Join a local community group.

- Learn a trade.

- Be curious.

- Learn to play golf, pick up tennis. Or an instrument. Or to speak a new language.

- Run a marathon, do a triathlon, try CrossFit, or take a yoga class.

- Share a hobby with a parent or grandparent (e.g., hunting, travel, etc.).

- Volunteer at an event, a gallery, or a charity.

After graduation is also a time to find another passion or two. Here are four things to consider when finding other passions in life postgraduation:

1. Revisit prior passions. Before sport was all-consuming to you, what else did you enjoy? Now that you will have time to explore other interests, an old passion may resurface.

2. To play an intercollegiate sport, you have to have passion for your sport. Your sport may be your ultimate passion, and that is okay, but figure out how to pursue that passion in another way after your athletic career: as a coach, fan, professional, volunteer, and so on.

3. When your sport is your identity for much of your life, a new passion will bring about new identity and excitement.

4. Trial and error will be required to find your passion. You might not hit it on the first attempt and you may not even be sure what precisely you are looking for. Try new things and see what keeps your interest.

Former student-athletes had a lot to say on the topic of passion.

Brooks Neal, former lacrosse student-athlete at Syracuse University and now Director of Corporate Partnerships at the Cleveland Cavaliers, told us, "For me, it sounds dorky, but I became an avid reader of books. I never read a book in my life for pleasure, honestly, unless I was forced by my parents or my school. I became an avid reader because I didn't know how to settle my mind or my body. It was a good way for me to calm down at night rather than being exhausted from athletics."

Neal also would "encourage you to take up triathlon training as it keeps that competitive fire going, or find something intellectually stimulating. I have teammates who have become elite-level CrossFitters or elite-level tri-athletes who realize that their athletic ability can be used in other ways outside of the sport they played. For athletes, it is filling that void in their life, and when you graduate, I think just going wide and going deep with experiences and interests can really help."

Hallie Olson, former student-athlete at Ohio University and now Manager of Corporate Development at the Chicago Bulls, said that volunteering was her passion, as it was a way for her to give back. "Your priorities change, and you realize there's more you can do outside of yourself. I was very selfish in school. I cared where I was supposed to be and it was always me, me, me. Now, it's me and my husband, and . . . and giving back to other people and really making an impact on my community here in Chicago."

Eddie Gill, former NBA player and now TV host for the Indiana Pacers on Fox, agreed that "volunteering in the community is one way to get outside of your comfort zone and do something different, while being a productive member of society. Throughout my career, I did a number of camps and things like that with kids so I knew that that was one of my passions. Being able to provide a service is a passion for me. The service component has translated to where I'm at now in the financial service industry. By being proactive during my career, I was able to find a passion to carry out a different career when basketball was over for me."

Drew Saylor, Minor League Manager at the Los Angeles Dodgers, mentioned curiosity, saying "curiosity is one thing that college should do for people from an athletics and from an education standpoint, and even just from a human being standpoint, you should always be curious. You should always sit there and find the "Why's?," you should always sit there and find ways to improve yourself on a day-to-day basis. Curiosity may lead to those new found passions you can improve on."

Kristen Brown, former student-athlete at Northern Illinois University, expressed that her "two passions in life are young people and mentoring," which led her to a career in college athletics following graduation.

So, what should you do to pick the right passion? How do you find yours?

Garrett Shinoskie was the former Director of Athletic Performance at Zone Athletic Performance in Scottsdale, Arizona. He was a Division III football player and is a believer in student-athletes finding additional passion(s) outside of sports and academics.

> Keeping an open mind is critical in all aspects of life! When you're exploring other interests, especially new interests, you have to walk into it with the mentality that you know nothing and are starting at the bottom. Putting unrealistic expectations on yourself will only lead to unnecessary pressure and disappointment. I would advise student-athletes to immediately explore new passions or potential passions with your new found time [post-graduation].
>
> Being able to check out multiple avenues of interests will be the key to separating passions that could lead to careers or are better left as hobbies. The best recommendation I can give for making a career out of a passion, is to get experience in the industry and ask questions.
>
> Whether it's interning, part-time employment, shadowing an expert in the field, check out the industry and ask the right questions. What are the requirements of the job, will you need more education, does the industry standard of income work for you, etc. If you think you have any interest in something, do your research and found out how to become involved and learn more. If you never try you'll never know.

Steve Watson, Athletic Director at Loyola University Chicago, talked about how he found the passion of working in college athletics. In our interview with him, he stated, "I had such a great experience as an athlete. I knew that as I was wrapping up the professional career that college athletics was where I wanted to be. I enjoyed my time as a professional. Watching the freshmen become seniors and coming back to campus as professionals out in the workforce, that is the best. To be able to experience that, it doesn't get much better than that."

Billy Lavelle, a former student-athlete in baseball, warned that finding a new passion is easier said than done. He recalled, "Since I was no longer able to identify myself as a baseball player, I was forced to try to find what my new identity would be and what I wanted to become. For the longest time all I knew was that I really enjoyed playing the game of baseball, but I never really thought about why I enjoyed it or why I was passionate about it [and how to figure out a new passion based on what I loved about baseball]. I loved the business side of it."

For those who want to work in college athletics after being a student-athlete, Terri Steeb-Gronau has some advice: "College athletics is still a part of higher education. If you are a person who wants to be involved in college athletics and you don't like teaching or coaching or mentoring, then college athletics is not the place for you. I tell people if you want to be involved in college athletics, there is a teaching component regardless of what you are doing. If you don't like working with young adults, it isn't the place for you."

Steeb-Gronau also mentioned that, "ultimately, you have to look inside yourself, and find what you are passionate about, outside of sport whether that is teaching, finances, environment, or working in the community. Is there something you look back on your life and say this is something that I enjoy, other than your sport? What energizes you? What gets you up in the morning? These are questions you have to ask yourself to determine what you're passionate about."

CHAPTER SUMMARY

Eddie Gill summarized the search for new passions perfectly with his favorite saying: "Get comfortable being uncomfortable."

Everyone has different passions, and some may have only one. Passions may come and go or completely change. No matter how many different passions you have, it is always good to find a new one and be open to finding a new one. However, passions can't be forced; it's all natural, as they say. Now that you are transitioning from being an athlete to the rest of your life, you need to find some other passions in your life, because life has a lot to offer.

Secret 15 Start Preparing in Your Sophomore Year

THE SECRET IN A FEW WORDS

Your sophomore year is the key time to prepare for your transition to life post-graduation. Sure, we get that it is three years away, but that also means you have only three years to prepare for your career launch, competition against other graduates in your chosen profession, or graduate program. Just imagine you are walking into a job interview for a position that you'd love to have. Early in the process, they ask you to describe the relevant experiences you have for the job. You don't have much, but explain that you were a student-athlete. You then hear that another candidate has a double degree, two internships, three international learning experiences, and two practicums with industry-leading organizations. How can you possibly compete?

START PREPARING IN YOUR SOPHOMORE YEAR

In doing the research for this book, the authors thought back to our collective experiences as student-athletes and found that everything pointed to the importance of the beginning of our sophomore (second) year. We were settled in the routine of college, had found our place on the team, had acquired a supportive social circle, and were comfortable with our choice of academic majors. It was the point to start focusing extra activities on finding a career (or obtaining entry to a graduate or professional degree) postgraduation.

If you're early in your sophomore year, now is the time to plan. This book can certainly help, as can your academic advisors, mentors, coach, parents, and classmates.

THE TRANSITION

When student-athletes graduate, they need to find a career or continue to progress toward one. In today's world, a college degree is a requirement for many careers and the number of people who hold one is very high. In the United States in the fall of 2016, according to the National Center for Education Statistics,[1] approximately 20.5 million students will attend US colleges and universities. About 3 million of these students leave college as graduates each year.

Importantly, for you, the next competition (for a career) is against the entire market searching for a job, not just other student-athletes. In many careers (e.g., accounting, electrical engineering), being a student-athlete has no impact on your "hireability." In fact, the time and effort put into practicing for your sport might represent an "opportunity cost" that detracts from your ability to win a job competition. Of course, you have the inside track on how to capitalize on your student-athlete experience to make sure you won't be in the situation of "only" having been a student-athlete.

THE CAREER

A career is not easy to find or to stay in. Industries change, jobs disappear. For example, in the 1960s, there were thousands of jobs in the printing industry. Those jobs no longer exist. Other fields, full of opportunity in the future, may not even exist yet.

You may choose a career path and decide shortly thereafter that you want to follow a different one. The Bureau of Labor Statistics reports that the average US working woman changes jobs every 4.5 years, followed closely by the average US working man, who alters his employment every 4.7 years.[2]

Matt Vansandt, a former track and field student-athlete and now Director of Championships at the Big South Conference, recalled his path: "I worked in real estate lending for the first three years out of college. I figured out I hated it and it wasn't what I wanted to do. I went back to grad school to pursue college athletics. Track taught me how to fail and keep getting back up again and again. That helped me with my career path in the sense that I failed at my first career path and had to get up and try something different."

There is no grand plan for a career, but it should be taken in steps. Some steps go forward, backward, or sideways, and sometimes you may feel like you are walking in circles. You don't have to decide what your whole life path is going to be, because you simply can't. Many aspects of life are unpredictable, and therefore you need to be equipped with more than one plan.

A career requires diligent planning and preparation and the ability—like sport—to beat other competitors seeking the same thing. Many coaches will say, "When you aren't getting better, you are getting worse because someone else is getting better." Make sure you prepare and plan for a career just like you do for your sport, because if you aren't getting better every day, you will fall behind others. Make it a goal to become better at one thing, even a little thing, every day.

SO, WHAT SHOULD YOU DO?

Step 1: Create a plan before your sophomore year

To ready yourself for success in life, figure out your plan and follow it. Truly activate your sophomore (second) year.

Here are the significant elements of your plan:

1. Get a career coach—if one is not provided by the university, find one.

2. Finalize your major, and study what you want to study, not what's easiest.

3. Schedule your classes so you have more freedom to gain experience in your junior and senior year.

4. Make a list of at least five postgraduation goals (e.g., go to law school, start my own business, get a job with a pro sports team).

5. Identify and build a relationship with a mentor/advisor in each of the areas noted in your answer to element #4.

6. For each answer to element #4, research and list the experiences, skills and aptitudes required for success in that pursuit.

7. Prioritize what is most important to you when making decisions about a job/career and its fit (things like salary, benefits, geography, proximity to friends or family, etc.).

8. Keep up on industry trends and career trends that will help you in your research as you develop a career plan and path. One way to do this is by getting involved on campus with an organization or club (if you cannot get an internship).

9. Gain as much knowledge as you can so you will make informed and educated decisions about career options.

10. Realize that finding a job or getting into a professional program (like medical school) is highly competitive, difficult, and requires years of preparation. Apply the same type of planning and preparation as you do in athletics toward your efforts to achieve the goals from element #4.

Step 2: Keep a realistic perspective on things

Many of the former student-athletes we interviewed highlighted the importance of having a realistic perspective. It is vital to have an open mind and be realistic about your upcoming decisions. Two interviewees below specifically help describe this step.

KRISTEN BROWN
(former basketball student-athlete at Northern Illinois University)

You have to look at it as one door shuts, another one opens. You have to change your perspective and your mentality, and look for an opportunity to make something happen."

. . . .

HILLARY (BACH) NELSON
(former softball student-athlete at Arizona State University)

Focus on controlling the controllables. For me, that was always attitude and effort. Looking back, I was most successful when I controlled my attitude and efforts toward practice, training, studies, and everything else. All I ever wanted was a national championship. I wanted to go to school. I told my coach when getting recruited. "I want to graduate in three years. I want to get my MBA and I want to win a national championship."

Coach Clint Meyers gave me all those things. At the end of the day, we were holding the national championship trophy above our heads, we went to bed that night and woke up the next day and then we started all over again. The next year, we just wanted to win a national championship all over again. Understanding that you'll never be fulfilled by that [big win] is important. Keeping things in perspective, happiness is the ultimate prize and it is not going to be a trophy or a piece of paper. It's going to be the relationships and the experiences you build with the people around you while you're a student-athlete.

CHAPTER SUMMARY

At this point, you should be very aware of the realities of going professional (or making an Olympic team) and you should have started your preparations for life after sports. The reason we suggest the sophomore year for this planning is, for many of you, the freshman year is for growing up and figuring out who you are. However, many wait too long to think about their future until it hits them square in the face at graduation. So, sophomore year is the time. We're not trying to scare you or be your therapist, just encouraging you to plan.

Secret 16 Invest in Yourself, Your Health, and Your Future

THE SECRET IN A FEW WORDS

One of the hardest aspects of transitioning from being an athlete to being a working professional is the change in lifestyle and habits. Retired athletes do not train like they used to when they were competing. When you, the student-athlete, are done competing, other responsibilities will take priority. Jobs, family, and many other endeavors will take priority over working out. Each individual has his or her own priorities, and there is no specific magical order that one must follow.

Throughout life, priorities change all the time, and your change in priorities as you first transition into life as a nonathlete is only the start. Nutrition not only becomes more difficult, but the eating habits you developed as an athlete most likely won't work for too much longer. During college, you could sleep in some days based on your class schedule, but when you have a job, your sleep schedule will likely change and you may find you need more and higher-quality sleep.

This secret is simple: It's necessary for you to invest in yourself, your health, and your future. All these changes in your lifestyle are just a few of the adjustments you will have to make as you start your career. At the end of the day, it is a lifestyle you create and you live by. Why not strive to make it a healthy lifestyle in hopes of healthy results?

INVEST IN YOURSELF, YOUR HEALTH, AND YOUR FUTURE

While you are competing and training, eating habits become a little abnormal due to the amount and type of food that you need to consume. In college, because of events and classes, you may eat at odd hours, creating bad habits for when you are not training (or training less).

Your daily student-athlete schedule is quite rigorous and can be a grind for those who take their academics seriously or who are enrolled in challenging or high-volume programs or majors. After you have finished your athletic career, many won't change their eating and nutrition habits. This can cause issues over the years because of potential changes in your training levels and your metabolism as you get older.

Yes, the transition from being a student-athlete to being a working professional isn't easy. No one said it would be. Having more money is a positive (and a prospect you are likely excited about!), but there are also downsides, such as the many aspects of our lifestyle that we may have to put on the back burner (or let slip from time to time) in order to maintain employment, family, parenting, home ownership, and other adult responsibilities.

Brett Fischer is a Licensed Physical Therapist, Certified Athletic Trainer, and Certified Strength and Conditioning Specialist. He has worked with the University of Florida, New York Jets, PGA & Senior PGA TOUR, and the Chicago Cubs. He currently provides sports performance training and rehab to MLB, NFL, NBA, NHL, and world-ranked tennis players. Fischer is also currently the staff Physical Therapist with the NFL's Arizona Cardinals. Over the years, he has dealt with many athletes and professionals, providing him with the experience to offer the following.

BRETT FISCHER

Student-athletes are usually given a program by a strength coach or some medical professional. All of the sudden, now it's over and there's no one there to tell them what to do and when to do it. They have to rely on what they were taught in high school or college then all of the sudden, they're on their own. From a principle standpoint, that's probably the biggest adjustment that student-athletes have to make during their transition into life.

From a nutrition standpoint, a lot of student-athletes face problems when transitioning because they were probably provided some kind of stipend, food plan, or prepared food... All of a sudden now your workouts aren't as long, you're not training as hard as you used to, and now eating the same way you used to eat back in college doesn't work. It's an adjustment because even in the NFL, I'll see guys post-career that are heavier a couple years later. I've seen some guys who were defensive backs who weighed 190 pounds, and they're 265 now, and you can't recognize them.

Athletes have been training so long and hard that it's something they use to get away from things. It's so much a part of their whole life. UCLA did research on Brain Mapping, and it showed whether you were in college or pro, when you no longer have a team to go to, the brain perceived that as being rejected. It's the same mechanisms that the brain detects as an injury. They lose their purpose of life. It's always been make it to the pros or be in the pros, and then one day it's over, now what? They don't have a team to go to. There's no schedule for them anymore. It's like you get divorced.

Mentally preparing and physically preparing for that transition is important, but so is emotionally preparing. College is different because they're not making money yet, but they'll still have that same soul-search as professional athletes do when they retire. I've seen that too where players didn't make the NFL and they put all of their dreams into playing a sport, and now they're no longer a part of a team and the locker room with all the guys and they're all alone. That's a big change emotionally as well as physically.

Your emotional health is going to affect your physical health, and you really can't separate the two from each other. The emotional struggle is the biggest part of transition struggles. They have no place to go. They feel like they're not a part of the team. They miss the locker room atmosphere. They miss their friends.

For many student-athletes, they've been told where to go, when to go and, in real life, that's not really the case. You're now in a situation where you have to make your own choices. What time do you eat? What time do you work out? What time do you go to work? Are you late? No one's going to be knocking on your door, making sure you wake up or giving you wake up calls. There's a transition of being responsible.

Louie Iglesias, a former Division I Tennis player at the University of Toledo who went on to a successful career in the sport business, offers his perspective as a former student-athlete.

LOUIE IGLESIAS (former tennis student-athlete, Director of Adult Programs at Southlake Tennis Center)

When I was competing, I didn't really watch what I ate because of the number of hours that I'd be on the court. At least three to five hours a day. I just ate and I was probably putting down about 5,000 calories a day. After my career was over and I stopped playing, the eating never stopped. I never trained myself to portion control or count calories or control carbs. At age twenty-two, I gained fifteen pounds in the first year that I had stopped playing. I wasn't burning the same amount of calories that I was burning previously, and I never conditioned my body to eat at a certain time of the day or be disciplined about my diet, which didn't help me when I stopped playing. When you start working, you don't have as much downtime as you did when you were an athlete, or certainly a student. When you're working, especially in your twenties, a lot of those first jobs out of college are where you're putting in sixty to seventy hours a week.

For a lot of those jobs, you're young, you're expected to put in a lot of hours and it's not uncommon to have a job where you only get thirty minutes for lunch. Then it becomes a matter of convenience. The average American between the ages of 22 and 29 will change jobs seven times. So, why is that relevant? It suggests that between the ages of 22 and 29 your schedule is going to be all over the place and at the very least, less stable.

When someone's schedule gets thrown upside down, the first thing impacted is always the diet. For an athlete, it's all about the routine. You want to get into your comfort zone and your routine because we are all "Creatures of Habit." It's almost like saving money, either you make it a priority or you don't.

When you enter that phase in your life where there's instability in terms of your schedule, what you need to do is plan the day around your meals. If you know that you only have thirty minutes for lunch, then pack a lunch. Everybody's a little bit different, but the main point is to create good habits and create a routine for yourself.

The biggest lifestyle change for me [following retirement as an athlete] was adjusting to the fact that I wasn't preparing for a tournament. I was a creature of habit. Every month of the year, I was always preparing for something. Tennis really didn't have an offseason, and there was always a tournament coming up.

Essentially when I graduated, it was like all of that stopped suddenly. All I knew how to do was to be a student and an athlete. I never worked at an internship in college. I never did any of that. I was just a student-athlete, and that's all I knew until I was no longer doing it. I found myself really behind the eight-ball, and really behind many people I went to school with. For me, I felt like a huge part of me died and there was a new Louie emerging that I didn't really know what to make of because I had no previous bearings to make any sense of it.

I got so much fulfillment in playing my sport, practicing for my sport, and working on my craft, that I didn't know where I was going to find my fulfilment now. Now I ask myself all the time, what do I want to aim for?

. . . .

CHRISTINA WRIGHT
(former student-athlete at American University, Lecturer of Sports Administration at Ohio University)

Christina Wright is a former Division I indoor and outdoor track and field student-athlete at American University (AU) in Washington, D.C. She currently holds the indoor and outdoor shot-put records, and is No. 2 on the AU All-Time Top Ten List for discus. She formerly worked at the NCAA in various roles. We asked her some pointed questions related to health following retirement as an athlete.

1. How did your diet and eating habits change for you as a non-athlete?

My diet and eating habits as a student-athlete did not change when I completed my eligibility in May 2007. Like many student-athletes, it was a bittersweet moment. For me it was no more lugging my throwing equipment on and off campus for practice, van rides with the men's team because my events always started early and ended late, scheduling everything and anything around my practice, class or competition schedule, it was freedom. But with this newfound freedom, I was still chained to bad habits. I had spent the past six years "bulking up" because throws are about physics.

I wasn't growing taller and getting longer limbs, so naturally, we focused on power and force. I went from two meals a day to five meals a day and mega carb-loading. I mean who doesn't eat a big bowl of pasta at least two days before a track meet, right? I kept eating at the same pace and portions as a student-athlete, but aside from a few club volleyball and softball games, I ceased all physical activity. I didn't handle the transition well—mostly because I love to cook and bake—and after living in the residence halls for four years, I finally had the freedom to cook and eat what I wanted, whenever I wanted.

I didn't drink much alcohol or soda during those years, but adding those items to already unbalanced eating habits didn't help. Instead of the freshman 15, I gained the retired student-athlete 30, and maybe even more.

2. What advice do you have for future student-athletes on learning to manage their diet while they are competing?

Almost a decade after the end of my student-athlete career, I was diagnosed with Type-I diabetes. Now I have to keep food and activity logs, just like I did in college, to help me manage my condition. If I could do it all over, I would have continued keeping a log because then I would have a visible accountability log showing me the caloric intake was way off-balance from my physical activity.

I am more conscious now of how my body reacts to certain foods—foods that make my glucose levels soar, foods that give me energy, etc. The other piece that would have helped me with the diet transition is the trendy concept of meal prep. This would have reduced eating out all the time and controlled my caloric intake with portioned meals appropriate for my age, health, and physical activity levels.

3. What was the biggest part of your lifestyle change when you finished competing?

Believe it or not, sleep. I finally was sleeping at least eight hours a night. In college I would average four to five hours at night and a two-hour nap, which I commonly referred to as siesta time. I look back and have no idea how I survived college without sleep. And then I think how much better a student and student-athlete I would have been if I had slept more regularly.

4. What advice do you have for future student-athletes on continuing to exercise after you are done competing?

I tried many different programs, even hired a personal trainer at one point. I found if I could blend exercise with some sort of social activity, that was the best motivation for me. I let myself fall into the trap of focusing on weight loss goals, and don't get me wrong, that's important; but when I was a student-athlete, setting realistic goals was key.

If I focused on weight, I didn't weigh myself every week. I focused on percentage lost and not number of pounds. My sport isn't one where I randomly pick up a discus and go into a backyard and throw. Post student-athlete days, my best workouts were thirty-minute intervals on an inclined treadmill, two to three times a week. Like anything else, you have to make it a priority for yourself. I was so eager to finally take a break that I lost the health benefits associated with playing sports.

5. What advice do you have for future student-athletes on making their exercise fun?

Friends, or at least an accountability partner or group. As much as we love our respective sports, our teams were our social support web. Why wouldn't we want to create a similar team post competition days? There are so many great options now: hot yoga, Zumba, CrossFit, etc. And when did 5K's, half-marathons, and marathons become so popular?

I hated running, probably because I associated it more with punishment than conditioning, but still, some people find running fills that competitive hole. Find something you enjoy and attach goals to it and that's the winning combination, as simple as that.

PREPARING FOR A HEALTHY TRANSITION

As your student-athlete days start to wind down, what should you do to prepare for a healthy life after competitive sport? We have a few suggestions based on our research and experiences.

1. Create a Structure Built around Physical Activity

As you've read, structure is a must as an athlete. Everything is scheduled, every day. Class, practice, training, competitions, tutoring, and all other aspects of your life are scheduled. After having been accustomed to so much structure, the majority of athletes struggle when there is no longer structure to their days and there are no longer professionals structuring their days for them. Having to create your own schedule based on your priorities is tough, especially when large stretches of time are now free, and scheduling is not a task you are used to doing.

For example, 24–35 hours a week of structured training and physical activity are all of a sudden gone. Having 30 hours a week to do whatever you want is quite the overload for athletes who don't know what to do with the time that was once part of a routine built around training.

Most athletes' motivation to maintain and continue training disappears after their athletic career is over. Thus, you need to build a structure that includes physical activity, social time, nutrition (based on current output), and sleep (expecting to move to a lifestyle based on a forty-hour work week or a variation thereof, depending on your professional aspirations).

Then within that structure, replace the former training (30 hours is certainly not necessary, but daily activity that burns calories is).

Brett Fischer suggested that you try to figure out what you enjoy doing:

Try different things. It could be rowing. It could be hiking. It could be something of a fitness nature to keep yourself going because you have to create endorphins.

Athletes hate to work out because they've worked out their whole life and they had to run sprints. We encourage former student-athletes to find those things they enjoy to do (and not running sprints anymore is just fine), but just find something else to do. There is just something about breaking a sweat that makes you feel good. Secondly, find something that's not going to hurt your body. Some student-athletes who may have had some injuries over the years playing college sports may not be able to run as much as they'd want to. Find yourself something to do just to keep yourself active.

2. Institute Portion Control in Your Diet and Be Aware of Nutrition

Brett Fischer advises that "with nutrition, you always want to continue with the proper proteins, carbohydrates, and fats along with portion control. It's easier to eat healthier in today's world . . . so there are no excuses because there are so many more options."

The keys as you transition from a calorie-burning athletic machine into a regular person are to reduce your portions, balance intake of food with calories expended, and remove or limit alcohol, desserts, and other sugary foods. Insure that you get enough fruit and vegetables daily (some guidelines suggest five a day is a good rule). Most important is portion control, which is the key for maintaining moderation. There are a number of methods to make sure this happens. Ask a nutritionist or do some online research to find out.

Mike Doehla, President of Stronger U, and NASM Certified Fitness Nutrition Specialist, gave us his take on nutrition for former student-athletes.

MIKE DOEHLA

The transition from student-athlete to postgraduation life can be quite the shock in some areas of life. However, in other areas it is more like a slow gradual evolution. In the case of nutrition and body composition, it is a mix. Immediately, your activity reduces, training changes, and external motivation may wane. Even though these changes are immediate, the impact on your body may not be evident for months or even a year or more. Because of these changes, former student-athletes often experience weight gain, muscle loss, and a deterioration of overall health. In my time as President of Stronger U working with hundreds of clients, many of whom were former athletes, I have developed a few guidelines that will help you avoid the pitfall of losing the muscle you have worked so hard for, gaining body fat, and starting down the road to poor overall health.

1. Be aware of overall caloric intake: With reduced activity, there is a lot less energy expenditure. Eating the same amount with less activity results in fat accumulation.

2. Watch your fat intake: Fat has the most calories at nine per gram and it's everywhere! Keeping your fat intake in check will automatically reduce your calories.

3. Eat a lot of protein: Protein will keep you full and help you preserve and build muscle.

4. Eat your veggies: Vegetables can be very filling, low on calories, and packed with nutrients.

5. Eat out less: If you keep meals out to a minimum, you can save a lot of calories (and money). Restaurants love fat and carbs. These foods are easy to overeat and quickly add up in overall calorie consumption.

6. Learn to cook: Learning to cook will help you choose foods that align with the food-related tips listed here. You control the ingredients and portions, and it's easy to cook a little extra and pack it up for lunch the next day.

Peter Rovinelli, a former wrestler and rugby player at Arizona State University, is the owner of Elite Wellness Solutions LLC and Be Elite Performance LLC. He provides his advice on portion control and nutrition based on the work he does with his clients.

First, he says here are three key principles to follow in achieving lifelong optimal nutrition:

1. Change your mindset: Move from "diet" to "nutrition" and understand the roles of food.

2. Change your awareness: Learn what foods are important and how much to eat.

3. Change your habits: Eat well most of the time, not some of the time.

Next, on sizing of portions, Rovinelli recommends that when you eat protein (chicken, steak, etc.), the portion should be about the size of your palm. For vegetables, about the size of a fist. For grains/starches/carbohydrates, about the size of a cupped hand. Finally, for healthy fats, the size of your thumb. Remember to modify these portion recommendations based on appetite, fullness, and individual nutrition goals. Also, remember that the same-sized portion of food might be a single serving for one person (a larger man) but two servings for another person (a smaller woman).

3. Sleep!

As noted, often with the new free time, less exercise, and less structure, it is easy to let sleep go. You might be tempted to stay up watching movies, socializing, or playing video games—lots of those things you weren't able to do before! This new freedom can be fun, but you need to show some restraint.

Fischer provides some good guidance:

> Sleep is a big part of a healthy lifestyle. There's a lot of things with sleep that are important. It's important to get six to eight hours every night and that's just to refuel the body. You want to find a place that's dark, and a place that's cool. Video games and cell phones really stimulate you before bed, so try to make sure you are in rest mode before you go to sleep. It's just stimulating your brain and your nervous system where it gets to the point where it's hard to turn it off. With professional sports teams, they research how much time guys are getting their sleep in and it's important that these guys get at least that six to eight hours. The good thing about sleep is you can make it up. If you had a short night, you can take a nap, and your body will make up for it. But if you keep doing that over and over, it puts a toll on your physical system as well as your mental system.

Here are five tips to help improve your sleep habits:

1. Don't eat too close to bedtime.

2. Limit exposure to light and electronics.

3. Wind down with reading, meditation, or prayer.

4. Don't keep your bedroom too warm.

5. Get seven to eight hours of sleep.

In a 2015 article, "A Recipe for Energy Management Success," Taylor Grayson interviewed Dr. Brian Hainline, chief medical officer at the NCAA.

Hainline said, "An often overlooked ingredient to a person's overall well-being is energy management." He further noted that "energy management can be broken into different aspects that all apply to well-being. The most important sector of energy management is often forgotten—not only by college athletes, but everyone: SLEEP. The average person should strive for about seven hours of sleep every night."[1]

To back up Hainline's point, an NCAA study published in 2016 released data showing that student-athletes clearly aren't getting enough sleep.

National Comparison Data on Days of Restful Sleep per Week (Enough Sleep to Feel Rested in the Morning)

Number of days	Athletes		Non-Athletes (NCHA-ACHA	
	Male	Female	Male	Female
0–3	52%	57%	55%	60%
4–5	31%	32%	33%	30%
6–7	17%	11%	12%	9%

NCAA Research. (January 2016). *Results from the 2015 GOALS Study of the Student-Athlete Experience.* Retrieved on May 22, 2017.

American College Health Association. American College Health Association-National College Health Assessment (2008–12). *ACHA-NCHA II, ACHA-NCHA IIb.* Hanover, MD. American College Health Association. Retrieved on May 22, 2017.[2]

4. Replace Your Support Services

As you move away from the tremendous support provided by your university and your athletic department, consider how you replace this. Do you need a psychologist, a physiotherapist, a sport medicine doc? These support services you took for granted (though you likely had some of the very best) will now be something you need to seek out, realizing that most health practitioners do not specialize in treating issues specific to high-performance athletes.

5. Consider Coaching

Fischer points out that coaching is a potential avenue (even as a volunteer kids' coach) to fill the "gap" when you retire. He notes that "you see so many players become coaches because they need to be a part of something. You can't wake up every day and say, 'I have nothing to do.' There has to be a purpose in your life."

6. Build an Exercise Plan

Number 1 on this list advised you to create a structure built around physical activity, and within that structure you need to build a plan for how to use the time you allocate for physical activity and training. You no longer have a coach, a manager, or a trainer to tell you what to do and when. You need to build some internal (intrinsic) motivation and keep healthy. Brett Fischer provides a helpful warning to get at it right away:

> I see a lot of former athletes who didn't take care of their body after playing as well as they should have, and ten years later, they aren't where they want to be. When they have a family, and they have kids, they don't have much free time to take care of themselves because they're working more now. They have different kinds of responsibilities.
>
> All of a sudden, now, you have to carve out time to work out. I get up at 4 *AM* every day to work out. If I don't do it then, I'll never get to it. I don't like getting up at 4, but I have no choice. I see that more with people who just get finished playing in college. It's just the progression of life and how much you still value the training aspect you were a part of as you were growing up? Some don't and they say they can't get to it and some do.

7. Balance, Balance, Balance

Secret 5 is of utmost importance here. Iglesias explains his approach:

I preach a balanced life. A life where you try to not let yourself be totally dictated by work, where you're working 70–80 hours a week, and then you can't exercise. It's all about healthy living. Money is important, but money is not the end all be all. Life is so much more than how much you make.

You have to look much more introspectively as to where is the happiness? Where is happiness central in my life? My own humble, personal opinion is that the happiest people that I have encountered in my life are those that have really managed balance in their life. Understanding what makes you happy in terms of the lifestyle that you want to live, that's the first step.

The second step is finding out who lives that kind of lifestyle? Try to pick their brain as to how they got to that particular lifestyle. Take a look at that lifestyle, and see if that's an actual fit for you. Just pick the brain of those who are living the lifestyle that is one that you would like to emulate. Pick some ideas from them and then use that as a road map on how to get you there.

8. Replace the Competition

One thing many former athletes miss (and crave) is the competition. But they are not likely to want to compete in their chosen sport, as their form has declined. Thus, a suggested tactic is to find a new pursuit (e.g., do a triathlon, join a Dragon Boat racing team) where you can be competitive but in a different arena.

Iglesias concurs: "I'm forty-seven now, and it's been twenty-five years since I've played my last collegiate tournament. That intense, burning desire to compete, I don't know if there's anything outside of actual competitions that truly fulfills you. You go out, you take up golf, you take up bowling, or what-ever activities you want along the way, because at some point, you'll never get as good in your sport as you once were, and your time has come and passed."

9. Have Fun When You Exercise!

Exercise is something that is built into our weekly schedule as athletes. We are extremely motivated to work out and improve our physical fitness levels in the hopes that it will improve our athletic performances.

As you transition into a different lifestyle, you may, like many others, struggle to maintain the motivation to work out, and many cannot find the time in their schedule to work out either because of work hours. Regard-less of the struggles, it is vitally important for your self-esteem, your overall health, and your confidence to continue to work out and exercise. You may not train like you did as an athlete, but finding ways to enjoy your time exer-cising is important in keeping a routine steady.

And, yes, fun is the key. Research shows that fun is the #1 reason why people do physical activity. So, instead of going for a daily morning run you despise, join a pickup basketball league or a co-ed soccer team.

10. Take Advantage of All Life Has to Offer

The last (but not least) of our ten steps is to invest in your future!

Working out, eating right, and sleeping well are important but there is much more to life than just those three things. We'd like to offer five additional pieces of advice to be sure you take advantage of more of life's opportunities:

1. Think big, but have short-term goals. Measure your life in two-year spans. Evaluate where you are, and what you want to do every two years during your career.

2. Take calculated risks in life. Try new things. Learn a foreign language. Study abroad during the summer or winter break.

3. Move around and explore the world while you are young. Living in new places and environments can help give you many different perspectives of life that you wouldn't have seen otherwise.

4. Get out of your comfort zone/bubble. Work at meeting and understanding people different from yourself.

5. Connect with many, because connections can open doors as you experience more in more places.

Iglesias has some useful advice on the keys to success for you to con-sider when investing in your future and taking advantage of all life has to offer. He says:

When transitioning out of your sport, you need to stay humble. There's always going to be someone bigger, faster, stronger, and better than you. If you cannot have success, don't look into blaming others, look at yourself in the mirror.

At the same time, that ability to overcome and be resilient, and the ability to overcome adversity is what we have all hopefully developed. It's not about the winning, it's about the journey. The whole point to being a student athlete is about the journey.

CHAPTER SUMMARY

Investing (as a concept) involves paying into a healthy lifestyle and doing the right things for your future. A healthy lifestyle is the first step in the right direction to a bright future and the rest will follow.

Our experts know that life is a process and the most important part of that process is preparing. Yes, your athletic career may be coming to an end (or already over), but your life isn't. Like most student-athletes reading this book, you have lived only a quarter of your life. If you have good genes, you may still have 75 percent of your life to live. How you want to live is up to you. Maintaining a healthy lifestyle will allow for a life full of opportunities.

Secret 17 Activate Your Student-Athlete Advantage

THE SECRET IN A FEW WORDS

Being a student-athlete is a great opportunity for those who have the privilege to compete. Student-athletes have a different college experience than the regular student does, but there are plenty of advantages that student-athletes can take from their experiences as they transition into life. Many people like to hire former student-athletes—that is no secret. But what are you going to do to give yourself an edge with prospective employers? How are you going to use your student-athlete experience to your advantage?

The real secret is that you need to "activate your student-athlete advantage."

ACTIVATE YOUR STUDENT-ATHLETE ADVANTAGE

Jason Elias is a former student-athlete baseball player who has worked in a variety of roles in the sports industry. During our interview with him, we covered several topics in relation to activating the advantages you have as a student-athlete.

JASON ELIAS (former baseball student-athlete at Baldwin Wallace University, Outreach and Sales Manager at IMG Academy)

I graduated from Baldwin Wallace University [as a student-athlete] and I thought I had a full-time opportunity with Fox Sports Ohio all lined up. It was a position that ended up being filled internally. I found out a week before I graduated as I walked off the NCAA baseball field for the last time. Even at that moment, I was still under the belief-structure that if I worked hard and competed well, academically, there was going to be some sort of position available, something that I was passionate about. That wasn't necessarily the case. It wasn't until probably almost a year and half later post-graduation that I had then gone to what I was comfortable with, and that was back to school. I was working on an MBA. It was then that I realized the significance of building a network.

Maximizing Your Student-Athlete Advantage

I would say most importantly; I don't think most student-athletes coming out of high school realize this enough, and I would even argue that unless they are in a formalized structure within their athletic program in college, they probably don't realize this: You are a part of a very elite fraternity as an athlete. I would say that from my own personal experience, as I was involved in college, I was an athlete, I was a baseball player that used a relationship with an alum . . . to eventually find [my dream job]. There were a couple of stops along the way, but I've traced everything that's happened to me in this industry back to a conversation I had with Jim Tressel [the alum] in 2005. Student-athletes need to understand that it's like being a part of any other group or any other fraternity or niche that you can find out there. It's all about the networking aspect. I think athletes need to understand that they have to be proactive, and they need to understand the power of relationships that they have that they may not even know exist. In many ways, they're unaware of what exists in their back pocket.

There are a couple terms that define a student-athlete, and these terms are also very attractive to a hiring manager. Athletes are resourceful. Athletes understand the meaning of work. Athletes tend to have excellent time management skills. Athletes tend to be adaptable, and collaborative. At times, they're risk takers, which some organizations would look at as a positive thing. Critical thinking skills tend to be very good. If you've been in a locker room, you tend to become more socially intelligent and I think that's an important skill to have. These are all aspects of the competitive and athletic experience . . . and an athlete may not consciously know that they've acquired these skills. The reality is that those particular skills/skill sets are very attractive to a hiring manager, and when you look at a general population of candidates, I can't say that nonathletes necessarily have the specificity of these skill sets.

Differentiate Yourself

Having the awareness of being a student-athlete plays a significant role, personal awareness. Understanding consciously that these skill sets exist will help those activate their student-athlete advantage. Student-athletes need to know that relationships and awareness of skill sets will be what creates the opportunity. Preparation within that opportunity is going to be what lands you the job. You can get the pick set for yourself through relationships and through skill-building. Once you get open, it's just a jump shot. Now hit the jump shot! You are going to be better prepared to hit that jump shot than the average individual because you've been through the competitive environment.

Another former student-athlete, Willie Patti, who has also been a coach and a scout professionally, agrees that an advantage exists: "I feel strongly that the opportunity to be a collegiate student-athlete has helped open the doors that have been there for me." We asked him to explain why.

> If it wasn't through the alumni of our university baseball program and fellow coaches I worked alongside of, I wouldn't be doing what I do now. You hear a lot about how being a college student-athlete helps get kids into college, or get a job after college, but never much after that! Being part of a very close-knit group of individuals who may be younger and older than you, never meant a thing to me besides that you were part of a brotherhood who would be willing to help in any way. The relationships I built up with those gentlemen really taught me as a young man who was going to be going out into the job world sooner than later. You have to build relationships with others because you never know when they may help you, or you can help them.

THE STUDENT-ATHLETE ADVANTAGE IS REAL

It is easy to take for granted the opportunity you have been given to be a member of an intercollegiate athletics team. Think about a regular classroom that holds sixty students. Maybe two are student-athletes, if that. In many classrooms around campuses, there are no student-athletes in that class. Of the remaining fifty-eight students in our hypothetical class of sixty, probably half of them wish they had the opportunity you are getting to play your sport, get an education, and receive all of the intangible skills that we have been highlighting throughout the various secrets presented so far in this book. Are you grateful? Are you activating the tremendous benefits that have been provided to you from your institution? Simply by being a student-athlete, you have an advantage over others as you transition from college to your professional life. But you are missing out on a big opportunity if you are simply satisfied with being a passive member of your team and the university community.

To get the most payoff possible from your experience in college, you have to be an active participant in the opportunities afforded you and be aware of how you can leverage them to your advantage. Jeff Rodin, former student-athlete and now a working professional in Major League Baseball, emphasized this and provides some words of wisdom:

> I would say as a student-athlete, you have a huge advantage. If you're a student-athlete and you work part-time and you're a double major, it forces you to manage a lot of different things and be disciplined. It can be the hardest thing you'll ever do, but it prepares you for life. You might not think you can handle it, but it prepares you and stretches you, allowing you to grow. Especially at the college and university level, you're talking about a huge transition and foundational-type situation. It's going to set you on a path with the relationships and the experiences that you encounter for the rest of your life. I could not encourage people enough to go through that process and do as much as you can, and get involved in as many different things as you can, because it allows for perspective on what your identity is and what your identity isn't, even more importantly, and creating that self-awareness. It's hard to put everything in perspective and balance that. Balance for me is different than might be balanced for somebody else. For me, when you commit to something, you commit 1,000 percent. You don't just dip your toe in it. It's pretty extreme, but that's also my personality. Do as much as you can, meet as many people as you can, hold yourself accountable, stay humble, and make yourself available to new opportunities because you don't want to miss anything.

WHY EMPLOYERS HIRE FORMER STUDENT-ATHLETES

Employers in both traditional professions and cutting-edge innovative areas are looking for the skills and abilities gained by being a student-athlete. A recent article in *Entrepreneur* (2016) highlights the fact that student-athletes have a strong work ethic, the ability to overcome failure, positive energy, and the ability to handle risks and responsibility. These are skills that other college students have to go out of their way to gain while as a student-athlete they are inherent in your sport participation and competition. Another article suggests that former student-athletes make great employees because they know how to work as a team, are leaders, excel at communication, and are driven (Capaletti 2014). A third article discusses the unique traits of student-athletes, including a competitive nature, handling pressure well, being coachable and willing to learn, having a great sense of discipline, understanding the importance of preparation, seeking and loving challenges, being self-motivated, and understanding the importance of time management (Ackerman 2015). You probably don't even realize you are gaining these skills and that they are specifically sought by employers. A 2014 study, looking at perspectives of employers hiring student-athletes, finds the four most important qualities and skills are a competitive nature, goal orientation, pressure handling, and work ethic (Chaflin et al. 2014).[1]

In a recent GOALS study done by the NCAA in 2015, student-athletes identified the qualities or skills that have been most positively affected by their student-athlete experience. Take advantage of these skills and develop them to be outstanding!

My college athletics experience has had a positive or very positive effect on the following skills/qualities in myself

	Division 1	Division 2	Division 3
Commitment to Volunteerism	67%	69%	61%
Leadership Skills	88%	88%	89%
Personal Responsibility	93%	92%	93%
Personal Values and Ethics	86%	87%	86%
Self-Confidence	79%	82%	81%
Study Skills	67%	67%	70%
Teamwork Skills	92%	91%	93%
Time Management Skills	81%	78%	82%
Understanding of Other Races	81%	82%	76%
Work Ethic	91%	90%	91%

Note: Top two scale points on a six-point scale

NCAA Research. (January 2016). *Results from the 2015 GOALS Study of the Student-Athlete Experience.* Retrieved on May 22, 2017.[2]

We asked Dan Butterly, Senior Associate Commissioner of the Mountain West Conference, to provide us with details about the process of hiring people and how student-athletes have an advantage if they have some experience under their belt. He advised:

> When I get a resume [from a job applicant], I look for if they have the degree. Then I look at their experience. I'm going to look to see what experiences they gained while they were on campus or since they graduated. Then I'm going to look at their references. I want to see who they have associated with. Who they are putting on their resume as people who have been influences in their life and will be there for them. That power of "who" is powerful. Those are going to be the key things, but it really comes down to the experience they gained. Once I've got the candidate pool and I've narrowed it down to phone interviews, it really is how they represent themselves on the phone. Can they show confidence without

a big ego over the phone? Do they know what they're doing, that they know the league, they know the position, and they know key things I look for in this opportunity? If they can do that, then I'm going to look at an in-person interview. In person, the first thing I'm going to look at is posture. Posture can show confidence. I've had people that come in who are just slouched shoulders and that kind of look grumpy with your slouched shoulders versus head up, shoulders back, and having a good handshake and saying hello, I mean those are big impacts and student-athletes definitely have a benefit as you can see in some of my answers. They know leadership, they know teamwork, they're driven for success. Those are the type of people that you want in any organization and I think that's a key driver. If I can get a student-athlete who shows the other factors that I'm looking at, then that's going to be my priority hire in many ways.

Brian Sanders, a former student-athlete and now an executive in Major League Baseball, supports Butterly's view and provides further advice on one thing you can do to help you activate that advantage on a resume: "Something that always catches my eye on the resume is some sort of catch phrase, or personal slogan. You have to get someone to give you that interview, and then you have to stand out and you have to compete. Just as you are competing on the field, you have to find a way to compete in the interview process. To stand out, say something a little off the wall, 'what's next?' Not enough young people in the workforce think about 'what's next.'"

HOW TO TRANSLATE LESSONS LEARNED THROUGH SPORT TO YOUR PROFESSIONAL WORK

From the job interview to your day-to-day life in your chosen profession, there are lessons from sport that you can translate to help your efficacy at work. But, and this is key, the ball is in your court. Nobody can activate your student-athlete advantage except you. Since no student-athlete experience is exactly the same as any other, you should be able to add to the list below that shares a few ideas on how to translate your sport experience to advantages in the workplace.

Here are just a few ideas to get you started:

1. *Interviewing*: Student-athletes are often provided training on how to interact with the media. What an amazing advantage in a job interview! Not only do you have on your resume the fact that you were a student-athlete, but you have specific knowledge and practice in an interview setting. Use this to your advantage. Kelsey Cermak, former student-athlete at Iowa

University, provides some useful advice here: "Figure out how to transfer all those skills you gain as a student-athlete onto a resume. Figure out what your weaknesses are and make them strengths. Try to fill up as many holes as possible. . . . I used to do mock interviews once a month during my senior year to prepare for interviews."

2. *Small Talk*: Your experience as a student-athlete is fascinating to most (or many, at least) people. It is a very easy way to start a conversation. Whether you start a conversation about your experience being a student-athlete or share a cool story from your time competing, most people will be interested. This comes into play at social events for work, at professional conferences, and when building your network.

3. *Creating Buy-In*: You probably do not realize that convincing an athletic team to do something (like practice extra to prepare for the game) with a good attitude is simply a combination of "selling" and "negotiating." This is especially true if you were a team captain or even assistant captain. And, now that you're heading to the work world, how about translating these skills into negotiating your salary, determining your job responsibilities, helping you lead a work team, or even actually informing your selling in the context of your job.

4. *Office Golf Outing or Softball Team*: If you have been around athletics your entire life, it is likely you have some skills in sports even outside the sport you played in college. More and more companies are creating opportunities for employees to be active and part of the office culture. If you can play golf, enjoy being on a recreational softball team, or generally want to keep being a leader on the field—this is an opportunity for you to stand out among your peers at work.

5. *Understanding Your Role*: Very few young employees understand how to lead, how to follow, and how to get out of the way when it's the right thing to do. Athletes understand this concept of changing roles. Moving from high school to college as an athlete, you probably went from one of the best on your high school team to being surrounded by a lot of good athletes in college. Many student-athletes learn to fill the role of starter one week and bench warmer the next—keeping a great attitude in either role. Athletes understand the value of each position on the team as well as the value of those who support the team from the bench.

Author Viewpoint—DR. HEATHER LAWRENCE

How did you activate your student-athlete advantage? Did your first jobs have other former student-athletes that you worked with? How did being a former student-athlete help you when you got your first job out of school?

Twenty years after finishing my career as a college diver, I am still activating my student-athlete advantage. It may sound crazy, but it is true. I am still introduced by colleagues with an additional sentence such as, "and she was an All-American diver at the University of Florida and a member of the United States National Team." How an introduction like that is perceived by others is not something I can control, but based on the high percentage of people I meet that want to talk more about my athletic career, I know it is of interest to people. It allows me to start the conversation with someone and then I can decide where to take the personal or business relationship from there. This might seem like an example that is years away for you, so let me back up and share with you ten times since college that I have activated my student-athlete advantage.

1. I graduated from college debt-free thanks to athletically related financial aid.

2. I chose to enroll in graduate school and study sports administration. My admissions essay reflected upon what I had learned as a student-athlete and, of course, my experience as an athlete played a huge role in the selection of my master's degree area of study.

3. I applied for a graduate assistantship to fund graduate school and was fortunate to be hired in the department of athletics at the University of Florida. I already knew the athletics director, my immediate supervisor, and pretty much everyone in the athletics department, making it easier for me to land that job.

4. I applied for postgraduate scholarships and was awarded more than one, thus, between the scholarships and my graduate assistantship I completed my master's degree debt-free.

5. I was hired full-time by the athletics department while still working on my master's degree. It was a new position for the athletics department, and the fact that I already knew the coaches and understood the sport was my advantage.

6. One of the work projects I had early in my career was extremely challenging, and I was terrified. But I distinctly remember relying on my ability to stay calm under pressure to and to "fake confidence" in order to get me through when I felt like I was in over my head. It was the same thing I had done in big competitions for years, I just had to translate it to my job and I ended up completing the project successfully.

7. I decided to take a job in a different state, and because I was so used to meeting new people through my travel in sport, it was an easy transition for me to acclimate to a new area, make friends, and be flexible as I got settled. In this situation, taking a risk to move and take a new job was comfortable to me as well because athletes are also used to being pushed outside their comfort zone and take on risk head on.

8. As a busy mom of two kids working full-time, I rely on my ability to thrive on little sleep and still get up early to work out to stay in shape. This may seem insignificant to some people, but staying active is critical to my ability to function well in other aspects of my life. I wake up at 4:20 a.m. most mornings and I got into this habit as a student-athlete. Experience, even a long time ago, balancing practice, travel, school, and a social life has prepared me for this time in my life balancing family, work, fitness, a social life, and other interests.

9. As a professor, I can choose to do the minimum required in my job just to get by or I can strive to add value to the University by helping my colleagues, generating new ideas, and putting in extra time and effort to help see projects through to success. Similar to how any high-performance athlete behaves, I choose to put in the extra time needed in everything I do. Whether that is preparing for class, creating new opportunities for students, or supporting others at work, I do this because it is what you must do to be successful. As a student-athlete, I learned this lesson and it has made me more valuable to every organization I have worked for—and my supervisors have told me that.

10. I have opportunities occasionally to speak to large groups of people such as audiences over five hundred. My mental preparation for these speeches is exactly the same as my preparation was for an important diving meet. Athletes understand that it takes hours of physical and mental practice before you are game ready. I pull on this experience on a regular basis, but when I am getting ready to speak before a large group I follow the exact pattern I used before big diving meets. I practice mentally, I practice physically, and then I do it again until I get it right every time.

Lastly, what should you do?

Step 1: Find an employer who also was a student-athlete

Hallie Olson, former swimming student-athlete at Ohio University, in her interview clearly supports this tactic: "If I'm looking at any resumes and I see that someone was an athlete, that's going to catch my eye, because I know that they've gone through the rigor and they have that work ethic to be successful."

Step 2: Understand what your experience is worth and why it is important

Step 3: Get your foot in the door somewhere . . .

Leverage Your Celebrity—EDDIE GILL
(former NBA player)

I think student-athletes should really look at doing a better job of leveraging their celebrity. If you're a collegiate athlete anywhere in the country, to some degree, you're a celebrity on campus. You want to start building those relationships with administration. When you go out to do community events, leverage your celebrity as an athlete because those people want to have a conversation with you. My advice to the young players is to embrace that role that you currently have. That doesn't mean you're being overconfident or cocky, but it's just being able to have a conversation with people and be friendly. Build that rapport, you never know what it's going to lead to.

My biggest piece of advice is to leverage your celebrity. I can't emphasize that enough. I've seen it. I'm guilty of it myself. I've done it as a collegiate athlete, and as a professional athlete. We do so many different things that are "mandatory," whether it's by the team, or by the league, or with your association. It's more than just being there. If you can really start forming relationships throughout that entire process, it can make your transition that much easier. If you're a professional athlete, maybe you go back to your university to do something, whether it's on campus or in that community. Those relationships that you build as a student athlete versus just going through the motions will differ in appearances throughout the community.

CHAPTER SUMMARY

Activating your student-athlete advantage isn't only a thing you do once you graduate just to get your first job, it is something you do for your whole life. Be thankful that you have the ability to activate this advantage for a lifetime of opportunities. Having the student-athlete experience in your pocket allows you to pursue so many opportunities that many people wish they could. Take advantage of the advantages you have because you may just get lucky. Thus . . .

Luck = Preparation meets Opportunity

Secret *18* Create Your Brand

THE SECRET IN A FEW WORDS

Brands are everywhere. We buy them, use them, cheer for them, and, whether you realize it or not, you represent one every day. A brand's image can change from time to time, and brands are created, not found or automatically provided. Many student-athletes, and many people in general, struggle with creating their brand and identity once they start a career. For student-athletes, their identity is no longer as a "player," but has to be created as something different. So the secret is to "create your brand."

CREATE YOUR BRAND

When asked how he created the most famous statue in the world, Michelangelo responded: "I just chipped away all the pieces that weren't David."

Your brand will help define and identify you to important relationships and stakeholders. Importantly, the name on your eventual business card will be much more important than the logo of the entity you are working for.

Branding is a highly developed and sophisticated field that has learned much about how to develop, activate, and grow equity in a brand or a suite of brands. This chapter outlines a multistep approach to brand specific to the context of the student-athlete.

Step 1: Strategies and Tactics

It has been said that if you can't see the finish line at the beginning of a race then you aren't going to get off to a very good start. It is critical to build your brand plan with the proper understanding of the differences between tactics and strategies. First, the definitions:

Tactic:

From the Greek *taktikós*: fit for arranging or ordering, equivalent to arrange, put in order.

Strategy:

A plan, method, or series of maneuvers or stratagems for obtaining a specific goal or result.

A plan for getting ahead in the world.

A particular long-term plan for success, especially in business or politics.

CREATE YOUR BRAND: HOW DO I GET THERE AND WHERE IS THERE?

How did you get here?

We would offer some insight based on a recent interview one of the authors was conducting. The candidate was asked, "Tell me about yourself. Tell me your story. Tell me how you got here." He said, "By car."

Exactly!

Was he serious? Absolutely serious.

Was he trying to be clever? Absolutely not. The interviewer has a very good wise-guy meter, but it was one of the best responses he had heard and he commented specifically about it in the context of his experiences.

Author Viewpoint—ANDY DOLICH

So, he said he got here by car!

Having spent forty-three years in the front offices of teams in the NBA (National Basketball League), NFL (National Football League), NHL (National Hockey League), MLB (Major League Baseball), NASL (North American Soccer League), NLL (National Lacrosse League), five years as the owner of my own sports consulting business, and two years with Tickets.com, I have learned well that there are a number of simple steps that, when followed, will greatly improve any new job seeker's chances of getting their high-priced athletic footwear in the door.

So I'll say I got here by car! How did I get here from sitting in an Ohio University classroom daydreaming about watching future Hall of Famer Mike Schmidt take ground balls at shortstop at that time? I remember saying, "You know, one of these days, he might be a decent minor league player and hopefully some day when I get out of the Sports Administration Program I might actually work for a team and get paid."

Little did I know back in the 1970s that Mike Schmidt would turn out to be one of the greatest third basemen in baseball history and, not on any kind of equitable level, that I would end up having a forty-five-year-and-counting career in sports, and there we were both in Athens, Ohio, dreaming about the future.

In those days before you could graduate you had to do a six-month internship, and mine was with the Philadelphia 76ers.

After three seasons with the 76ers I took a step back to take two forward and joined the Maryland Arrows to the Washington Capitals (NHL) to the Washington Diplomats (NASL) to the Oakland Athletics (MLB) to the Golden State Warriors (NBA) to my own business consulting group to Tickets.com to the Vancouver Grizzlies, who became the Memphis Grizzlies, to the San Francisco 49ers and back to my own sports business consulting firm. That's kind of a compressed time capsule of close to six decades, which never ceases to amuse and amaze me.

If I can do this, so can you. I am the official poster child of possibilities in building a career brand in sports.

One visual reminder of my dream-come-true ride since 1971 after graduating from Ohio University: I have a plaque on my wall, which has every single one of my business cards along the way. I was the beneficiary of a number of informational interviews way back when, as I was going through the internship process at Ohio University, and I show that to everybody that comes through me looking for advice on getting a job in the "high paid, low hour" business of sports, whether it be in the pros or the brave new world of collegiate sports.

I'd say it's not quite as easy as you might think looking at somebody's resume or reading about them or having Googled them. Look at this plaque and spend a few moments seeing the different zip codes while I was also trying to raise a family, find my competencies, and get paid fairly.

When people come to my office they say, "You know, I need to do one of those." It's not complicated. You don't need a patent. Just take your business cards and go into "Frames-R-Us."

In creating your brand, you may be a leader as a student-athlete, and you may continue to be a leader in the next chapter of your life. However, there are many types of leadership. What kind of leader will you be?

YOUR LEADERSHIP DNA: WHAT STYLE WILL YOU USE?

Personal and business leadership skills are defined by the ability to navigate the uncharted waters created by today's society. Implement your leadership skills and keep your brand nimble, focused, and healthy by becoming an expert on the uses of the eight "scopes":

1. *Microscope:* To view and understand every minute detail of your business.

2.   *Telescope:* To look beyond the given and create road maps to unexplored territories.

3.   *Stethoscope:* To listen to the heart of your organization and the people in it.

4.   *Proctoscope:* To take you to places that people don't want to go, but necessary to protect the long-term health of the enterprise.

5.   *Gyroscope:* To keep everyone centered in times of crisis. In today's world, crisis is the new normalcy.

6.   *Periscope:* To give you the ability to stealthily see what your competitors are up to.

7.   *Kaleidoscope:* To help you visualize and appreciate the ever-changing business patterns and human interactions of your enterprise. Without diversity we have no teamwork.

8.   *Horoscope:* To develop bold plans for the future using a tool of science and symbolism.

Successful leaders who have devoted themselves to their careers share a common thread of DNA. But if you Google "Theories of Leadership" there are only about 8,300,000 links to choose from.

Role models don't always make great leaders. We care more about the latest skinny on *Jersey Shore*'s Snooki and *Keeping Up with the Kardashians* than doing something about the growing epidemic of childhood obesity (or adult obesity, for that matter). We spend more time breaking down player scouting reports for our upcoming fantasy league draft than building up a broken educational system. We live in a world of nanosecond affirmation and even speedier deconstruction. It would have been instructive to hear what John Wooden might have thought about the antics of the LeBron James "Decision."

When successful organizations go under the microscope, you will see that there is consistent high-quality leadership and brand mission at all levels.

Successful individuals brand themselves with a DNA strain composed of the Eleven T's. Think of the any industry's best and brightest—these should fit them to a T.

1.   *Affinity:* The hours and pressures of the job mean that you can't fake the way you get along with colleagues. The compatibility factor always shines through between leaders and their coworkers when times are the toughest.

2.   *Agility:* Today's world calls for incredible changes of pace and direction to keep up with changing market conditions. If you can't go to your left, then work on that move. If you are a winner-take-all negotiator, try enticing your opponents with a carrot every once in a while instead of beating them with a stick.

3. *Creativity:* Business is defined by a herd mentality. A good idea causes the line to form. Leadership shouldn't get stuck in a "Groundhog Day" thinking. Changing how you approach the business of your business is critical. Look to the outside world of creative business solutions, not just the best practices of your industry.

4. *Hilarity:* A career is a marathon, not a sprint, whether it is a job at one company or a career made up of many jobs in many places. A career is full of serious goals and objectives, bottom lines, wins and losses, hirings and firings, promotions and demotions, elation and deflation. In the end it is only a game. Many leaders lose their way by weaving a web of woe. Show a sense of humor and a bit of wackiness every once in a while. It will lighten the load for everybody.

5. *Honesty:* The most respected leaders tell the truth—good, bad, or ugly. Think of the hardest teachers you had in high school or college. They never let you slide as you cursed them under your breath. A few years after graduation you realized they gave you the best education. The same is true with great leaders: They can pat you on the back and kick you in the gut without compromising the organization's view on how to succeed.

6. *Humility:* One of the many potential hazards that befall leaders is defining themselves by what they do, not who they are. When they lose their way they can take their organizations over the edge. Your business card and title should never control your true sense of self.

7. *Loyalty:* Leaders ask their staffs to invest their loyalty for the greater good of the organization. When a season, a campaign, a project goes wrong there is usually collateral damage in the form of terminations. Loyalty Street should always be a two-way avenue for the organization's success.

8. *Mobility:* Mobility is leadership by walking around. Many executives barricade themselves in their office castles with a moat, a closed door, and a fire-breathing executive assistant. The simplest way to lead is to walk around the office every day. The two-minute face-to-face is usually more productive than the ninety-minute conference room agenda-driven meeting.

9. *Opportunity:* As a leader, everyone is going to want a piece of you. Think of those who mentored or spent time with you when you were coming up! Every young person in your organization who wants to spend a few minutes with you deserves your attention.

10. *Simplicity:* Between multitasking, social media of the day, meetings by the moment, and crisis management, the life of a leader is growing more and more complicated. The great ones create simplicity without dumbing down the product. If you can't explain what you are up to in two or three sentences, it probably isn't worth explaining.

11. *Unity:* Most sport organizations are split into quarters with ownership, business operations, team operations, and finance existing on different planets. "Ubuntu" is an African term that is generally defined as unselfishness and team unity. The spirit of Ubuntu that teams on the field strive for can become even more powerful if the entire organization lives it.

No one knows which of those eight million-plus leadership styles guarantees success. There are no magic wands, lanterns, or carpets, no silver bullets, secret handshakes, codes, Rosetta Stones, catchy phrases, or best-selling books that guarantee leadership success. It stands the test of time that human beings working together have accomplished far more than the sum of their individual efforts and capabilities. They have committed themselves to something larger than the individual. Leaders live teamwork every day, and the great ones make it happen.

Regardless of whether you go work in sports, education, real estate, medicine, or law, these T's can apply to any type of career you pursue. The lessons and concepts are the same.

BECOME AN ETHICAL BEING IN CREATING YOUR BRAND

There are many areas that make up a person's ethical foundation. Here are the top ten in our view:

1. Empower others (do not micromanage: trust others, when trained, to do the job).

2. Maintain a positive attitude especially when the environment is negative (negativity is rarely the answer).

3. Demonstrate high character (make good decisions, think of (all) others, consider your environment).

4. Be willing to lead (do NOT be that critic on the sideline who is first to complain or nitpick, be the one who steps up to help when a leader is needed).

5. Strive to be a leader (leadership is a hard-earned status; do not be in a rush).

6. Remain teachable and coachable (listen to advice you get and be willing to adapt your ways of doing things based on what you hear).

7. Be accountable (take responsibility for your mistakes and stand up for your colleagues).

8. Be fully prepared (never attend a meeting or presentation without being ready for it).

9. Never quit (adapt your timelines, not your goals).

10. Respect your coworkers (treat others, both higher- and lower-ranking than you, as you would like to be treated yourself).

WE ADVISE YOU TO RUN TO CHAOS AND DISASTER!

Most neophytes in the career search process look for the most successful technology brands, marketing agencies, and sports teams they can find and send blind letters to the owner or CEO right after they have won a championship. (Wrong, wrong, wrong.) You want to reach out to the lepers, disasters, car wrecks, and toxic dumps. Find brands, organizations, teams, and properties that people are running away from. That's where you want to go.

Let's give you an example. It is again from the sports industry and is about coauthor Andy Dolich, who has thrived for many years in that world. By pure good luck, Dolich's first job in sports was with the Philadelphia 76ers in 1971. Trivia experts would know that this team had records that stood for nearly forty years. In the 1972–73 season when he was Administrative Assistant to the GM, the club went 9–73. That's right—they could not even get into double figures in wins!

In the same season, they had noncontiguous losing streaks of 13, 14, 15, and 20 games. The two longest losing streaks were interrupted by a two-point win which, if they had lost, would have given the club a depressing 33 losses in a row. It was a glorious time in that Andy was able to take responsibility for areas that he would have had to wait years to experience otherwise because the organization was in such disarray. He was learning on the job, and fast. Look for chaos, disaster, unrest, change that creates opportunity. That's where you are going to learn and move up the fastest.

. . . .

To provide extra advice on creating your brand as you transition out of sports and into a career, we have interviewed experts to help you out.

We interviewed longtime professional sport executive Fred Claire, who provided some valuable insights on brand from his fifty-plus-year career in the sport business, including a very senior role with the Los Angeles Dodgers.

FRED CLAIRE
(legendary former Executive VP and General Manager of the Los Angeles Dodgers, and cofounder of Scoutables)

In my Dodger days I had a philosophy that I believe works, and it applies to athletes and others: everything we do, everything we say, everything we write, every exchange we have with another person or a group—*how comfortable will you be* when this becomes fully public?

Because it will be public, believe me, particularly for one who lives in the public world. And with technology and social media of today we all live in a public world. So as an athlete or any individual we don't need to create anything or hire anyone to establish our identity. We need to live every minute and every day of our lives in a manner that gives us self-worth and makes our family and friends proud and the universities or schools or companies we represent proud. One doesn't need a "professional" brand; it rings false. Athletes and others should be dedicated and work every day to be the best they can be; to listen to their family and coaches; to be a great teammate; to set a true and proven example for younger people; to inspire others with inspirational acts. We can't change our basic talent, only improve through daily dedication. Along the way we all fall short and we are left to acknowledge shortcomings and always be totally honest and transparent. We are left to get up and continue the journey. At the end, we are not a "brand," we are who those who knew us best with the full disclosure of facts and time know or knew us to be. For all of us there is a legacy. We, and indeed the athletes of today, are writing that legacy *every single day* of our lives.

· ·

JONI LOCKRIDGE (former softball student-athlete, and former Director of Digital Strategy at the PGA Tour)

We talk about "creating yourself, not finding yourself."
What did you do to "create yourself" and what does your "brand" represent?

Right or wrong, I believe that the construction of personal brand can be simplified into two tasks: defining who I am, and defining who I am not.

This process requires a willingness and openness to continually evaluate and decide. It's not easy, and it never ends. The idea of a final state of "me" implies that both my own characteristics and the characteristics of the situation and the people around me never change. Knowing this to be untrue, former athletes must recognize that unlike that final buzzer in which the score stands, the act of creating ourselves will span our full lifetime.

How did your brand change as a student-athlete compared to being a working professional?

As a student athlete, I wanted to be known as the hardest-working individual on the team. I wanted to take more reps than anyone else so I could have that edge that every competitor desires. I thought that if I did this, I could turn my brain off. I could shift from "try," to relax and do, and excel through will power and physical control.

As a working professional, I want to be known as the smartest working individual in the organization. I try to design my time around when my brain can be "on," and my will power now drives my focus more than my feet.

One difference that age has brought—I'm more likely to be able to break or throw away what is already in working order to improve. Considering I work to create digital experiences, this is critical in my job. Had I applied these principles more often as a student athlete, I would have achieved more success throughout my career.

With your role in the digital world, what suggestions do you have for future student-athletes on how to represent themselves on social media?

I have three suggestions:

First, be smart with your security settings.

Second, remember that your digital personality is a representation of more than just you. Make sure you are willing to accept the consequences for any digital statement you make.

Third, as you work on both your offline and online identity, don't lose your individuality.

Hallie Olson, commenting from her experiences as a student-athlete swimmer turned graduate student turned working professional, noted:

> You are a brand. At peak of what your brand used to be [as an athlete], your entire brand used to be athletics, and now it's not anymore [as a graduate retired athlete]. It [the athlete part of your brand] will always be a part of you, but it's just not something that is at the forefront anymore. Now it's just developing what's the next chapter? What is the next chapter of your life? What are you looking to achieve? Once I started feeling successful somewhere else, when I got a job, or when I was doing things in graduate school where I felt like I was making an impact, that's when I started feeling like I don't have this crisis, I'm not going through this brand-identity crisis anymore.

She went on to describe, very specifically, how she felt about her "brand" as a professional versus having formerly been a student-athlete.

Being a student-athlete, you are held to a high standard because you're representing your university. When you're in a professional workplace, you are representing a company. When you're at the professional stage, there are many more expectations and everybody is replaceable. The professional world is more cut throat. In swimming, we had a three-strike system, if you mess up three times, then you're out. At the professional stage, everybody is replaceable, and you could be gone [fired] in a second if you do something wrong.

In building a brand, Christa Mann, MLS professional and former student-athlete, advised the student-athlete about to become a young professional to "identify yourself for all of the skills that you embody. There will come a day when you are no longer a student, you're no longer an athlete, but you are who you are and it's important to learn who that person is while you are in school. When you are out of school, away from sports, or wherever life takes you, you are still that person."

Finally, Steve Cobb, another former student-athlete, noted: "I think if you are going to create your own brand, you've got to know what a brand looks like in your area of expertise. Create your brand by learning from those people who are in the industry. Find out where you fit. Ask yourself, "What is it that I enjoy, when push comes to shove, why am I here, what's my passion about?" in whatever it is you are doing. I think you develop your brand by realizing what other people's brands are. I'm not suggesting you go and be like somebody else."

CHAPTER SUMMARY

This chapter provides secrets to creating and managing your own brand. Think about what you want your brand to represent, why and how. Think about how you want to be perceived by others. As you create your brand, you will have to decide if you are going to be a leader, and if so, what kind. Your brand will continue to change and shift throughout life, but there will always be a foundation of your brand that we believe will be created after you are no longer an athlete.

Many former student-athletes lose sight of what their brand really is after they finish competing. Many search or try to find their brand instead of creating it. You control your life and you create who you are. Stop searching and start creating. Just as we tell you to create your brand, we advocate for you to "Create yourself, don't find yourself."

Secret *19* Be Fiscally Smart

THE SECRET IN A FEW WORDS

You may think you have a handle on your finances, but you still have a lot to learn as you grow. If you have never had to worry a day in your life about money, you definitely need to treat this secret as extra special. As we've mentioned, being a student-athlete puts a lot of stress and pressure on you in many ways. Once you get out into the real world, you will have new stresses and potentially even more of them, but if you take this secret to heart, you will have less stress financially. Not having financial stress can make so many relationships and aspects of your life better in multiple ways.

This is a REAL secret, one you should pay close attention to and one you probably thought was not about you, a student. Well, you are wrong. It is now that you need to start building very good behaviors and attitudes around money, spending, and saving. Very small amounts saved and not spent can easily translate into very large sums when you're in your sixties or seventies and don't really want to work anymore. Thus, this secret is all about being wise about what you have, limiting what you have to borrow, and seeking to build a few assets (or at least a good credit rating) along the way.

BE FISCALLY SMART

The world is changing right before our eyes economically, socially, and politically. Traditional supply chains and communication methods are declining and new ones emerging every day. Your investment in your four years of college, if you followed the earlier secrets, should have led you to a point

174

where you are graduating (have graduated) with a degree in a field where employment is possible, if not probable.

Along the way, as a student-athlete, you were likely on scholarship (at least partial), which may have reduced the financial stress of your experience by providing support for accommodation, meals, books, sport costs, and more. If you were on a full ride, this may have meant very limited stress here. However, the downside might be that you did not have the chance to develop the ability to manage finances or think about investments or use of assets. So, now is the time! And, these skills will come in handy when you buy a car, get a mortgage, go to grad school, or have children.

As a student-athlete, you are likely to be familiar with studying and following game plans, whether it be as part of a team or figuring out what you are going to do in one-on-one competitions. However, as a student-athlete, your time isn't necessarily your own and strategies for developing a financial plan might not be at the top of your list. You need to understand when to finance a purchase and how. You need to know what to do with extra money. You need to understand debt and payment plans. You need to project and plan for major purchases or expenses that will come.

PERSPECTIVE OF PROFESSIONAL ATHLETE FINANCIAL MANAGEMENT: WHAT CAN WE LEARN?

Bob Boland, Athletics Integrity Officer at Penn State University

Why so many professional athletes seemingly retire in or quickly develop some form of hardship—financial, social, or medical—and what can be done about this is an important question for the survival of the sport industry. In studying this question, the answer is elusive. The problem of broke and broken former athletes doesn't run exclusively along racial, social, class, or sport lines. The amount earned over a career can positively influence success in retirement, but there remain cautionary tales out there of famed athletes who have burned through or lost giant fortunes. The ability to save certainly can help, but realistically, how does a league or an agent talk about retirement with athletes in their early twenties, whose greatest asset personally and professionally is the confidence to believe they are the exception to all rules. And frankly, athletes would have to save so aggressively that the lifestyle they are seeking in playing professionally would never be in reach. What fun would that be?

Rather, the key to having a successful retirement for athletes, especially at an age when most people's careers are just getting started, lies in lessening the downward slope of their personal lifetime earnings curves. What we have seen help that in the case of successful sports retirees is to look at the transition holistically.

Instead of focusing on spending or savings, [concentrate on] what aspirations does the individual have, what impediments in terms of savings, medical issues, and education does that person possess and figuring out a strategy for having a purposeful, engaged, and meaningful postathletic career. While the ex-pro athlete's earnings may never match their earnings as a pro, they can manage the downward slope of that curve and enjoy their second lives.

The same facts generally hold the key for the postcollegiate athlete, too. Except ideally their earnings curve will look like that of a successful college graduate and peak in their fifties or even later. What factors help the professional person's earnings curve lengthen are easy to calculate. First, education is statistically the most important factor. Yes, I am a college professor and yes, I am deeply invested myself as I am still paying off my law degree.

Some question the efficacy of this educational debt, and in fairness debt should always be carefully considered, but I pay about as much now for my law degree as I do for either my satellite TV or my monthly wireless data plan, a small cost for something that lets me earn a competitive salary and have portable skills.

Second, while education is important demographically, athletes graduating now are entering into a world where their bachelor's degree isn't as marketable as it once was because so many people against whom they are competing have the same degree. So that puts an extra focus on skills. You need the degree as a symbol, often just to get in the door, but you need skills to be successful.

Too many athletes have an aspiration gap. This seems counterintuitive because an athlete likely has endured years of intense training and practiced unmeasured amounts of self-discipline in getting to their athletic goals, so how can they lack aspiration? New goals, new game. We've found that the way student athletes are segregated from their communities, their student bodies, their potential competitive sets, means that they struggle to develop postathletic aspirations. Circling back, where does one go to work on aspiration? Usually work or school, and, if you have a degree or a skills gap, getting either a career-making job or profession or advanced degree that provides lifelong earning power can become a vicious cycle.

Boland's perspective is most valuable and his point on needing skills is key for you to consider. Yes, it is true, due to the high demands of the athletic portion of the student-athlete experience, many athletes lag behind their classmates in terms of skill development when it comes time to go on the job hunt. A number of previous secrets address this around using your time wisely to build skills.

A point that is often overlooked is that time management can be just as critical as money management as you build a career game plan. There is no one size fits all equation. Each and every person's situation is unique. Never follow someone else's plan unless you are absolutely sure it fits your financial circumstances and your personality.

Knowing you need a plan is one thing. Coming up with that plan is another. And actually putting your custom plan into action (a plan designed just for you on your reality) is another thing altogether.

BUILDING YOUR FINANCIAL PLAN—WHERE DO YOU START?

- Assess your current financial situation. How much do you have in the bank? Do you have a savings/retirement account? Does your employer offer a retirement plan? Will your employer match your contributions? Do you have debt? What's the interest rate on that debt? Do you know exactly where you are financially? Is anyone in your family helping you out financially or paying some of your costs?

- Know your cash flow. Do a cash flow analysis. Simply said, how much money do you have coming in and going out? Are you "liquid" (i.e., will you have enough money to pay the bills throughout the year)? Yes, cash flow, the dreaded "budget" word. Oh, and if you've never taken an accounting course, do one and learn to do a cash flow statement and analysis.

- Create a credit rating if you don't have one. A good tactic here is to start buying things that you can afford (e.g., clothes, electronics, computer) with a credit card, pay it off in full, and see your credit rating improve (and ability to borrow money).

- Have a realistic conversation with your parents and/or spouse to make sure that everyone is on the same financial page. Consider succession, retirements, death, children, and all factors. Are you still on your parents' payroll or do you have financial freedom? Cutting the money cord to your parents can be a scary scenario but a necessary one.

- Check reality! If you think the pros are going to be your ticket to financial independence, just look at the odds.

CREATE YOUR BUDGET

Personal finance isn't something you master at a certain age or after passing a class. You have to work on it over time and adjust as your situation changes. You have to update the documents regularly and track your spending. Financial planning is just like your daily workout or practice. The more you put in, the more you benefit when it's game time.

Your short-term focus may be paying down student loans. But in a few years, it could be buying a house and starting a family, bringing on another unique set of financial circumstances. Perhaps you'll move to another country and be paid in another currency and have to file taxes in a new jurisdiction.

DON'T SPEND MORE THAN YOU EARN!

Former student-athlete Eddie Gill, from whom we've heard a few times, now sends a clear warning to new graduates:

> The first mistake student-athletes make out of college is spending their entire first check on whatever it may be. They think, I got it, well now I have to spend it. If you start that, maybe that becomes a habit for you. I know another check is coming, I'll spend it knowing another one is coming.

A few years back, the Oakland A's had a player who went to salary arbitration. The night before his hearing the media asked him how he felt. "Tomorrow I'm going to wake up rich or richer!" Well, he won his multimillion-dollar arbitration, but there was a major flaw in his plan, which was his lack of a long-term financial plan. Within a year he had spent more than the value of his contract. Within a few years he was out of baseball and had declared bankruptcy. Simply stated, he spent more than he earned and never even thought about creating a financial game plan.

CREDIT RATING

If you don't have one, get started with a credit rating agency. Create a solid rating as soon as you can. Your credit score is more important to your future than how many points you scored as an athlete. All you need is a social security number and a credit card (which you then pay off in full each month, on time) to get started.

PAY OFF YOUR CREDIT CARD DEBT

Once you get started on that credit rating, you have to prioritize paying off your credit card bill in full on time each month so that you don't get charged interest or late fees on an outstanding balance. Yes, there is no point in putting any money in savings while you are paying interest on credit card debt. The best savings accounts pay under 1 percent currently, while the lowest credit cards charge 6 percent, and more likely upwards of 20 percent. The lower your credit rating and the fewer assets you have (common for former/ current student-athletes), the higher the credit card interest rate normally is. While it may feel more responsible to start saving, if you already have accumulated credit card debt, eliminate your high-interest debt as fast as you can. Put the maximum amount of money you can toward this debt every month until it's paid off. On other debt, such as mortgages and car loans (which can be as low as 0 percent, at least for an initial period), you can look at the benefit of putting the money in savings versus the costs of carrying that debt.

So, what to do? Well, start by paying off the credit card with the highest interest rate first. As you get them paid off, cancel any cards that charge annual fees. There are so many credit options out there, there's no reason for most people to pay an annual fee.

Former student-athlete and former MLB pitcher Seth Etherton provides some insight and advice:

> Obviously, you want to eliminate debt as fast as you can. Once you finish college, you are financially responsible regardless of your parents helping you out. You need to simplify your life and live within your means. There are a lot of things that we want, but we can't always have them. Determine what is really important to you, and start to make some goals on what is most important from a financial spending perspective.

BUILD AN EMERGENCY FUND

Once you have your high-interest credit card debt paid off, the cards that charge annual fees canceled, and your remaining credit card bills paid on time and, if possible, in full each month, it's time you stay there. Build up three to six months of savings in an emergency fund (in case you lose your job, have a bad investment, etc.). Find the highest interest rate savings account you can, and start putting money there. Today, there are many online savings accounts that pay much higher interest rates than do "regular banks." Don't go crazy with a traditional savings account though, because interest rates are so low these days.

A good rule of thumb for the size of your emergency fund is that it should be equivalent to three months' salary.

PLAN FOR RETIREMENT

This is a challenging goal to tell someone just coming out of college. We debated about it, and given its importance to the planning theme that is so strong in the book, we have included it.

Retirement planning can seem extremely hard, because you're not sure you'll ever see the money again. It's not fun to take money you could use for entertainment or other discretionary spending now and put it aside for later. But you can't count on social security or pensions. The amount of money that can be made on compounding an investment over thirty years is enormous. Also, retirement savings become another asset you can tap in times of extreme need. The most important thing with retirement planning at your stage is simply to acknowledge it, consider how you might want it to look and get an "idea" of what you will ultimately need to make that happen. It may help you to start investing or saving to get ahead of the curve that is coming. If you have the ability to do so, get an IRA started as soon as you can and consistently contribute to it.

Gill again provides some sound advice: "Once you get your first job, you would definitely want to look into what your company is doing in terms of if they have a retirement savings plan for you. That's the easiest way to save. It depends on the company. There's a lot that will match up to X amount of dollars you put into it, so it essentially is free money for you."

As a start, this can be as simple as building up a small nest egg of dollars in a savings account to move to a larger apartment, save for a down payment on a home, build up dollars for a trip you want to make or bike you want to buy, etc. Perhaps you need to buy a new car for a new job or your family is having a once-in-a-lifetime wedding on a Caribbean island and you want to go. You need some money to cover these things. Get ahead.

OPTIMIZE YOUR TAXES

This may be a bit cart before the salary horse from a job but you need to get some sound tax advice once you start making money to a level where you are paying significant levels of tax. A good benchmark is anything over $30,000 annually. Learn some accounting or get some accounting advice. Once you start thinking about family, homes, children, etc., tax deductions and decisions make a big impact.

START INVESTING

This is the most complex part of a financial plan and can make you debt free or in debt based on the investments you choose. This is another area to seek a trusted professional advisor who has a proven track record. Consistency and diversity are key. As you consider investing, make sure that you have an idea of what your goals are. Obviously there are many different avenues to investing, whether it is high interest/no-risk savings, high reward/risky investments, buying real estate, etc.

INSURE WHERE APPROPRIATE

It is probably a good idea to get long-term health care insurance as well as disability insurance, along with car insurance and insurance on personal property. These policies are often inexpensive and a good hedge against the worst.

Spend a moment and think about how much time you have devoted to your sports and education. Now is the time to bring that enthusiasm, focus, hard work, and teamwork to becoming fiscally smart!

PRACTICAL APPLICATIONS

Most student-athletes don't receive "full rides" and don't have enough time to get a job to pay for tuition otherwise. Therefore, the majority of student-athletes may have some amount of debt from loans that they will have to pay back after they graduate. You'll likely also need to get a car, an apartment in an urban setting, and maybe a new computer and phone. Yes, that new paycheck will get split quickly.

At the end of the day, you should follow the five steps below as a start:

Step 1

Create a checklist of "needs" and "wants." Needs are things like utilities, rent, transportation, clothes, food, necessary travel, and more. Wants are things like a phone upgrade, a new video game, trendy clothes, and trips. Keep these separate and only dip in the 'wants' when you have the needs under control, your emergency fund in place, and confidence in future revenues.

Step 2

Start a financial budget template on Excel, Numbers, or other spreadsheet software. Don't do this informally or haphazardly. Build a good and easy to update budget template. Keep all old data so you can track your budget versus reality the year later. Most bank accounts and credit cards now have very detailed online systems with your records that you can draw from.

Step 3

Use technology and apps to help you track your spending, investments, and credit cards. There are many great tools out there now to control your spending (e.g., max of $15/week on coffee, how many days you go out for lunch, etc.). Use them if you are not disciplined enough (like many of us are!).

Step 4

Create financial goals for yourself and set yourself boundaries and limits on your spending. Like many of the other secrets in the book, a plan and clear objectives and priorities are needed!

Step 5

Within your means, understand what "lifestyle" you are going to and can afford to live. Be smart. An apartment closer to work where you don't need a car but is a few hundred dollars more may be a better investment than a cheaper apartment far away. Include your extracurricular activities around a balanced and healthy life in these decisions.

CHAPTER SUMMARY

As we tell you to be fiscally smart, don't think it is so easy and that it will all take care of itself. As we mentioned, you need to:

- Build yourself a financial plan
- Create your budget, and spend only what you can afford
- Create a good credit rating

- Pay off your debt and build an emergency fund
- Acknowledge your eventual retirement, optimize your taxes, and start investing
- Insure yourself and be practical

All of these will change as life changes, and it only becomes more complicated if you add a spouse and children to the mix. Educate yourself, and take control of your finances. Don't let them get out of hand or out of sight.

It may not be the first thing on your mind as you are mostly worried about your tuition and when your next meal is, but take some time to learn and think about what is ahead of you.

Secret 20 Prepare for the Future by Tracking Trends

THE SECRET IN A FEW WORDS

Since this is The Final Secret, we thought it had better be a good one. In fact, it's kind of a summary secret because it combines elements of Secrets 1, 8, and 11: Create and Follow Your Student-Athlete Plan, Your Major Really Matters, and Face Reality in Sports and Life. Tracking trends may sound boring . . . like some kind of research assignment for a class you didn't really care about. But there's a big difference for this particular research, this quest, because the class is YOU. And if you aren't interested in YOU . . . well, then you should toss this book away.

So here's the secret: If you want to live that life you've possibly imagined . . . the one where you live comfortably and work at a job you like . . . you have to prepare for that future and you have to follow the societal and business trends that influence the world around you. Presidential elections suddenly matter because they might influence the creation of new jobs. New inventions matter because they might create entire industries. So, too, popular culture, economic realities, and real-world threats.

No one goes into a big sporting event without some kind of a plan for achieving victory. The reason coaches study game film is to spot the trends the opposing teams employ and to make predictions on what those players (and their coaches) will do in the next game.

You've got to start spotting those trends in life in order to win.

PREPARE FOR THE FUTURE BY TRACKING TRENDS

As this book draws to a close, there is one last secret to share. It's a simple one but something every student-athlete who won't turn pro in sports should learn: how to know who and what is out there . . . and then . . . how to prepare for the future by spotting the road signs, those big neon indicators. You need to come to grips with the fact that the year you graduate, more than 100,000 student-athletes who didn't sign pro sports contracts will simultaneously enter the job market, and many of them will be looking for the same jobs you are seeking.

Trends are usually slow moving, but graduation ceremonies happen with perfect regularity every May, June, and December. That means regardless of what attractive new industry (technology, fashion, electronics, broadcasting, engineering, military, entertainment, social media, and an endlessly changing list) is suddenly emerging, it is one that hundreds of thousands of other graduates will be targeting.

So you need to be quick getting off the blocks and you need to know where to look. In other words, you need to know who "those guys" are. You have to try (and it takes training) to get a step ahead. To know what's coming.

Have you ever participated in a scavenger hunt? Small teams compete to be the first to gather all the items on a list containing a crazed range of objects (e.g., a lug nut, a box of Lucky Charms cereal, an Ohio State baseball hat, the front page of the *New York Times*). Some scavenger hunts give vague or mysterious clues, which sometimes simply lead to other clues. A scavenger hunt is usually a fun, competitive race that takes the players on a wild search for the strange objects on the list. Team members have to work together and use their ingenuity to find the items required, and they need to do so with urgency.

That's one way of thinking about spotting and tracking trends. You probably have some rough sense of what is happening in the world but are not sure what it all means. If you're like most people reading this book, politics and big business may or may not have been your thing. You've simply been trying to manage classes, your coaches' expectations, and a social life.

Suddenly, someone tells you that you won't be "going pro" and you have to think about working (ugh!) and earning a paycheck. When that thought kicks in (the whole job thing), you may find yourself racing around (if you haven't lined up a job during your senior year) and trying to match up what you like doing with a company that looks like a good fit.

Think of it this way: You probably like playing sports and you should know that Nike, Under Armour, Warrior Sports, and Sports PT were created by student athletes (Phil Knight ran track at Oregon; Kevin Plank played football at Maryland; Dave Morrow played lacrosse at Princeton; Lynn Steenberg was a trainer for the football team at Ithaca). You would probably also think that working for a company that creates products for athletes would involve staying close to elite competition and might also be fun.

But what do you really know about Nike, Under Armour, Warrior Sports, and Sports PT? What trends are influencing those brands? What challenges do the CEOs of those companies face? What are the new frontiers in sport apparel or footwear? Where is lacrosse equipment headed in the future? How is technology changing the way sport is played? Why is physical therapy for injured athletes booming as a business?

Naturally, everyone who likes sports can't get hired by a sports company. But everyone can get better at spotting trends and making projections. Famed hockey player Wayne Gretzky once said that he didn't skate to where the puck was . . . he skated to where the puck was going. Translation: the greatest hockey player of the modern era scored more goals by anticipating where he needed to be in order to get the job done (i.e., to put the puck in the back of the net). He didn't skate directly at the action. He skated to the place where the action would end up.

If you are only skating toward your collegiate sport, you won't end up where the puck (your career after college) is going. You may talk a good game about your sport, team, or campus, but you won't know what is going on in the world.

TECHNOLOGY AND CAREER MANAGEMENT TRENDS

Dan Butterly, mentioned a few times in the book already, a senior associate commissioner at the Mountain West Conference, provides his insights and advice for current and future student-athletes on the topic of technology trends and tracking changes that will affect your career.

DAN BUTTERLY
(Senior Associate Commissioner at the Mountain West Conference)

1. What impact do you see technology making on the future of the student-athlete, and how will that affect the way student-athletes will need to prepare for their transition?

Technology has advanced training, not only in the equipment that is used, but also in nutrition, health, physical fitness, sports medicine, and medical procedures. Student-athletes are dealing with continual changes in technology in their own lives, inclusive of social media, digital content, internet availability.

It is helping to make lives more efficient, but is drastically hurting such entities as the retail store industry in how we buy products and services. Managing our personal finances has changed from going to the bank, to using our mobile devices. Why do you need a financial advisor these days when you can chart, research, and invest all through mobile devices? All college students must evaluate their career fields and look at how technology and innovation will impact their opportunities for career growth. Will you be an innovator, or will innovation take over your career?

2. What trends have you seen with student-athletes over the years that may continue in regards to preparing for their future?

Student-athletes continue to be outstanding leaders. That has not changed over the years. There are tremendous traits student-athletes have that many times they undersell on their resume or job interview. Team building, how to deal with adversity, excellent health and wellness, leadership traits, and a zest for success.

One of the great trends I have seen from this generation of student-athlete compared to previous student-athletes is how they venture outside their own sport, come together with student-athletes in other sports, and have created a significant voice and leadership group not only to make the NCAA better, but by leading, to make their generation better too.

When I was an undergrad, I heard student-athletes from other teams often complain about all the great resources football and men's basketball received. Now, many of those same benefits are available to all student-athletes, because of the voice this generation of student-athletes has put forth.

3. What impact will technology have on the job market for graduating student-athletes?

Technology is changing the way the world works. I have worked in marketing and sales since I started my career in the early '90s, and the inventory we sold, or mediums we used to promote our brands, are no longer the key mediums. Print, radio, and television have been replaced with the internet, social media, and such digital broadcast channels as YouTube.

This has changed not only marketing and sales, but how businesses do business. Students must always look toward "what's next" and look to be innovators in their field. Soon, streets will be filled with self-driving cars. Social media has changed the "we" to "me." Student-athletes will be key leaders moving forward, as they know how to work within teams and drive success.

Snapchat is the perfect example of "me" versus the "we." When I was going to school, you were focused on core curriculum, and you focused on your friends. Now, you're doing things via social media that we never would've done with an older fashion camera. . . . When you're talking about the potential impact of selfies and that personal mobile device, the things that you're doing when you post rants on a Facebook page or via Twitter are unacceptable.

How that will impact students, not only student athletes, but students as they go into the working world, as they go into interview space or get the potential to even interview for a position would surprise you. Putting your resume together is one thing and, obviously, having a digital profile on LinkedIn is another. It's very easy for me to hire a background firm to search through your social media accounts to determine if there's anything negative that may impact your job status or the potential of me interviewing you for a job situation here at the Mountain West Conference, or any place I may be.

I just don't think people nowadays, specifically the high school, early college generation that have grown up with mobile devices, realize the impact that a selfie or a statement that you put up at the age of seventeen or eighteen may have on the future of your job potential.

4. What trends have you seen with the job market and how student-athletes can best prepare themselves for trending industries?

In my experience, students can best prepare by taking courses or trying new experiences that challenge them beyond their current major or sport. Life experiences, and finding what you truly enjoy, while developing critical thinking skills, are the fundamental benefits of college. Innovators are working daily to find new ways to change old industry via technology. People are more mobile than ever before.

Look at ways the career field you choose can do business in a new way that our mobile society can engage. If you are an accounting major, take some technology courses and learn how to develop apps or new ways to communicate. If you want to head into the sport field, how can you best engage fans, sponsors, boosters, season ticket holders, etc. so they want to continue to spend hundreds or thousands of dollars to get to your events? In-stadium attendance is trending down, not up, and mobile technology is a key driver.

Chris Dawson is an associate commissioner at the Pac-12 Conference and a former women's basketball player at the University of Virginia. Through her many years in college athletics and her student-athlete experience, she has expertise about the future of student-athletes and what they can do to prepare for the biggest pending changes.

CHRIS DAWSON (former student-athlete, Associate Commissioner at the PAC-12 Conference)

I think the biggest potential change in intercollegiate athletics will probably come from the litigation that's still pending. The other things that make it a different world from even when I competed or I would say twenty years ago is the amount of money that's involved, like television money, all the things that people now think you "have to have" to be successful. You have to have a shiny locker room on par with professional locker rooms.

You have to have the next big thing in facilities and I think that there's a financial breaking point that's going to hit and it's already hit some places. In my opinion, the path between athletics as an educational enterprise with a lot of money involved and the legal challenges that come with will be the most difficult thing in the next five to ten years. Student-athletes will have to deal with fewer opportunities across different sports if things get scaled back. Who are the people who are not going to have the opportunity to compete at the Division I level that they have now?

The other aspect for students on campus will be continued pressure to win and perform at a high level academically and athletically all the time. It all depends on the institution, the competitive level, the kind of institution, the preferred major, and the designated major of the student. I think more schools now are aware of the need for mental health services for people.

JOB PLACEMENT

Jim Kahler is a former Division I swimmer at Xavier University who went on to work in the sports industry for many different organizations, including the Cleveland Cavaliers. Kahler is currently the executive director of the AECOM Center for Sports Administration at Ohio University. He provides his insights in the box below on what you need to consider and prepare for when starting a career and looking for a job. He focuses his advice around the five pillars of job placement.

FIVE JOB PLACEMENT PILLARS

Sports business is like most other traditional industries; however, you need to have an open mind with regard to relocation in order to advance your career. If your end goal is to work for the hometown team you may never get your foot in the door and can find it next to impossible to grow from an entry-level position to the CEO's office. Most sports organizations are small in scale with low turnover rates inside successful companies. To advance your career you need to perform at a level that will get you noticed by your current supervisors, other organizations, and recruiters. When it comes time to make a move, you need to carefully evaluate each opportunity and not let the excitement of being recruited cloud your vision. At an early age I was once given some great advice by a recruiter when she said, "Sometimes in sports you become better known for the jobs you turn down as opposed to the ones you accept."

Over the years I have developed a rubric for new opportunities, even if it's your first job, that I refer to as the Five Job Placement Pillars. Listed below, in no particular order of importance, are five elements that you need to research and factor in before accepting any new positon:

- *Geography*—How will this job meet my needs when it comes to the geographical location? You will need to be able to answer the following questions:
  - If I need to make a trip home in case of an emergency, how long will the trip take me?
  - How expensive is a roundtrip airline ticket?
  - Can I drive the distance in a reasonable time?

- Are my parents in good enough health to travel in for a visit?
- Is the location one that would be attractive for family and friends to visit?

- *Organizational Culture*—I know I will end up working long hours in sports, but what's the organizational culture going to be like? Every organization has its own culture and it's incumbent on you to do your research so you will be able to answer the following questions:

    - What's the real goal of the organization that I am going to be working for?
    - What's the management style of the organization—micro or macro?
    - Does the organization consider its employees to be the most treasured possession of the organization? This organizational style is often referred to as the Baseball Team Culture.
    - What are the processes and procedures like with the organization?
    - How does the organization feel about training and developing its employees?

- *Direct Supervisor*—The person who is your direct supervisor will have a tremendous impact on your level of job satisfaction. In challenging times your direct supervisor can become your greatest ally or your worst enemy. So how can you get a read on your new boss during the interview process?

    - Do your homework to determine if your supervisor is a developer and someone who enjoys working with their direct reports (i.e., employees) or a grinder and someone who is only concerned with net results.
    - Take advantage of LinkedIn and see if your new boss has recommendations from former employees or customers.
    - Ask yourself if your new boss is going to be with the organization for a while or are they ready to make their next move in the sports business industry, which will more than likely end up with a move to another organization.
    - Does your direct supervisor have balance in their life or are they a workaholic?
    - How does your new boss define success?

- *Room for Growth*—Will the responsibilities that you are given with your new position provide you with new experiences and challenges? Room for growth doesn't necessarily mean internal growth within the organization as opposed to having the opportunity to develop new skills that will make you more valuable in sports. Some companies talk a good game when it comes to training and executive education. Your direct supervisor might be a great manager and developer but will higher management provide the budget and permission that allows you to attend conferences and networking events?

- *Compensation*—While you will undoubtedly have to pay your dues and be patient in the sports business industry, compensation has to be one of your placement pillars. If you can't afford to live in a great city, sooner or later you will be looking for that next job and you do not want to get the reputation of being a job hopper (someone who takes a new job every eighteen months to two years). Oftentimes energetic and hard-charging employees are willing to take below-entry-level wages and end up expecting a larger-than-life raise after the first year on the job. Please remember if your boss offers you a 10 percent increase after your first year on the job and tells you that you just received the largest percentage increase in the organization that simple math still applies. Ten times nothing (1.1 x a low entry-level salary) will still equate to a low salary unless you find yourself in a sales positon that has applicable commissions.

In addition to these five pillars that will help you form the foundation for a good decision you also need to ask yourself what else matters and will drive your final decision. We all have different challenges and situations in life, but I do believe these five basic pillars will come into play every time you make a move in your career. It's also very important to realize that the priority order of your placement pillars will change every three to five years in your life. As you get older, compensation and geography will probably become more important than when you first graduate. You also will be more likely to take a greater risk with organizational culture at the start of your career just to gain experience.

FIVE PLACEMENT PILLARS / RUBRIC

Geography
Organizational Culture
Direct Supervisor
Room for Growth
Compensation

Placement Pillar in Priority Order	Placement Value	Total Score
1.	25–30 points	
2.	20–25 points	
3.	15–20 points	
4.	10–15 points	
5.	5–10 points	
Total Score		

FIVE PLACEMENT PILLARS / SCORING SYSTEM

Letter Score / Total Points	Do Your Homework	Suggestions
A+ / A– = 90–100 points		Accept the offer
B+ / B– = 89–80 points		Proceed with a plan after two years
C+ / C– = 79–70 points		Proceed with caution and a short-term plan
Below 70 points	X	Turn down the offer

While the scoring system that I have outlined above may seem unrealistic, you need to do your homework prior to accepting any new job. Oftentimes the grass will seem greener on the other side of the fence, but you need to be careful and run your current job through the same rubric above before making a change. Early in your career, compensation jumps into a priority position (1–3) when you leave your first job for the second one. Don't let your salary be a bigger issue than it needs to be, as most people tend to let their egos get in the way of continued career development. Don't be in a hurry to leave a supervisor who has a proven track record as a developer of talent or a company that has an excellent organizational culture.

YOUR PERSONAL AUDIT

What have you been given and how does it fit with your life after college?

It's an important question and gives you a reason to conduct a personalized audit. Would you write down any of the following or would you list other things?

- A college degree
- A major (or minor) you selected and liked
- Course specialization that is relevant for the world you will move into
- A chance to practice and play sports in college (regardless of whether you started, played, or walked on . . . and regardless of whether you played DI, II, III, NAIA or any other form of organized collegiate sport
- A competitive spirit
- A teamwork orientation (i.e., you know what it takes to be a good teammate)
- Physical reliability
- Emotional strength (drawn from hard work and close contests)
- A few inspiring professors
- A happy childhood

- A childhood filled with challenges that you overcame
- A life filled with challenges you are still working on
- Wealth, poverty, or something in between
- The knowledge that your life wasn't easy but you've made the most of yourself
- A vision of what you are still capable of achieving

Your potential and your merit are what matters and both of those lead to a discussion of market forces and market demand. Spotting trends is about knowing what is influencing a market and knowing what employers are looking for in new hires.

You've learned the "college system" (how to register for classes you want, how to get into certain buildings after hours, etc.), so why can't you master the next system?

Lynn Steenberg, the CEO of Sports PT, was mentioned earlier in this chapter and frequently guest lectures at Syracuse University on sport industry leadership. She often tells a story about her father and how he taught her what he called the seven-option rule.

"That was important," Steenberg recalls. "In his business, whenever they were faced with a challenge, my father's business partners would force themselves to come up with at least seven options. I asked Dad: Why the number seven? He said: 'It forces you to think beyond the obvious. It's easy to come up with two or three options. It isn't so easy to come up with seven.'"

Steenberg goes on to say that a lot of times, the first option for many folks is doing nothing. And the second option is way at the other end of the spectrum and virtually impossible if not highly improbable. "But then you work to fill in the middle five. It forces you to think broadly."

Spotting trends may be like that. At first you may only see the obvious things or you'll predict things so far into the future you won't be alive to see them happen. But building a capacity to understand how the world works and what is driving the change you see all around you is important because it can shape your future success.

CHAPTER SUMMARY

We've made this chapter's secret sound easy to master, and that is perhaps a disservice to readers. If all of us could spot trends (think of the stock market or gambling), everyone would know what to do next. The truth is that many trends are not that easy to identify and some are extremely hard to put into everyday words. You might sense something but not know how to explain it. You might see something new and believe it is going to be the next big thing. Some days it is, most days it isn't.

But our secret—and it's a valuable one—is letting you know that the most successful people are the ones who have a sense of what's coming next.

They have that ability to look around the corner without sticking their necks out. The can correctly guess "fast ball, down and away" or that the player shooting on goal will go "upper left." They are moving to block the shot before it happens.

These prognosticators hold an advantage when they look at what's going on around them. It's the difference between being focused only on self and instead looking at everything else. And that proactive, initiative-taking inspiration is a valuable trait to develop.

Many of us develop that skill early when we know someone will be mad at us before the other person even hears the whole story about how the window got broken. Or the dog got out. Or the door got left open.

But switch this habit from the negative to the positive and try your hand at guessing which business sectors might grow or which companies might be hiring in the future. Which "friends" in your network can really help you and which ones can only talk a good game. Get in the habit of predicting which new social networks or apps will catch on and which will fail. Work on telling the difference between a short fad and a bankable trend.

And don't get down on yourself if you get predictions wrong. All of us swing and miss at a lot of pitches and we do so all the time. But as in sports, you get up, dust yourself off (or wait for the next at bat), and try to figure out how to win the next situation.

The End—Your Road Map: It's Not a Secret

Now that you have read our twenty secrets, our final chapter is to ask you to sincerely create and then follow a road map toward personal success. This road map incorporates those twenty secrets and will help you out along your journey.

As you create and follow your road map, you need to keep learning in everything that you do. Always strive to continue to learn because for every one thing you learn, it will open your eyes to three things that you don't know. Your education is something that no one can ever take away from you. As some will say, "Be a sponge and soak everything up."

We believe your career path and life path shouldn't be separate from each other. The two may intersect at the right time and move forward from there, but both paths need to incorporate compatible goals and coexist. Therefore, provide yourself with a road map that gives you guidance to your paths.

To provide you with advice on what to plan and how to navigate through your transition, we interviewed Azure Davey.

AZURE DAVEY (former lacrosse student-athlete,
Director of Academic Affairs and Membership at the NCAA)

The Plan

All strategies and approaches to preparing yourself for life after sport boils down to one master plan—know yourself to the greatest degree possible, commit to learning more about yourself and your abilities, and use that knowledge to determine your next steps.

You must take a hard look at what your interests are, what your skills and abilities are, who you know, what foundational elements you learned along the way and meld it all to create a personalized blueprint. It's not a perfect science—it's meant to evolve and you need to be fluid. However, if you aren't thoughtful about your passions and gifts and refine your pursuit of those passions, you may end up feeling as though you are floating though this transition and the others that will come later in life.

Skills to Prepare for Any Future Career Transition

- *Proactive Thinking and Vision.* Proactively think about where you would like to be in the future and how what you do today may best support that vision. For almost everyone, this vision must be something other than professional sport. Even for those who will go pro, there will be another life, another career. You need to learn about yourself and your personal and professional interests as soon as possible.

- *Flexibility and Adaptability.* The only guarantee in preparing for transition to "real life" is that not everything will go according to plan. Be prepared to both capitalize and pivot when curveballs are thrown your way. Hurdles can sometimes be the best tool to help you define where you want to go.

- *Clear Articulation of Your Skills and Abilities.* One of the most important skills is being able to describe your skill set and articulate why it is valuable. In the case of athletics, what have years of playing a sport taught you and how are those skills transferrable *and* valuable to future employers? Being able to articulate and help others draw the connection is vital. If you can't articulate it, why should you expect others to get it?

Preparing Yourself for the Transition

The day will come that, when asked to describe yourself, you'll need to use labels different from "athlete" or "potential professional athlete." You need to think about what those other descriptions are sooner than your junior or senior year of college. Ideally, you're thinking about those descriptions when you select your school, identify potential co-curricular activities, and prepare for future jobs. The sooner you start using those other descriptive terms to describe yourself, the better. That doesn't mean you don't identify and describe yourself as an athlete—you just need to know what your other gifts, interests, and skills are.

You'll still be an athlete, and chances are many of you will continue to be active throughout life, but knowing that you have other talents and that those talents are just as important as your athlete status is important to transitioning and getting involved in other facets of life.

Why Preparation Eases the Transition

It's likely that for years you've primarily thought of yourself as an athlete. If you continue with that sole mindset, you might flounder with the next steps.

By thinking about yourself in other contexts besides athletics and cultivating those thoughts with action, the transition is less dramatic and your identity and future are open and ready for the next thing—the future you!

Jeremy Foley just recently retired from being Athletic Director at the University of Florida. Foley was the AD there for twenty-five years, and worked in the athletic department prior to becoming the AD. Foley was also a football and lacrosse student-athlete in his days at Hobart College. Foley provides a unique perspective on how you should become a successful person in life outside of being a successful student and athlete.

JEREMY FOLEY (former football and lacrosse student-athlete, retired AD, University of Florida)

Creating the Road Map

You are going to have to create your own road map and you may not find it right away. All of your life, your road map has been given to you, and you have been guided along the way, but now you have to take the lessons you have learned as being a successful student-athlete and take those into the next chapter of your life.

If you transfer what you have learned, continue to evolve, and don't be discouraged, you will be successful. A lot of student-athletes spend time in the past, and the past is gone and done with. Records are shattered, people are replaced, and that is how it will always work. It is important to take those lessons that you have learned from the past with you, but while looking forward.

Figure Out What Is Important in Life

The process is this; none of us know what your journey is going to be. I ended up spending forty years at Florida, who knew that was going to happen. You have to let the world come to you, but you still have to put in the work, get your degree(s) and network. I think that a lot of people put too much pressure on themselves to control the game of life. You can't get discouraged because you may not be where you want to be right away, and you can't put false pressure on yourself. Being out in the real world is not going to be as easy as you want it to be. You may not get a job you like right away, and you may not get the job you apply for that you really want, but don't let any of that discourage you. You use the lesson you learned as a student-athlete of getting back up and continuing to work, and keep going.

Throughout my forty years, whenever my alarm clock went off, I never once thought that I "had to go do" my job. I always thought that I "get to go to do" my job, regardless of what that day was going to look like, good or bad. My point with that is that if there is something that you really love to do, then go chase it. Regardless of your road blocks in between, go do it, because I can't imagine having to settle to do something you don't necessarily want to do all the time.

Top 10 Qualities of a High Achiever

1. High integrity and ethics
2. Outstanding work ethic
3. Ability to listen
4. Ability to make decisions
5. Control over temper
6. Being a people person
7. Loyalty
8. Common sense
9. Toughness
10. Ability to smile and have fun

Too many times, people take shortcuts. The end justifies the means. Winning is the end all be all regardless of the path to get there, and I don't think that is ultimately what it is all about.

Being able to listen to other people makes you a more effective leader. If you aren't listening, people won't give you input. At the end of the day, it's about getting the best input to make the best decision as a leader.

8 Aspects of Becoming a Successful Professional

1. Learn how to treat people with respect
2. Learn and develop the value of respect
3. Understand the value of people
4. Be known for the having the highest of ethics and personal integrity
5. Be the most honest person you can be
6. Be humble
7. Have a strong work ethic
8. Learn how to lead

You need to be humble. A lot of people that become successful get big egos or it becomes all about them. At some point in time, the success you may be achieving is going to take a hit. You aren't always going to be at the top. People like being around humble people, not I people, or me people.

In staying humble, you have to know that what you are doing is much bigger than you. At the end of the day, this isn't about us. It is all about "the place." At Florida, we are just a part of a great institution. We represent the University of Florida, "we" being the whole department. Every decision we make needs to be made in the best interest of "the place." If the motivation is about ourselves, then we will make bad decisions.

Having a great work ethic is something you can control. I've seen people that have been successful, but at some point in time they stop working because they think they have made it, or they just cruise at what they are doing. I think that the more successful you become, the harder you have to work.

If you want to be really successful, you have to learn how to lead. I think leaders are made, not born. Leading people and motivating people is a key part of being successful. You need to self-evaluate yourself on that level every single day. Leading people changes every day and you have to continue to learn.

I always had a fear of failure. I didn't want to fail because it meant that the University of Florida failed. I used that as motivation, and continued to work harder. As Athletic Director at Florida, the thing that kept me motivated the most was the ability to impact people's lives. I love winning, and I love being in the front row for a lot of special events, but the most important thing to me has been the ability to impact and change people's lives. Changing someone's life is much more important than winning a ring.

· ·

That's all, folks (an old line from an old cartoon). Those are the twenty secrets. Finito. No tests. No homework assignments. Just our sincere hope that this book helps you handle the complex process of playing sports in college while getting a high-quality education.

Get busy living. And enjoy your time. Many nonathletes out there would do anything to be you for just one day. Know it or not, you are a hero in someone's eyes. Stay strong.

Afterword

Pat O'Conner,
President of Minor League Baseball

Transitioning from athlete to former athlete involves more than having your uniform taken away from you. The very nature of your life will be altered at some level. It is an exciting new beginning in your life and nothing more detrimental than a rite of passage to maturity as a person. With a couple of caveats, successful transition is incumbent on you making smart decisions and committing to this new path with the same zeal and intensity with which you competed as an athlete.

I am a firm believer in dreaming big. One of humanity's greatest flaws is the willingness to settle for too little. Do what makes you happy and chase your dreams in the process. Do not expect anyone to believe in you, or your dreams, if you do not believe in yourself and those dreams. Never look to someone else to accomplish something you should do. As the saying goes, "Don't let good get in the way of great" and never shy away from an honest day of hard work. People will notice hard work.

I had a college professor who often warned us against "sitting down at breakfast and starting to think about lunch." The moral is to stay in the present. Commit to the task at hand, give it all you have, and the next opportunity will present itself at the appropriate time. Work with all your heart and might in the position you have and you will learn a skill, build a good reputation, and become an attractive candidate for the next big opportunity.

Finally, I encourage you to make sure your job is what you do and not who you are. Our job is an important part of what defines us as individuals, but it is not everything. In my case, I had to overcome being known as "the baseball guy" and regain my identity as "the guy who is in baseball." Never lose sight of your faith, family, and friends as you strive for excellence as a professional.

Appendix A

NCAA Student-Athlete Success Data

Estimated Probability of Competing in College and Professional Athletics

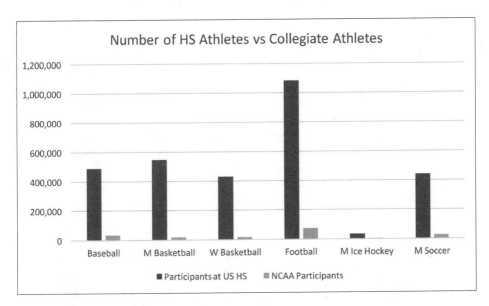

Number of HS Athletes vs Collegiate Athletes

NCAA Research. (2017 March 10). *Estimated Probability of Competing in College Athletics.* Retrieved on May 22, 2017.

(continued on next page)

Estimated Probability of Competing in College and Professional Athletics

(continued from previous page)

NCAA Research. (2017 March 10). *Estimated Probability of Competing in Professional Athletics.* Retrieved on May 22, 2017.

Male Identity by Division (Athlete/Student)

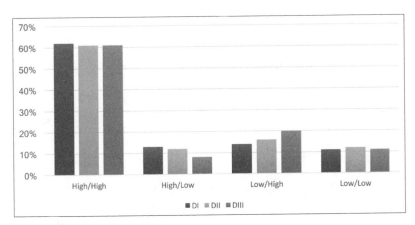

Female Identity by Division (Athlete/Student)

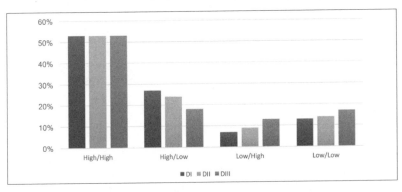

NCAA Research. (August 2013). Do NCAA Student-Athletes View Themselves as Students or Athletes? Retrieved on May 22, 2017.

Estimated Probability of Competing in Professional Athletics

	NCAA Participants	Approximate # Draft Eligible	# Draft Picks	# NCAA Drafted	% NCAA to Major Pro	% NCAA to Total Pro
Baseball	34,554	7,679	1,206	695	9.1%	--
M Basketball	18,684	4,152	60	44	1.1%	19.1%
W Basketball	16,593	3,687	36	35	0.9%	4.9%
Football	73,660	16,369	253	251	1.5%	1.9%
M Ice Hockey	4,102	912	211	51	5.6%	--
M Soccer	24,803	5,512	81	75	1.4%	--

NCAA Research. (March 10, 2017). *Estimated Probability of Competing in Professional Athletics.* Retrieved on May 23, 2017.

Male Opinion of Likeliness of Going Pro

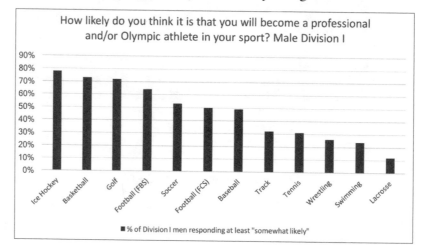

NCAA Research. (January 2016). *Results from the 2015 GOALS Study of the Student-Athlete Experience.* Retrieved on May 23, 2017.

Female Opinion of Likeliness of Going Pro

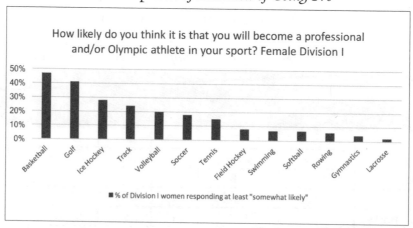

NCAA Research. (March 10, 2017). *Estimated Probability of Competing in Professional Athletics.* Retrieved on May 23, 2017.

Estimated Probability of Competing in College Athletics

	Partici-pants at US High Schools	NCAA Par-ticipants	Overall % HS to NCAA	% HS to NCAA Division 1	% HS to NCAA Division II	% HS to NCAA Division III
Men						
Baseball	488,815	34,554	7.1%	2.1%	2.2%	2.8%
Basketball	546,428	18,684	3.4%	1.0%	1.0%	1.4%
Cross Country	257,691	14,412	5.6%	1.9%	1.4%	2.3%
Football	1,083,308	73,660	6.8%	2.6%	1.8%	2.4%
Golf	146,677	8,676	5.9%	2.0%	1.7%	2.2%
Ice Hockey	35,155	4,102	11.7%	4.6%	0.5%	6.5%
Lacrosse	109,522	13,466	12.3%	2.9%	2.3%	7.1%
Soccer	440,322	24,803	5.6%	1.3%	1.5%	2.8%
Swimming	133,470	9,455	7.1%	2.8%	1.1%	3.2%
Tennis	157,201	8,092	5.1%	1.7%	1.1%	2.4%
Track and Field	591,133	28,334	4.8%	1.9%	1.2%	1.7%
Volleyball	55,417	1,899	3.4%	0.7%	0.8%	1.9%
Water Polo	21,857	1,014	4.6%	2.6%	0.7%	1.3%
Wrestling	250,653	7,075	2.8%	1.0%	0.8%	10%
Women						
Basketball	429,380	16,593	3.9%	1.2%	1.1%	1.6%
Cross Country	222,516	15,958	7.2%	2.7%	1.8%	2.7%
Field Hockey	59,793	6,032	10.1%	3.0%	1.2%	5.8%
Golf	74,762	5,293	7.1%	2.9%	2.1%	2.1%
Ice Hockey	9,514	2,289	24.1%	9.0%	1.0%	14.0%
Lacrosse	88,050	11,375	12.9%	3.8%	2.6%	6.5%
Soccer	381,529	27,358	7.2%	2.4%	1.9%	2.9%
Softball	366,685	19,680	5.4%	1.6%	1.6%	2.1%
Swimming	166,747	12,356	7.4%	3.3%	1.1%	3.0%
Tennis	183,800	8,933	4.9%	1.6%	1.1%	2.2%
Track and Field	485,969	29,048	6.0%	2.7%	1.5%	1.8%
Volleyball	436,309	17,119	3.9%	1.2%	1.1%	1.6%
Water Polo	20,230	1,136	5.6%	3.3%	1.0%	1.3%

NCAA Research. (March 10, 2017). *Estimated Probability of Competing in College Athletics.* Retrieved on May 23, 2017.

Appendix B

Other Resources

Health and Safety Resources from the NCAA website
  http://www.ncaa.org/health-and-safety/health-and-safety-resources
NCAA Sport Science Institute
  http://www.ncaa.org/sport-science-institute
NCAA Research Center
  http://www.ncaa.org/about/resources/research
January 2016 GOALS Convention
  http://www.ncaa.org/about/resources/research/ncaa-goals-study

STUDENT-ATHLETE CAREER RESOURCES

NCAA After the Game Career Center: http://www.ncaa.org/student-athletes
  /former-student-athlete/careers
NCAA Former Student-Athlete Employment: http://fsacareercenter.ncaa.org
  /jobseekers/
Teamwork Online: www.teamworkonline.com
Grit Scale: http://angeladuckworth.com/grit-scale/
Career Personality test: http://www.humanmetrics.com/personality/career-choices
LinkedIn: www.linkedin.com
Athletes to Careers: http://athletestocareers.com
Athletes Touch: http://www.athletestouch.co
Athlete Network: https://www.athletenetwork.com

RELEVANT JOURNAL ARTICLES

Bukstein, S. 2016. "Practical Strategies for Thought Leaders in College Athletics and
  Higher Education: Developing a 'Meaningful Education and Career Preparation
  as Compensation' Model." *Journal of Higher Education Athletics & Innovation*
  1(1), doi:10.15763/issn.2376-5267.2016.1.1.61-72.
Chalfin, P., et al. 2014. "The Value of Intercollegiate Athletics Participation from
  the Perspective of Employers Who Target Athletes." *Journal of Issues in Intercollegiate Athletics* (8): 1–17.

Comeaux, E. 2005. "Environmental Predictors of Academic Achievement among Student-Athletes in the Revenue-Producing Sports of Men's Basketball and Football." *Sport Journal* 8(3).

———. 2007. "The Student(less) Athlete: Identifying the Unidentified College Student." *Journal for the Study of Sports and Athletes in Education* 1(1): 37–44.

Comeaux, E., and C. K. Harrison. 2011. "A Conceptual Model of Academic Success for Student-Athletes." *Educational Researcher* 40(5): 235–45.

Comeaux, E., L. Speer, M. Taustine, and C. K. Harrison. 2011. "Purposeful Engagement of First-Year Division I Student-Athletes." *Journal of the First-Year Experience and Students in Transition* 23(1): 35–52.

Fuller, R. D. 2014. "Transition Experiences out of Intercollegiate Athletics: A Meta-Synthesis." *Qualitative Report* 19(46): 1–15.

Gayles, J. G., and S. Hu. 2009. "The Influence of Student Engagement and Sport Participation on College Outcomes among Division I Student Athletes." *Journal of Higher Education* 80(3): 315–33.

———. 2009. "Athletes as Students: Ensuring Positive Cognitive and Affective Outcomes." In J. D. Toma and D. A. Kramer, eds., *The Uses of Intercollegiate Athletics: Challenges and Opportunities (New Directions for Higher Education,* no. 148): 101–7). San Francisco, CA: Jossey-Bass.

Gayles, J. G., A. B. Rockenbach, and H. A. Davis. 2012. "Civic Responsibility and the Student-Athlete: Validating a New Conceptual Model." *Journal of Higher Education* 83(4): 535–57.

Harris, H. L., M. K. Altekruse, and D. W. Engels. 2003. "Helping Freshman Student Athletes Adjust to College Life Using Psychoeducational Groups." *Journal for Specialists in Group Work* 28(1): 64–81.

Harrison, C. K., J. Stone, J. Shapiro, S. Yee, J. A. Boyd, and V. Rullan. 2009. "The Role of Gender Identities and Stereotype Salience with the Academic Performance of Male and Female College Athletes." *Journal of Sport and Social Issues* 33(1): 78–96.

Leonard, J. M., and C. J. Schimmel. 2016. "Theory of Work Adjustment and Student-Athletes' Transition out of Sport." *Journal of Issues in Intercollegiate Athletics* (9): 62–85.

Marx, J., S. Huffmon, and A. Doyle. 2008. "The Student-Athlete Model and the Socialization of Intercollegiate Athletes." *Athletic Insight* 10(1).

Melendez, M. C. 2006. "The Influence of Athletic Participation on the College Adjustment of Freshmen and Sophomore Student Athletes." *Journal of College Student Retention: Research, Theory & Practice* 8(1): 39–55.

Miller, P. S., and G. Kerr. 2002. "The Athletic, Academic and Social Experiences of Intercollegiate Student-Athletes." *Journal of Sport Behavior* 25(4): 346–67.

Osborne, B. 2014. "The Myth of the Exploited Student-Athlete." *Journal of Intercollegiate Sport* 7(2): 143–52.

Potuto, J. R., and J. O'Hanlon. 2007. "National Study of Student-Athletes Regarding Their Experiences as College Students." *College Student Journal* 41(4): 947–66.

Watt, S. K., and J. L. Moore. 2001. "Who Are Student-Athletes?" In S. Watt and J. Moore, eds., *Student Services for Athletes,* special issue of *New Directions for Student Services* (93): 7–18. San Francisco, CA: Jossey-Bass.

Yopyk, D., and D. Prentice. 2005. "Am I an Athlete or a Student? Identity Salience and Stereotype Threat in Student-Athletes." *Basic and Applied Social Psychology* 27(4): 329–36.

RECOMMENDED BOOKS

The 7 Habits of Highly Effective People, by Stephen R. Covey. New York: Simon & Schuster, 1989.

Outliers: The Story of Success, by Malcolm Gladwell. New York: Little, Brown, 2008.

Grit: The Power of Passion and Perseverance, by Angela Lee Duckworth. New York: Scribner, 2016.

Pitch Perfect: How to Say It Right the First Time, Every Time, by Bill McGowan and Alisa McGowan. New York: HarperBusiness, 2014.

A Career in Sports: Advice from Sports Business Leaders, by Michelle Wells, Andy Kreutzer, and Jim Kahler. M. Wells Enterprises, 2010.

Start with Why: How Great Leaders Inspire Everyone to Take Action, by Simon Sinek. New York: Penguin, 2009.

The ONE Thing: The Surprisingly Simple Truth behind Extraordinary Results, by Jay Papasan and Gary Keller. Austin, TX: Bard Press, 2013.

The Subtle Art of Not Giving a F***: A Counterintuitive Approach to Living a Good Life, by Mark Manson. New York: HarperOne, 2016.

What Color Is Your Parachute? 2017: A Practical Manual for Job-Hunters and Career-Changers, by Richard N. Bolles. New York: Ten Speed Press, 2016.

Good to Great: Why Some Companies Make the Leap . . . and Others Don't, by Jim Collins. New York: HarperBusiness, 2011.

Great by Choice, by Jim Collins and Morten T. Hansen. New York: HarperBusiness, 2011.

Wooden: A Lifetime of Observations and Reflections On and Off the Court, by Coach John Wooden. New York: McGraw-Hill, 1997.

The Power of Now: A Guide to Spiritual Enlightenment, by Eckhart Tolle. Novato, CA: New World Library, 1999.

The Talent Code: Greatness Isn't Born. It's Grown. Here's How, by Daniel Coyle. New York: Bantam, 2009.

The Power of Failure: Succeeding in the Age of Innovation, by Fran Tarkenton. Washington, DC: Regnery, 2015.

Drive: The Surprising Truth about What Motivates Us, by Daniel H. Pink. New York: Riverhead Press, 2009.

Off Balance: Getting Beyond the Work-Life Balance Myth to Personal and Professional Satisfaction, by Matthew Kelly. New York: Hudson Street Press, 2011.

Mindset: The New Psychology of Success, by Carol S. Dweck. New York: Random House, 2006.

Appendix C

Contributors to the Book

Contributor	Title	Sport	School
Alexis Pinson	Sales and Service at San Francisco 49ers	Volleyball	Arizona State University and Ohio University
Anson Dorrance	Head Coach–Women's Soccer at University of North Carolina	Soccer	University of North Carolina
Azure Davey	Director of Academic Affairs and Membership at NCAA	Lacrosse	Hamilton College
Bill Shumard	CEO of Special Olympics Southern California	N/A	
Billy Lavelle	Premium Service and Sales at Phoenix Suns	Baseball	University of Redlands
Bob Boland	Athletics Integrity Officer at Penn State University	Football	Columbia University
Brett Fischer	Owner of Fischer Sports Institute, Physical Therapist for the Arizona Cardinals	N/A	
Brian Sanders	SVP of Stadium Operations at Los Angeles Angels	Baseball	Chapman University
Brooks Neal	Director of Corporate Partnerships at Cleveland Cavaliers	Lacrosse	Syracuse University
Chris Dawson	Associate Commissioner at Pac-12 Conference	Basketball	University of Virginia
Christa Mann	Manager of Communications at MLS	Soccer	Georgia State University
Christina Wright	Former Assistant Director of HR at NCAA, and Lecturer in Sports Administration at Ohio University	Track and Field	American University

Colby Targun	Management Council, NFL Commissioner's Office	Football and Baseball	Texas State University
Connor Hancock	Assistant Manager, Digital Sales Administration at NBCUniversal Media	Baseball	University of Redlands
Dan Butterly	Senior Associate Commissioner at Mountain West Conference	N/A	
Danny White	Director of Student-Athlete Development at Virginia Tech	N/A	
Dawn Buth	Associate Director of Sport Science Institute at NCAA	Swimming and Dive	University of Florida
Drew Saylor	Minor League Manager at Los Angeles Dodgers	Baseball	Kent State University
Eddie Gill	Former NBA player, Wealth Management Advisor at Wells Fargo Wealth Management	Basketball	Weber State University
Erik Price	Associate Commissioner at Pac-12 Conference	N/A	
Fred Claire	Former GM of Los Angeles Dodgers, cofounder of Scoutables Inc.	N/A	
Garrett Shinoskie	Former Director of Athletic Performance at Zone Athletic Performance, now real estate agent	Football	Capital University
Glenn Schembechler	President at GES Advisory	Football	Miami (OH) University
Gracie Frizzell	Graduate student of Physical Therapy at Arkansas	Basketball	University of Mississippi
Hallie Olson	Manager of Corporate Development at Chicago Bulls	Swimming	Ohio University
Hillary Nelson	Partnerships Manager at Positive Coaching Alliance	Softball	Arizona State University
Immanuel Kerr-Brown	Assistant Director of Development at Penn State University	Wrestling	Duke University
James Biddick	Assistant Director of Graduate Management and Career Coach at Ohio University College of Business	Field Hockey	New Zealand
Jamilah Ali	MSA graduate student at Ohio University	Gymnastics	Bowling Green State University
Jason Elias	Outreach and Sales Manager, IMG Academy	Baseball	Baldwin Wallace University
Jeff Rodin	Director of Community Outreach and Development at Arizona Diamondbacks	Baseball	University of Illinois–Chicago
Jeremy Foley	Former Director of Athletics at University of Florida	Football	Hobart College

Jim Kahler	Executive Director of AECOM Center for Sports Administration at Ohio University	Swimming	Xavier University
John Nowicki	Senior Account Manager at ISC	Lacrosse	University of Detroit-Mercy
Joni Lockridge	Former Director of Digital Strategy at PGA	Softball	Furman University
JR Reynolds	Area Scout, Cincinnati Reds	Baseball	Ohio University
Kelsey Cermak	Assistant Director, Championships & Alliances at the NCAA	Basketball	University of Iowa
Kevin Brice	Analytics Assistant at Los Angeles Angels	Baseball	Pomona College
Kevin Hall	Doctor of Physical Therapy at Mayo Clinic in Scottsdale, AZ	Baseball	Wichita State University
Kevin Hurd	Field Marketing Manager at Mike's Hard Lemonade	Baseball	University of Northern Colorado
Kristen Brown	Associate AD–Administration at University of Maryland	Basketball	Northern Illinois University
Liz Woerle	Stewardship Coordinator at University of South Carolina Athletic Department	Soccer	Drake University
Louie Iglesias	Former Sales and Service for Dallas Cowboys	Tennis	University of Toledo
Matt Engleka	Owner of LEJ Agency	Baseball	Ohio University
Matt Vansandt	Director of Championships at Big South Conference	Track and Field	Augustana College
Mattie White	Associate AD–Academic Services at Indiana University	N/A	
Max Dittmer	Associate Business and Store Planner at Under Armour	Swimming	University of Iowa
Mike Doehla	President, Stronger U, NASM Certified Fitness Nutrition Specialist	N/A	
Nick Manno	Pro Scout at Seattle Mariners	Baseball	Mount Union
Oliver Luck	Executive VP of Regulatory Affairs at NCAA	Football	West Virginia University
Pat O'Conner	President of Minor League Baseball	Baseball	Wittenberg University
Peter Rovinelli	Owner of Elite Wellness Solutions LLC and Be Elite Performance LLC	Wresting and Rugby	Arizona State University
Pim Thirati	MSA graduate student, Ohio University	Golf	University of Illinois
Rob Smith	Head Baseball Coach at Ohio University	Baseball	Indiana University
Rod Baker	Assistant Coach at Philadelphia 76ers	Basketball	College of Holy Cross

Ryan Sollazzo	Director of Sponsorships at Major Leaague Baseball	Football	FAU and Stony Brook
Scott White	Jacksonville Area Account Director at Super Fit Foods	Baseball	Ohio University
Seth Etherton	Minor League Pitching Coach at Cincinnati Reds	Baseball	USC
Shauna Happel	MSA graduate student at Ohio University	Soccer	Northern Iowa University
Steve Cobb	Director of the Arizona Fall League	Baseball	Wooster College
Steve Watson	Athletic Director at Loyola University Chicago	Basketball	Bowling Green State University
Terri Steeb-Gronau	Vice President of Division II at NCAA	Volleyball	UAB
Wally Ritchie	Former MLB pitcher	Baseball	N/A
Willie Patti	National Scout, NSCA	Baseball	University of LaVerne

Appendix D

About the Authors

RICK BURTON is the David B. Falk Distinguished Professor of Sport Management in Syracuse University's Falk College of Sport and Human Dynamics. At Syracuse, Burton serves as the University's Faculty Athletics Representative (FAR) to the NCAA and Atlantic Coast Conference (ACC) and is a member of the NCAA's Women's Basketball Competition Committee. He also chairs the ACC's Infractions and Sportsmanship Committee, is a member of the ACC Finance Committee and a member of the conference's Autonomy Committee. Previously, Burton held a number of progressive industry positions, including Chief Marketing Officer for the US Olympic Committee, and Commissioner of the Sydney-based Australian National Basketball League. He consults, speaks, and writes extensively. This is his fourth book.

JAKE HIRSHMAN is a former student-athlete in the sport of baseball, and now a professional in that sport. He attended the University of Redlands, where he played baseball as a student-athlete and received his bachelor's degree in Business Administration. He also played baseball, then coached, at Ohio University during his graduate work, completing two master's degrees. Throughout his career to date, Jake has worked for the Rose Bowl, the Seattle Mariners, the Inland Empire 66ers, Special Olympics Arizona, the Arizona Diamondbacks, and the Arizona Fall League.

DR. NORM O'REILLY is recognized as one of the leading scholars in the business of sports. He is the Richard P. and Joan S. Fox Professor of Business and is Chair of the Department of Sports Administration at Ohio University's College of Business. He has authored or coauthored eight books, fourteen case studies in the Harvard/Stanford series, and more than 100 peer-reviewed journal articles. At conferences, he has won twelve Best Paper awards. In 2015, Dr. O'Reilly was awarded the Career Achievement Award by the American Marketing Association's Sport Marketing Special Interest Group. As Partner Consultant with the T1 Agency, he works with industry clients regularly. He is active as an expert witness in legal cases and is often quoted in media interviews. In 2016, Dr. O'Reilly was Assistant Chef de Mission for the Canadian Paralympic Team at the 2016 Paralympic Games.

ANDY DOLICH brings over five decades of front office executive experience in the sports industry, including positions in the NFL, MLB, NBA, NHL, and pro soccer and lacrosse. His vast experience includes executive positions such as Chief Operating Officer of the NFL's San Francisco 49ers, President of Business Operations for the Memphis Grizzlies and Golden State Warriors of the NBA, as well the Oakland A's during their run of success in the 1980s and '90s. Currently, Dolich runs a sports business consulting firm in the San Francisco Bay Area and is the cofounder of the virtual reality firm VHere. He is senior advisor to 3Ball, a 3×3 basketball league launching in the summer of 2018, advisor for *TBT: The Basketball Tournament* on ESPN, and owner of *Project Fanchise*, the first-ever fan-run sports league, the eFL (indoor football). He is Entrepreneur in Residence at Menlo College.

DR. HEATHER LAWRENCE is an Associate Professor of Sports Administration, Associate Dean of Graduate Programs, and Robert H. Freeman Professor of Business in the College of Business at Ohio University. Prior to beginning her academic career, Dr. Lawrence was an All-American diver at the University of Florida and worked in various administrative positions within intercollegiate athletics at Southeastern Louisiana University and the University of Florida. Dr. Lawrence has also served as a visiting professor at Instituto de Empressa in Spain, taught in the Hamdan Bin Mohammed Program for Sports Leadership in Dubai, and been a faculty member for the UPG (India)/Ohio University Certificate in International Sport Management. Heather has received numerous teaching awards, including the University Professor Award at Ohio University and the Outstanding Teacher Award in the College of Business at Instituto de Empressa. Dr. Lawrence has published and presented extensively in the areas of intercollegiate athletics finance, gender and sport, intercollegiate athletics leadership, and premium seating. She is also coeditor of the textbook *Event Management Blueprint*. She was inducted into the University of Florida College of Health and Human Performance Alumni Hall of Fame in 2009.

Notes

SECRET 1: CREATE AND FOLLOW YOUR STUDENT-ATHLETE PLAN

1. See Appendix A for NCAA reports supporting the 99 percent figure.

2. Example: J. T. Edwards and M. Washington (2015), "Establishing a 'Safety Net': Exploring the Emergence and Maintenance of College Hockey Inc. and NCAA Division I Hockey," *Journal of Sport Management* 29(3): 291–304.

SECRET 2: UNDERSTAND WHO A STUDENT-ATHLETE IS

1. There exists a vast body of research that shows how college student-athletes take on different roles, behaviors, and risk-taking actions than college students in general. A good source is N. R. Mastroleo, N. Scaglione, K. A. Mallett, and R. Turrisi (2013), "Can Personality Account for Differences in Drinking between College Athletes and Non-athletes? Explaining the Role of Sensation Seeking, Risk-Taking, and Impulsivity," *Journal of Drug Education* 43(1): 81–95.

2. See Appendix A for reports on NCAA student-athletes.

SECRET 3: RIDE YOUR SUCCESS WHEEL

1. There is much research on this topic—for more detail, see R. M. Southall (2014), "NCAA Graduation Rates: A Quarter-Century of Re-branding Academic Success," *Journal of Intercollegiate Sport* 7(2): 120–33.

2. E. Comeaux and K. C. Harrison (2011), "A Conceptual Model of Academic Success for Student Athletes," *Educational Researcher* 40(5): 235–45

SECRET 8: YOUR MAJOR REALLY MATTERS

1. This table is sourced from a 2015 study by the NCAA on goals. The study comes from NCAA internal documents—shared with the researchers by the NCAA on September 29, 2016, and reproduced by permission.

SECRET 12: MENTALLY MOVE ON AS A SENIOR

1. R. D. Fuller (2014), "Transition Experiences out of Intercollegiate Athletics: A Meta-synthesis," *Qualitative Report* 19(46): 1–15.

SECRET 13: IDENTIFY WHO YOU ARE

1. J. Leonard and C. Schimmel (2016), "Theory of Work Adjustment and Student-Athletes' Transition out of Sport," *Journal of Issues in Intercollegiate Athletics* (9): 62–85.

SECRET 15: START PREPARING IN YOUR SOPHOMORE YEAR

1. http://nces.ed.gov/fastfacts/display.asp?id=372.
2. http://www.bls.gov/news.release/archives/tenure_09182014.pdf.

SECRET 16: INVEST IN YOURSELF, YOUR HEALTH, AND YOUR FUTURE

1. Study Source: NCAA internal document shared with the researchers by the NCAA on September 29, 2016; from http://www.ncaa.org/student-athletes /former-student-athlete/recipe-energy-management-success.

2. American College Health Association, *National College Health Assessment* (ACHA-NCHA), Fall 2008, Spring 2009, Fall 2009, Spring 2010, Fall 2010, Spring 2011, Fall 2011, Fall 2012 [ACHA-NCHA II, ACHA-NCHA IIb] Hanover, MD: American College Health Association; (2013–10–31).

CHAPTER 17: ACTIVATE YOUR STUDENT-ATHLETE ADVANTAGE

1. P. Chalfin et al. (2014), "The Value of Intercollegiate Athletics Participation from the Perspective of Employers Who Target Athletes," *Journal of Issues in Intercollegiate Athletics* (8): 1–17.

2. This table is sourced from a 2015 study by the NCAA on goals. The study comes from NCAA internal documents—shared with the researchers by the NCAA on September 29, 2016, and reproduced by permission.